RELIGION IN VOGUE

Religion in Vogue

Christianity and Fashion in America

Lynn S. Neal

NEW YORK UNIVERSITY PRESS

New York

NEW YORK UNIVERSITY PRESS
New York
www.nyupress.org
© 2019 by New York University

References to internet websites (URLs) were accurate at the time of writing. Neither the author nor New York University Press is responsible for URLs that may have expired or changed since the manuscript was prepared.

Library of Congress Cataloging-in-Publication Data
Names: Neal, Lynn S., author.
Title: How God got on a dress : a history of fashionable religion in America / Lynn S. Neal.
Description: New York : NYU Press, 2019. | Includes bibliographical references and index.
Identifiers: LCCN 2019009445 | ISBN 9781479892709 (cl : alk. paper) |
ISBN 9781479813599 (pb : alk. paper)
Subjects: LCSH: United States—Church history. | Christianity and culture—United States. |
Popular culture—Religious aspects—Christianity. | Popular culture—United States. |
Fashion—United States—Miscellanea.
Classification: LCC BR517 .N43 2019 | DDC 261.5/7—dc23
LC record available at https://lccn.loc.gov/2019009445

New York University Press books are printed on acid-free paper, and their binding materials are chosen for strength and durability. We strive to use environmentally responsible suppliers and materials to the greatest extent possible in publishing our books.

Manufactured in the United States of America

10 9 8 7 6 5 4 3 2 1

Also available as an ebook

In loving memory of my father, K. Barry Neal

Fashion is not something that exists in dresses only. Fashion is in the sky, in the street, fashion has to do with ideas, the way we live, what is happening.
—Gabrielle "Coco" Chanel

CONTENTS

Color insert follows page 186

LIST OF FIGURES

Introduction

Fashion History Is Religious History

In November 1988, Anna Wintour, newly minted editor of American *Vogue*, shocked the fashion world with her debut cover.[1] It featured Israeli model Michaela Bercu in a casual pose with her hair down, her eyes almost closed, and her midriff showing. She wore jeans and a black Christian Lacroix jacket adorned with a large bejeweled cross. The cover differed markedly from the norm of close-up, formal portraits featuring perfectly coiffed and made-up models. Wintour's cover, in contrast, displayed an unfamiliar casualness for the magazine with Bercu's relaxed pose, unstyled hair, and fifty-dollar acid-washed jeans. Bercu also, according to Anna Wintour, sported a few post-vacation pounds. The jeans, in fact, became part of the shoot because the matching Lacroix skirt did not fit. Further, the dominance of the cross symbol on this seemingly secular fashion magazine (and an Israeli model) shocked some and prompted them to wonder if it "was a religious statement."[2]

While Wintour denied any such intention, she would not be able to deny that *Vogue* and the fashion industry more broadly do make religious statements. In the years since that inaugural cover, such statements have become commonplace on the fashion runway, from Gianni Versace's designs featuring the Virgin Mary in the 1990s to Dolce & Gabbana's collection inspired by the Cathedral of Monreale in the 2010s. Even more notable, Jesus, part of the Christian godhead, appeared on numerous items in Karla Špetić's Fall 2013 "Faith" collection. These garments and frequent headlines proclaiming the controversies surrounding fashion's use of religious symbols and figures in designer clothing shape the central question of this book: How did God get on a dress? Or, put another way, how did Christianity and Christian symbols become such a prominent part of the fashion industry?

Figure I.1. Anna Wintour's debut *Vogue* cover
featuring a cross-embellished jacket by Christian
Lacroix, *Vogue* 178 (November 1988): cover;
photograph © Peter Lindbergh, courtesy of Peter
Lindbergh and Condé Nast.

Designer Data for Religious History

Answering the question of how elements of the Christian imaginary
began appearing on designer clothing necessitates foregrounding history, specifically fashion history. My focus is on fashion since World
War II, as this global event simultaneously disrupted the international
fashion industry and introduced significant changes in the American
religious landscape. However, since examinations of the relationship
between religion and fashion do not appear in any significant way in
either religious or fashion histories of the period, I had to turn to other
historical sources. Fashion magazines, which function simultaneously
as a gateway to and gatekeeper of fashion, provided a way to discover

this discourse—what religion looked like and meant in fashion over this time period, albeit from a particular lens. *Vogue* (US), supplemented by *Harper's Bazaar*, became primary sources for constructing the broad contours of this history.[3] In these pages, long before bejeweled crosses adorned the cover of *Vogue*, I found the writings of Catholic Bishop Fulton Sheen, advertising images of angels and churches, and haute couture inspired by monks' cowls. These numerous instances of religiously oriented articles, images, symbols, and apparel suggested an alternative source and perspective on religious history.

I have focused on *Vogue* because, of the many fashion magazines available, it leads the way in terms of status and circulation. Established in 1892 as a New York society weekly, it became a national women's magazine when purchased by publishing executive Condé Montrose Nast in 1909. Nast had worked at *Collier's* and increased its annual advertising revenues from approximately $5,000 to more than $1 million dollars in ten years through his innovations, including the use of color, two-page spreads, and special issues. He brought this expertise to *Vogue* and sought to make it "the technical adviser—the consulting specialist—to the woman of fashion in the matter of her clothes and of her personal adornment."[4] He raised the price of each issue and charged more for advertising, as the magazine reported on and sought a high-society clientele. Nast's counterintuitive marketing strategy worked, as the circulation of *Vogue* went from fourteen thousand in 1909, when bought by Nast, to more than 1.2 million in 2014. Today the average reader is a thirty-eight-year-old woman with a median household income of $60,536, and a full- or part-time job (almost a quarter of which are in management).[5] The magazine now has editions in more than fifteen countries.

Vogue showcases the aspirational—the clothing and lives desired by many but worn and achieved by few.[6] It presents a high-class, predominantly white and whitewashed world, beyond the reach of most readers. Yet, by inspiring and teaching these mostly female readers about a host of topics, the magazine promises the potential and proximity of this beautiful life.[7] Issues, averaging 350 pages, overflow with advertisements and feature articles to help guide and orient the reader.[8] Regular features include the latest fashion collections and trends, advice on health and beauty, as well as information on those making a name for themselves in the fashion industry. These articles encompass both the international and American fashion scene, providing an American take on a global phenomenon. Alongside these fashion-oriented articles are regular stories on political trends, women's issues (sexuality, marriage, careers), and cultural events (art exhibits, photographers, popular literature).[9]

More than fashion, *Vogue* sells a vision of the good life, a vision dominated by the world of high culture and haute couture. It focuses on idealized representations of and rhetoric about this idyllic realm. This makes sense, as fashion magazines hope to sell advertising space and the centrality of fashion to people's lives. Fashion magazines are, as Leslie W. Rabine notes, "well known as instruments for consumer capitalism," but as she and other scholars remind us, "fashion eludes a purely economic explanation."[10] While the glossy pages filled with images, articles, and advertisements hope to sell products by presenting a beautiful world in which people go to art exhibits, travel internationally, and wear designer clothes, they also encourage readers to cultivate particular attitudes and practices. Nast and his magazines, argues his biographer Caroline Seebohm, "showed Americans how to appreciate modern art, music, photography, and illustration, and in making an intellectual standard of art acceptable to society, he elevated American taste."[11] *Vogue* and other fashion magazines set the standard for taste and class. They contain a wealth of information about prescribed ideals and practices that can illuminate broader trends in American culture.

In terms of fashion, *Vogue*'s focus on the aspirational provides the researcher with a historical guide to popular trends, lauded designers, and valued topics in different time periods. As a prescriptive source, fashion magazines teach the reader "how to look," or, to use the words of scholar David Morgan, a "way of seeing."[12] They train readers how to see and practice fashion, what to wear, how to wear it, where to buy it. Assuming a kind of "trickle-down" approach, fashion magazines rest on the idea that the fashion ideals and products set forth and associated with the upper class will eventually be imitated by the middle and lower classes.[13] As such, using fashion magazines as primary source material informs scholars about what designs, values, and ideals the modern fashion industry hopes will find their way into potential consumers' wardrobes and lives.

Yet fashion magazines do more than prescribe fashion tips and etiquette rules. Perhaps somewhat surprisingly, they also teach readers how to look at religion. They remind us that "in principle, anything, from language to the body, from book to computer, from sculpture to icon can become a religious medium."[14] When I first sat down with a hefty volume of *Vogue*, I wasn't sure what I would find, but as I flipped through countless pages, I saw the concept of religion defined in terms of Christianity and mediated in multiple forms—textual, visual, and material. Words, such as "heavenly," "divine," "prophetic," and "miracle," denoted Christianity, as did symbols, including angels, crosses, and Eve's apple. These words and symbols appeared in advertising copy and illustrations alongside feature articles and photographs on religious topics. Settings ranging from churches to mosaics, clothing designs that resembled nuns' habits, and models with their hands clasped in prayer all evoked the Christian imaginary. From these sources, I was able to sketch the broad contours of how fashion utilized Christianity; however, they also identified central moments, trends, or designs that demanded further examination and more sources.

Thus, in addition to fashion magazines, I examined historical newspapers. Fashion columns and features provided important details about trends, designers, garments, and their reception. Newspapers also enhanced my understanding of fashion's impact on and interpretation within American culture. Further, as Christian designs and symbols became a more frequent part of high fashion apparel, I went beyond fashion magazines and researched designers inspired by and incorporating elements of Christianity. Biographies of designers, books featuring photographs of designers' collections, along with digital archives of these collections and videos of runway shows all became valuable resources for examining how Christianity came to constitute such a regular part of the high fashion industry. Through these additional sources, I was able to flesh out the contours of the Christianity and fashion relationship drawn from *Vogue* and construct a narrative that traces how God got on a dress—how conceptualizations of Christianity shifted from the textual and visual discourse surrounding fashion (articles and advertisements) to its increasing materialization in fashion (jewelry and apparel).

This book, then, is not a traditional or standard religious history. It does not privilege religious sources, recount religious debates, or foreground religious subcultures. Nor is it an ethnographic account of the religious garb people wear or what people do with religiously inspired fashions. Rather, it focuses on how the fashion industry has constructed a vibrant textual, visual, and material discourse on Christianity—through articles, advertisements, accessories, and apparel—that exists alongside and intersects with those discourses that scholars have traditionally deemed religious. Examining fashion's construction of this Christian discourse illustrates how the industry does more than depict angels or nuns' habits; rather, it illuminates how fashion generates a specific vision of the Christian tradition.[15]

I use the term "fashionable religion" to capture this generative vision and perspective. The *Oxford English Dictionary* defines "fashionable" as "good-looking, stylish," which reflects its common usage today. But "fashionable" also means "capable of being shaped or moulded." This word, then, highlights how the fashion industry "shapes and molds" the concept of Christianity in particular ways to produce a vision of religion that it deems "stylish" and "of good appearance."[16] The fashion industry then normalizes this religious perspective and reproduces it in various ways.

Further, even though Christian ideas and images dominate the pages of *Vogue* and the symbols that find their way into the accessories and onto the apparel of the fashion industry, I use the broader concept of "religion," rather than the more specific "Christianity" to capture this generative process. This choice emphasizes the ways in which the fashion industry actively shapes and constructs popular conceptualizations of religion and the religious, while my examination focuses on one particular tradition. Studying fashion does not simply provide a window into Christianity; rather, it represents an important and powerful way for scholars to examine how religions are constituted and evolve.[17] Thus, I hope others will be prompted to analyze diverse fashion mediations of "religion," even as this book focuses on how the fashion industry draws upon, reshapes, and embellishes Christianity.

Specifically, I argue that in the latter half of the twentieth century the modern fashion industry constructed an aestheticized vision of Christianity deemed fashionable. By "reprocessing" elements of Christianity—decontextualizing them from their theological and institutional contexts and recontextualizing them within the sartorial realm[18]—the fashion industry accustomed people to seeing it in bits and pieces. This aestheticized perspective modeled how to approach the Christian tradition and its heritage in ways that emphasized the seeking individual over the religious institution, the sensual reaction over contextual knowledge, and the local experience over global systems.[19] This, in turn, helped to construct a fashionable religion that envisioned Christianity as a diffuse and benevolent supernatural force that inspired beautiful artistic wonders and bestowed enchanted gifts that offered moments of awe that could transform people's lives. It blended historical Christian elements with modern liberal Protestant values and Catholic iconography in ways that offered the possibility of being religious while avoiding the unfashionable stigma of being a religious conservative or "primitive." As such, it provided progressive Catholics, liberal Protestants, and spiritual seekers—groups separated by a "blurry" if not porous dividing line[20]—an alternative and stylish way of being religious.

An Altered Approach to Religion and Fashion

In foregrounding how elements of Christianity became part of couture designs and the fashionable religion produced by the fashion industry, I confronted longstanding patterns in scholarly and popular conceptualizations of the relationship between religion and fashion. In many ways, the seeds of scholarship and popular thinking about fashion were sown in the Garden of Eden. Church "fathers" and Christian theologians have labeled the events of Genesis 3 as the "fall of man." Not only does this passage record the "original sin," but it also makes a statement about fashion. It introduces clothing as one of the results of sinful behavior. Eve's eating of the fruit and her sharing it with Adam produced knowledge of their nakedness. "Then the eyes of both were opened, and they knew that they were naked; and they sewed fig leaves together and made loincloths for themselves" (NRSV Genesis 3:7). The image of Adam and Eve adorned with fig leaves has become iconic, while dominant interpretations of this passage imply that in a perfect and pre-fallen world, clothing was unnecessary.

Over time two seemingly antagonistic discourses, religion (dominated by Western Christianity) and fashion, would grow from these biblically rooted seeds.[21] Framed as binary opposites, religion represents that which is spiritual, serious, and substantive, while fashion is material, silly, and superficial. Religion focuses on the interior, while fashion adorns the exterior. Religion focuses on the divine, while fashion centers the self. Men lead religions, while women consume fashions. Religion is sacred; fashion is profane.

Historical sources demonstrate the pervasiveness of this framework in Christianity. For example, in the thirteenth century, to deter the sins of vanity and pride the Dominican and Augustinian religious orders forbade their members from wearing coral, amber, and crystal paternosters (a string of beads used for prayers).[22] Apparently, though, not all agreed with or abided by these restrictions, which necessitated admonitions against such practices. "By the end of the 15th century a reforming preacher in France was even giving sermons where paternosters were cited along with worldly wealth and mistresses as things to be renounced by the pious."[23] Within Protestantism in the eighteenth century, John Wesley, in *Advice to the People Called Methodists, with Regard to Dress*, urged his followers to adopt neat and plain dress, by which he meant cheap and grave (as opposed to airy), and to not wear gold, pearls, or precious stones. By doing so, he hoped to distinguish "good" Christians from the "singularities" of Quaker dress and the indulgences of "the world."[24] Similarly, Martha Finch's investigation of the "Old Clothes Controversy" that plagued one sixteenth-century Separatist congregation shows how fashion symbolized the sin of pride for some church members. Finch explains that for congregant George Johnson "his sister-in-law's pride was so offensive because it was so publicly and extravagantly displayed upon her body, in velvet, lace, whalebone, and gold."[25] These sources show how Christian leaders emphasized the antagonism between the spiritual and the sartorial, a trend that continues in some religious circles today.

The modern fashion industry often reinforces this interpretation. Upholding art for art's sake and its freedom from conventional authorities, including religion and religious institutions, the fashion system frames itself as secular, progressive, and avant-garde. Wintour's *Vogue* cover featuring a cross-embellished jacket, then, appears as surprising and cutting-edge, and perhaps controversial, but garners little more thought. Given the dominance of this binary thinking and rhetoric, inclusions of religion appear occasional and exceptional, rather than as part of a larger historical trajectory.

This dominant, antagonistic framework helps to explain why textbooks in both fashion studies and religious studies neglect one another. Religion remains absent from standard texts, such as *Fashion Today*, *A History of Costume in the West*, and *20th-Century Dress in the United States*. According to the indices, *Reforming Women's Fashion, 1850–1920* mentions Christianity on one page, while the index to *Survey of Historic Costume* refers readers to religious dress—Egyptian, Greek, and Roman. These narratives suggest that the sacred realm rarely impinges upon fashion and that religion, once upon a time, shaped the attire of more "primitive" people, but no longer.

Similarly, fashion, costume, and dress occupy little more than a footnote in textbooks of American religious history, implicitly reinforcing the sacred/profane dichotomy. Book-length studies and articles on religious dress helpfully highlight the history and significance of clothing in religious life, often utilizing a Durkheimian approach that emphasizes the distinction and hostility between the "sacred" and "profane" realms.[26] For example, Linda B. Arthur's edited volume *Religion, Dress and the Body* examines the distinctive forms of dress donned by religious subcultures, including Amish and Mormons, Hasidic Jews, and Catholic nuns.[27] In doing so, it employs Durkheim's ideas as Arthur explains: "The binary opposition of the sacred and the profane are intentionally used to separate these religious groups from the larger culture."[28] This approach helpfully highlights how these communities used dress to reinforce theological norms and create community distinctiveness.

Subsequent historical and ethnographic studies focused on religion and fashion have challenged the dominant Durkheimian dichotomy. Jenna Weissman Joselit's *A Perfect Fit* focuses on how the relationship between clothing and character shaped collective identity in the United States in the late nineteenth and early twentieth centuries.[29] Joselit's cultural history emphasizes the connections between religion and fashion. Similarly, in her article "The Robes of Womanhood" Pamela Klassen shows how nineteenth-century African American Methodist women used forms of fashionable dress to claim religious leadership and challenge white male privilege.[30] Recent ethnographic studies, such as Emma Tarlo's *Visibly Muslim* and Elizabeth Bucar's *Pious Fashion*, highlight Muslim women's spiritual and sartorial agency, as well as the creation of Islamic fashion. Bucar's fieldwork in Tehran, Yogyakarta, and Istanbul highlights the diverse and evolving aesthetics of Islamic fashion(s), while Tarlo focuses on the Islamic fashion scene in Britain and the complexities involved in "looking Muslim."[31] These studies helpfully problematize Durkheim and highlight the interplay between religious identity, dress, and fashion. In doing so, they demonstrate, as Colleen McDannell argues, "the scrambling of the sacred and the profane" that has occurred throughout the history of American Christianity, and religion more broadly.[32]

Yet, the current scholarly lens only focuses on how religious individuals and groups use dress and fashion. It has not expanded to provide a model for or explanation of the data I found in fashion magazines, fashion columns, or designers' collections. It does not account for numerous references to Christian symbols and elements that appeared over time and across various dimensions of the fashion industry with little comment or controversy. As a result, I kept asking and assembling a way to answer: What does American Christianity look like if we shift our attention to fashion sources?

These fashion sources provide an alternative perspective on American Christianity. In a 1964 article for *Harper's Bazaar*, socialite and fashion icon Gloria Guinness wrote an article entitled "Eve and the First Dress." She proclaimed in this slightly humorous piece that "It is Eve who started it all." According to Guinness, a bored, intelligent, and imaginative Eve sought something more, something new. "Without thinking, but trying to do so, Eve picked a large beautiful leaf, and concentrating on thinking began to pass the leaf over her face and hair, and then lower and lower along her body, until suddenly, the hand stopped. And Eve knew. And from that moment on the textile industry has ruled the world."[33] In this twist on the "fall of man," Guinness highlights the significance of clothing, the intellect of women, and the power of fashion. Rather than lament Eve's sin, Guinness's article celebrates Eve's imagination and creativity. This fashionable retelling of the biblical account provides one example of how Christianity is woven into the fabric of the modern fashion industry. It exemplifies how Christianity is *a part of*, not *apart from*, fashion.

By conceptualizing Christianity as a part of fashion, I incorporated the "scrambling" of sacred and profane utilized by other scholars, but, at the same time, altered its focus from "religious" to "nonreligious" sources and from demand to supply. Put another way, this book focuses on fashion's circulation of and communication about religion, rather than that of religious practitioners and practices. This shift in perspective foregrounds how religious ideas, symbols, and gestures appeared in and moved through the fashion industry. By attending to the ways that the fashion industry infused its products with dimensions of Christianity, we can see how fashion, along with other forms of popular culture, constitutes a form of religious communication.[34] Thus, fashionable religion not only reflects existing elements of American Christianity, but it also constructs new and altered "expressive forms, discourses, moods, and modes of debate."[35] It shapes how we look at, see, and experience the Christian tradition.

Conceptualizing fashion as a form of communication builds on a dominant scholarly trajectory in fashion studies. This trajectory highlights not only the relationship between wearer and worn but also the ways clothing provides insights into broader culture. For example, Malcolm Barnard explains, "clothing as fashion, as communication, are cultural phenomena in that culture may itself be understood as a signifying system, as the ways in which a society's experiences, values and beliefs are communicated through practices, artefacts, and institutions."[36] Similarly, Fred Davis argues that fashion symbolically conveys "images, thoughts, sentiments, and sensibilities."[37] Numerous studies of religion and dress rely on this perspective to understand religious practitioners; however, it has not been applied more generally to the fashion industry and the ways it creates and circulates Christian ideas, symbols, gestures, and more. This book analyzes this discursive realm.

Further, in framing fashion as communication I do not restrict my analysis to the written word. Colleen McDannell, in addition to her "scrambling" of Durkheim's categories, highlights the importance of examining the material dimensions of religious life. She explains, "People learn the discourses and habits of their religious community through the material dimensions of Christianity."[38] McDannell and other scholars since have persuasively shown that "meaning production is not disembodied and abstract, but deeply sensorial and material."[39] Thus, throughout this book, I attend to illustrations and photographs as well as words and captions. Symbols and gestures, as well as props and backdrops, matter. Clothing designs and embellished garments matter. David Morgan argues, "pictures [and objects] are not merely illustrations of nonvisual events" but rather a "powerful way in which" things, including religion, "happen."[40] Studying these sources, then, provides us with a way to understand how religion "happens" visually and materially. Fashion illustrations, designer garments, and advertising images featuring religious elements cultivate a particular way of seeing Christianity, which, in turn, communicates fashionable religion.[41]

A Haute Couture Vision of American Christianity

Examining this fashionable religion deepens our understanding of American Christianity in the latter half of the twentieth century. At midcentury, the idea of Christianity, its meaning, shape, and manifestations, was changing, and these changes laid the foundation for the religious shifts that would dominate subsequent decades. Robert Ellwood emphasizes that popular religion at this time focused on addressing individuals' "yearnings" and helping them achieve personal power and happiness.[42] Similarly, Wade Clark Roof states that "a new cultural context for religion was emerging, one in which faith was increasingly psychologized and viewed as a matter of one's own choice and in keeping with one's own experience."[43] He explains how this "expansive self" necessitates "an unending search for moments of transcendence." In this cultural milieu, people become "spiritual omnivores" hungry for new and ever more meaningful experiences.[44]

Robert Wuthnow's findings reinforce this understanding, but he uses a different metaphor. He argues that religious life in the United States was shifting from "dwelling" to "seeking." The once dominant mode and mood of Christianity, focused on the church, the home, and the nation, was changing to one of religious seeking, characterized by individual exploration and negotiation of "new spiritual vistas" that offered "sacred moments," rather than sustained faith.[45]

This changing religious landscape helped shape the fabric of fashionable religion even as the structures and norms of the fashion industry embellished and tailored it in particular ways. The fashion industry trained people to see Christianity in terms of extractable visual elements that could be interpreted and experienced individually in nonreligious contexts. Roof's description of the emerging spiritual marketplace of the time helps make sense of this interpretation. "Casting religion in subjective terms meshes well with a highly individualistic, inward-looking culture, and particularly its emphasis upon spiritual openness and expansion. Symbols are selectively retrieved and interpreted or re-interpreted, in the creation of alternative universes of meaning."[46] Roof further explains that this communication is predominantly visual as religious symbols are "lifted out of one cultural setting, and 're-embedded' into another."[47] Fashionable religion communicated, assumed, and utilized many of the symbols of Christianity in ways that simultaneously reinforced, expanded, and altered existing religious trends.

Within this changing religious context, the Christianity evoked and produced by the fashion industry not only wove together these threads of individualism, sacred seeking, and visual culture but also incorporated the ethos of liberal Protestantism with elements of the Catholic "sacramental imagination."[48] Tracy Fessenden persuasively demonstrates how in the nineteenth and early twentieth centuries a "Protestantized conception of religion control[led] the meanings of both the religious and the secular."[49] She urges scholars to consider "the consolidation of a Protestant ideology that has grown more entrenched and controlling even as its manifestations have often become less visibly religious."[50] Similarly, N. J. Demerath argues that even as mainline, liberal Protestant denominations declined in the twentieth century, their values—individualism, freedom, pluralism, tolerance, democracy, and intellectual inquiry—"triumphed" in American culture.[51] These liberal Protestant values are integrated into the fabric of fashionable religion.

At the same time, though, heavily influenced by the fashion industry's roots in a Western Europe steeped in Catholic history, this fashionable religion also embraced elements of Catholicism. Cities such as Paris, Milan, and Rome shaped the lives of many esteemed fashion designers. Further, their rich visual and material Catholic heritage epitomized notions of "taste" and "high culture," while also fostering a sense of sacramentality. This sensibility emphasized God's presence and grace in the world; it highlighted how divine potential infused the mundane and material realms of life.[52] Numerous Protestant converts to Catholicism described how "the beauty," "the sensuality," and "the grandeur" of Catholicism provided an "antidote" to liberal Protestant rationality.[53]

In addition, from 1945 through the early 1960s, Catholicism became a more prominent and respected part of the American religious landscape. Historian Sally Dwyer-McNulty demonstrates that Catholics occupied a "visual high point" at this time and explains that "Catholic clothing became a fixture in the American imagination."[54] Catholicism's aesthetic heritage, its more affirmative position on the material world, and its increasing visual presence in the mid-twentieth century not only influenced the fabric of fashionable religion but also provided it with a culturally familiar repository of symbols to retrieve and refashion.

By fusing the values and ethos of liberal Protestantism with the aesthetics and visual iconography of Catholicism, fashionable religion became a stylish participant in the emerging spiritual marketplace. Through supplying a familiar yet altered set of religious ideas, symbols, and artifacts, fashionable religion shaped the conversation about Christianity, and religion more broadly, in the latter half of the twentieth century. Religion, Kelly Besecke argues, is about not only social institutions or individualized beliefs but also "societal conversation about transcendent meanings." She explains: "By recognizing communication about transcendent meanings as a primary dimension of religion, we can begin to comprehend the 'religion' that takes place in otherwise 'secular' settings such as bookstores, lecture halls, movie theaters, and cafes."[55] As part of the conversation, fashionable religion simultaneously reinforced and shaped existing religious trends in ways that upheld Christian assumptions and dominance even as Christianity's meanings grew more diffuse and mainline Protestant institutions declined. As the American spiritual marketplace expanded, fashionable religion modeled tasteful ways of thinking about and adapting to the changing religious landscape. Simultaneously, the textual and visual contributions of fashionable religion provided those interested fashion followers with ways to customize and tailor their religious experiences through cultivating their appreciation of religious art or purchasing a particular product. It also offered those in marginalized religious traditions a model of what "good" and "tasteful" religion should look like if they wanted to "fit in" to the dominant religious scene.[56]

This fashion-oriented approach to American religious history since 1945 builds on and adds to current studies of post–World War II religion.

By focusing on fashion sources, which privilege visual and material forms of religion, we can see how, as Wade Clark Roof writes, "since midcentury especially, the images and symbols of religion have undergone a quiet transformation."[57] Scholars and others often comment on this transformation and decontextualization of religious symbols, especially when bejeweled crosses appear on the cover of *Vogue*. Such uses are often understood as part of the diminishing role of religious institutions and the rise of spirituality—where people seek "authentic inner life and personhood," rather than "group identity and social location."[58] These insightful studies utilize sources such as survey data, religious literature, personal interviews, and field observation to demonstrate this profound shift in the religious landscape. From these studies and others, we know the political, legal, and religious contours of this topographical change. They do not, however, map how God got on a dress. Put another way, they do not foreground how the circulation, meaning, and mediation of Christianity changed through the linguistic, visual, and material apparatus of the modern fashion industry. The rise of seeker spirituality revolved around increasing religious diversity, experimentation with alternative belief systems, and the creation of hybrid religious identities. However, it also occurred through and included a strong visual and material dimension not examined in the existing literature. Chronicling this neglected dimension better positions scholars to understand the current religious landscape and the multiple resources from which people are constructing hybrid religious worlds.

The fashionable religion promoted by the fashion industry is perhaps best described as idealized. Like the fashions that permeate the pages of magazines or walk the runway show, this fashionable religion celebrates beauty and wonder, innovation and enchantment. It would be tempting to dismiss the beautiful Christianity presented by fashion as nothing more than rhetorical flourishes and symbolic accessories designed to increase publicity and sales. Others might want to dismiss it as a superficial or trivial spirituality. The story of fashionable religion is not, after all, one steeped in the religious institutions (churches, synagogues, mosques), religious people (ministers, missionaries, mystics), and religious values (sacrifice, justice, depth) that scholars of religion expect and typically value. Yet, examining American Christianity through the lens of the modern high fashion industry helps scholars gain a more complicated understanding of the numerous religious transformations that have occurred since 1945.

Reading *Religion in Vogue*

The overall organization of this book is broadly, but not strictly, historical. Each chapter focuses on a different form of religious mediation in fashion—articles, advertisements, jewelry, and designs—that emerged as prominent in a particular time period.[59] This structure highlights how fashion's incorporation of Christianity occurred and evolved over time. While the various forms highlighted in each chapter do not disappear after the time period under study, other forms emerged that expanded the ways fashion shaped and mediated Christianity. Examining this historical process reveals how fashionable religion became more materialized over time, as this evolution eventually included not only texts and images but also cross jewelry and then clothing inspired by religious dress and later garments embellished with religious figures. This increasing materialization personalized fashionable religion, as people could purchase what they liked and wear it on their bodies.

The first two chapters focus on the same time period but examine different sources to establish the historical and dominant ways fashion envisioned Christianity from 1945 through the 1960s. Chapter 1, "Designing New Ways of Seeing Christianity," analyzes the most explicit and common ways of seeing the Christian tradition constructed through fashion magazine articles.[60] These texts provide an important entry point for thinking about the relationship between Christianity and fashion, and they help outline the fashionable religion promoted. Religion-oriented articles did not stop in the 1970s, as fashion magazines addressed the Religious Right and abortion rights, as well as the rise of New Age spiritualties in the 1980s; however, their frequency did decline over time. During this same time, advertisements, the focus of chapter 2, "Making Over Christianity," appeared alongside articles on religious topics. While more implicit, advertising utilized religious language, symbols, and gestures that reinforced a vision of Christianity, and a conception of religion, as supernatural yet sophisticated, beautiful yet attainable and practical. Such ads and visual cues continued beyond the

1960s, but in the late 1960s other religious mediations in fashion appeared on the scene. The addition of new mediations, though, did not mean the disappearance of these older forms (articles and advertisements referencing Christianity continued) but rather demonstrated the increasing breadth of fashionable religion.

The remaining three chapters attend to these increasingly material religious mediations and advance the book's chronology. Chapter 3, "Accessorizing the Cross," traces the rise of cross jewelry as a fashion trend that occurred with little controversy through its more controversial reappearance in the 1980s. Examining the early emergence of this trend also highlights a central shift in how fashion mediated Christianity. Prior to this, fashion's incorporation of Christianity focused on the textual and visual and constituted part of the discourse surrounding fashion. With the popularity of cross jewelry, fashion's mediation of Christianity became more embedded in the material forms of fashion. Fashionable religion was transformed from something you could see—a church, an image in a magazine, a short story—to something you could wear in a stylish and sophisticated way. Chapter 4, "Innovating Religious Dress," addresses fashion's next popular religious mediation—fashion designs (forms and shapes) inspired by religious dress. This chapter focuses on when, how, and why fashion designers found inspiration in Catholicism. Beginning in the late 1960s and emerging periodically thereafter, the garb of monks, nuns, and priests inspired fashion designers, which reinforced a way of seeing Christianity based on decontextualized religious symbols and garments. Attending to this history highlights how fashion constructed visual and material ways of seeing Christianity that focused on the supernatural and experiential.[61] Through the late 1980s, religious mediations in fashion designs referenced Christian symbols, such as the cross, or forms, such as nuns' habits. However, they shied away from pictorial representations of Christian figures, such as Jesus, Mary, and the saints. This changed in the 1990s when high fashion designs began to incorporate such representations. Chapter 5, "Fashioning Holy Figures," chronicles this trend toward increasingly figural representation and its predominant focus on the Virgin Mary. Examining these garments, as well as the controversy surrounding them, further demonstrates fashionable religion's emphasis on visual and material forms. Tracing this evolution of the relationship between religion and fashion highlights how fashion has shaped ways of seeing Christianity in the United States.[62]

The conclusion, "Putting God on a Dress," chronicles the emergence of the Christian God and Savior, Jesus, as the focus of fashion collections in the twenty-first century and examines the implications of this inclusion for fashionable religion and the wider religious landscape. We can better understand the individualistic and unaffiliated trends in contemporary US religious life by analyzing the varied and profound ways the modern fashion industry has shaped conceptions of Christianity and religion. Fashion designer Coco Chanel famously said, "I don't do fashion. I am fashion."[63] In a similar way, then, this book demonstrates that fashion does more than use Christianity; it also helps create it.

1

Designing New Ways of Seeing Christianity

Amid advertisements for makeup and perfume, photographs of the latest designs from Paris, and advice on beauty regimens, a full-page color photograph of Joseph, Mary, and the infant Jesus being watched over by an angel captures the reader's attention. A close-up of exquisitely crafted crèche figurines, the photograph visualizes the religious significance and atmosphere of the season—December 1950. This image accompanies "The Light in the Dark," a Christmas rumination by Anglo-Irish writer Elizabeth Bowen published by *Vogue*. In her musings about the holiday, Bowen explains how Christmas provides a light amid the darkness of daily life. "This reaching out, this signaling through the dark, is for something more than the communication of fears and loneliness: man joins man so that together, they may lift up their hearts . . . from the first, there has been our need for the miracle. As creatures, we are formed to adore and marvel. In answer, we have been given Christmas."[1] The language of miracle continues as Bowen ponders the meaning of the manger. "Is it not, also, the miracle of the scene that supernatural and natural should so sublimely merge?"[2] Christmas, she writes, is "a time when magic joins with holiness."[3] In the person of Jesus and in the season, these two disparate worlds, natural and supernatural, mingle. According to Bowen, such a miraculous occurrence gifts us with a different "sort of vision." With our Christmas eyes, we are able to find joy and delight, experience the innocence of childhood, celebrate with children, revel in mystery, "perceive the especial dearness of what is dear to us," and help others.[4] Neither God nor religion is mentioned in "The Light in the Dark," but it makes a statement about both.

This chapter examines the religion-oriented articles published by fashion magazines from the mid-1940s through the 1960s. In many ways, these articles present an unlikely point of departure. They do not talk about fashion or mention clothes, nor do they quote religious leaders commenting on the latest style trends. Yet, in trying to figure out how God got on a dress, these articles provide a valuable starting point for understanding how fashion conceptualized and presented Christianity in the mid-twentieth century, which shaped the subsequent ways that the modern fashion industry mediated religion.

As purveyors of modern style, current events, and cosmopolitan values, fashion magazines acknowledged the importance of Christianity in the nation and in the lives of readers. In this way, fashion magazines participated in the larger religious and publishing trends of the time. Religion-oriented articles were not featured in every issue of *Vogue* (US) or *Harper's Bazaar*, but they did appear *at least* annually, most often at Easter and Christmastime.[5] These articles demonstrate how Christianity constituted an accepted and expected topic to be covered by fashion, rather than an antagonistic foe. As a result, these articles help scholars see how religious trends were distributed through and adapted by "secular" sources. More than ministers, sermons, and inspirational books purveyed theological and spiritual ideas. Christianity circulated through various sources in American culture, including fashion.[6]

These articles also illuminate the complicated and dynamic relationship between Christianity and fashion. While Elizabeth Bowen identified a different "sort of vision" that occurred at Christmastime, analyzing religiously oriented fashion magazine articles demonstrates how the fashion industry constructed a particular "way of seeing" Christianity. According to David Morgan, this concept entails examining images and the "visual practices" that accompany them as a way to understand how "religion happens visually."[7] Morgan's work highlights how religious traditions construct different visual worlds. This chapter extends Morgan's "ways of seeing" to fashion magazines and the modern fashion industry to analyze the fashionable religion produced and promoted.

Through stories about Christianity and photographs of Christian art and symbols, these magazine articles constructed a fashionable religion that aligned spiritual experience and wonder with the modern and sophisticated sensibility of imagined readers. This fashionable religion revolved around the experiential and the miraculous, the sensual and the mysterious, the individual rather than the institutional. It promised readers spiritual experiences to help move beyond reason, commercialism, and anxiety to feelings of enchantment and experiences of joy—if only they would have the eyes to see, the ears to hear, and the heart to feel.[8]

This fashionable religion, though, facilitated particular ways of seeing Christianity.[9] The promise of extraordinary spiritual experiences
rested on a series of assumptions, attitudes, and practices woven into
the religion-oriented articles that appeared in *Vogue* and *Harper's Bazaar*. While intersecting with one another, I discuss these assumptions,
attitudes, and practices separately below for clarity and to highlight the
nuances of each.

First, fashion magazines published spiritual advice from elite
sources—Ivy League chaplains, Pulitzer Prize–winning authors, esteemed photographers, renowned artists, and aristocratic aesthetes, both
Protestant and Catholic. Not only did the status of these author-artists
imbue their article contents and artistic creations with a sense of sophistication, it also taught readers how to identify the types of religious leaders to whom they should listen—credentialed, educated, and explicitly
or implicitly "liberal" in some regard.[10] Articles avoided any discussion
of Protestant fundamentalism or popular evangelical leaders, such as
Carl Henry and Harold Ockenga, and Billy Graham only merited a very
brief mention.[11] These religious relatives "were at best regarded as unsophisticated and unenlightened cousins without benefit of world-class
theological education, at worst as bigoted zealots."[12] Instead, fashionable
religion instructed readers to embrace cultured Christian leadership.

Second, these religiously oriented fashion magazine articles reinforced the broader trend toward religious individualism gaining popularity at midcentury. The spiritual leaders published in fashion magazines
highlighted the centrality of the individual and her development through
the cultivation of taste and the curation of experiences. This, in turn,
reinforced the increasing emphasis on an "expansive self" enhanced by
the acquisition of particular attitudes and goods.[13] By highlighting the
individual, these religious elites downplayed the significance of religious
institutions and theological dilemmas. At the same time, the vision of
Christianity fostered by fashion magazines combined elements of liberal
Protestantism, including individualism, pluralism, and tolerance, with
features of the Catholic "sacramental imagination," including art, architecture, and ritual.[14] By combining elements of both religious worlds,
this fashionable religion avoided the sterility of Protestant rationality
and the conservatism of Catholic theology.[15] This blending of elements
produced a more diffuse Christianity that appealed to, and blurred the

already fuzzy lines separating, liberal Protestants, progressive Catholics, and spiritual seekers.[16]

Third, fashionable religion promoted sensory experience and spiritual transcendence, but it did not sanction giving in to excessive emotionalism or irrationality—traits implicitly deemed unsophisticated. Instead, fashion magazine articles emphasized human, rather than supernatural, sources for and explanations of these religious experiences. Modern art, photography, and literature, not divine disruptions of the natural world, provided people with ways of moving beyond the mundane. By mediating Christianity through these sophisticated art forms, this fashionable religion offered readers moments of spiritual "delight," rather than religious "delusion."[17] As Bowen put it in her Christmas story, this brand of religion merged the supernatural and the natural. Photographs of "miraculous churches" and firsthand accounts of sensual Catholic processions evoked feelings of wonder and enchantment based on artists' compositions. They created a sense of proximity by drawing the reader in through full-page color photographs and accounts rich in description. At the same time, though, they also established a sense of distance and detachment, as the reader could enjoy "miraculous churches" or Holy Week in Sicily through the pages of a fashion magazine and, within that, through the lens of a photographer or the words of a Pulitzer Prize–winning writer.[18] This distancing allowed the reader-viewer to see herself as "respectable and superior by substituting observation for participation," which, in turn, infused the depicted religious ideas with a sense of class.[19] Thus, fashion magazines provided readers with a fashionable religion that wove together visions of the supernatural with the logic of modernity.

Fourth, fashionable religion encouraged reader-viewers to see Christianity in bits and pieces. Religion-oriented articles in fashion magazines offered readers access to the wonders of the Christian heritage, art, symbols, and sites, with little contextual framing. For modern people, "reality and authenticity," Dean MacCannell argues, "are thought to be elsewhere: in other historical periods and other cultures, in purer, simpler lifestyles."[20] This kind of tourism rests on extracting elements "from their original natural, historical and cultural contexts," so they can be discovered, seen, and experienced by sightseers.[21] MacCannell highlights patterns that can be seen in fashion magazines' treatment of

Christianity. In the pages of fashion magazines, reader-viewers could discover and see the "authentic" Christianity of others. They could then use these bits and pieces to aid in their individual spiritual journeys. In an increasingly active spiritual marketplace, religious dwellers became "spiritual omnivores" hungry for "sacred moments" and "new spiritual vistas," which could be found in the pages of fashion magazines.[22]

Fifth, as fashionable religion promoted the idea that "real" religion was out there to be discovered and experienced, it invoked the concept of "a universal religious sentiment." This promoted the idea that a common religious essence "lay behind the institutions, scriptures, and creeds of particular religions and that preceded such formal expressions in order of importance."[23] As the United States became more religiously diverse in the 1960s, this concept not only opened up the possibility of learning from other religions but also emphasized the importance of cultivating tolerance, a liberal Protestant value that was increasingly becoming an integral part of broader American mores.[24] Fashionable religion suggested that the cosmopolitan Christian and spiritual seeker were, at the very least, tolerant of religious diversity.

These ways of seeing Christianity were woven into the fashionable religion presented in these articles and contributed important ideas to the larger societal conversation about how religion looked, felt, and worked at midcentury.[25] To highlight this grain in the fabric of fashionable religion, I organize my analysis thematically, rather than chronologically. The first section examines how religion-oriented fashion magazine articles diagnosed the dominant religious mood at midcentury and how these ways of seeing Christianity helped provide the cure. The subsequent sections provide a more in-depth examination of the ways fashion magazines presented and hoped to instill these ways of seeing in three commonly featured topics—Christmas, church, and pilgrimage.

Seeking Faith in Fashion Magazines

At midcentury, profound shifts occurred throughout the American religious landscape. In the aftermath of World War II, Americans struggled to make sense of the war's brutality and its political implications. The Cold War began, and McCarthyism emerged. As the United States fought against "godless" communism, many Americans sought to reaffirm their national and Christian identity. Church building boomed and church attendance soared, peaking in 1955 and again in 1958. During these years almost half of the US population, approximately 47 percent, attended church services.[26] Sunday schools overflowed, media exalted the nuclear family, and "under God" was added to the Pledge of Allegiance.

Patriotism, revivalism, and conformity characterized the 1950s; yet, it was also a decade of intense anxiety. "If wartime terror was the dominant emotion of the early 1940s," writes historian Patrick Allitt, "a more diffuse anxiety seemed to be the dominant emotion of the decade's later years."[27] Headlines confirmed the extent of this malaise. In February of 1950, the *New York Times* reported that "mental health" was "this country's 'No. 1 health problem.'"[28] During this decade, the number of mentally ill people in both Europe and the United States increased and peaked at mid-decade.[29] In 1955, the *Chicago Daily Tribune* proclaimed that mental illness remained "the nation's No. 1 health problem," and that "at least 10 million Americans—one in every 16—are now suffering from some form of mental aberration."[30] By 1959, the Deputy Surgeon General of the United States' Public Health Service pronounced that American society was "living near [a] mental abyss."[31]

Numerous people warded off the feelings of fragmentation and the "mental abyss" by attending church and participating in what Erin A. Smith calls the "cult of reassurance." This religious trend "repackaged American faith in the individual and his boundless capacity for achievement in psychological and theological language."[32] Religious self-help books by popular religious leaders, such as Fulton Sheen, Norman Vincent Peale, and Rabbi Joshua Loth Liebman, dominated best-seller lists and "periodicals of every stripe were increasing their coverage of religion."[33] Advice columns and "self-help books . . . promised readers escape from spiritual emptiness through the fusion of religion and psychology."[34] The success and scope of these publishing endeavors emphasizes the complex combination of anxiety and hope, insecurity and promise that characterized the era.

In keeping with broader publishing trends, fashion magazines also acknowledged people's proximity to the "mental abyss,"[35] and offered spiritual reassurance by publishing the works of elite Christian leaders and award-winning authors. For example, in 1950, Columbia University Chaplain James A. Pike's article title, "A God-Shaped Blank in Man's

Heart," captured the "dark" described by Bowen—the sense that something was amiss. Pike described the troubled cultural mood and invited readers in by acknowledging the problem. "An increasing number of people show the marks of insecurity. What are they? Anxiety, sense of guilt, loneliness, sense of frustration, despair."[36] Similarly, Princeton University Chapel's Dean Emeritus, Robert Russell Wicks, highlighted the culture's "confused state of mind." "Our faith," he explained, "claims that under the Providence of God life has a meaning. But with wars and atomic explosions there is enough going on in the world to make it all look senseless."[37] Despair and anomie characterized the atmosphere,[38] and Pulitzer Prize–winning author René Dubos acknowledged that "the concept of perfectibility and progress has deteriorated."[39]

In addition to introducing readers to credentialed and cultured religious leaders skilled in diagnosing the current cultural malaise, Vogue's featured elites also provided ideas about a cure. These articles fostered a way of seeing Christianity focused on the individual and her development.[40] They assured readers that Christianity held the answers to their problems. In doing so, they embraced liberal theological tenets, psychological theories, and engaged readers through a personalized style that fostered intimacy with readers.[41]

Vogue published purveyors of the "cult of reassurance," such as Bishop Fulton Sheen, known for his best-selling Peace of Soul, as well as his work in radio and television. Immensely popular, the Catholic Sheen, similar to liberal Protestants of the time, embraced psychology and framed "problems in modern language for modern people."[42] He acknowledged the fraught political-religious climate, yet entitled his piece "Hope"—an encouraging word for readers perched on the edge of the "mental abyss." His article explained to readers that "hope is possible only when matters are hopeless. This, then, should be an age of hope." Citing the lessons learned by the wayward Prodigal Son, rather than dogma of the Catholic Church, Sheen encouraged readers to help others and reassured readers that "hopelessness *is* the beginning of hope."[43] Sheen and other popular writers published in fashion magazines insisted on Christianity's continuing significance in and answers to an anxious age.

Pike's 1950 essay "A God-Shaped Blank in Man's Heart" made this promise clear by highlighting Christianity's embrace of science. His discussion combined psychology—the unconscious mind, psychosomatic illness, schizophrenia, and inferiority complex—with Christianity. He focused on the individual's often misguided negotiation of her spiritual life. Anxiety, he reasoned, resulted from individuals relying on the unreliable. "It is this suspicion—the suspicion that our 'god' will not meet our full needs—that leads us to erect other gods to meet our needs." Ultimately, the problem, Pike explained, was idolatry, which resulted in a type of polytheistic schizophrenia. The cure to such a malady, then, was belief in one God accompanied by self-acceptance. Jettisoning any language of sin or denomination, Pike assured readers of God's acceptance of the striving individual.[44]

Two years later, Princeton's Robert Russell Wicks echoed Pike's diagnosis of the problem, as well as his message about anxiety and idolatry. "The peril of the world today," he explained, "is not that there are unbelievers but that there are too many who believe in the wrong things." Like Pike, Wicks emphasized liberal Protestantism's increasingly accepted tenets, including adaptation and religiously based progressivism.[45] For religion to be helpful, he argued, people needed to separate "the timeless truth of the message from the particular situation in which it emerged. To be transmitted alive, the eternal essence must come to life again in the experience of the present."[46] This claim simultaneously diminished the significance of religious institutions and encouraged readers to actively look for and cultivate skills in separating "truth" from "form." This position, in turn, encouraged people to look for manifestations of "a universal religious sentiment," that would offer spiritual reassurance and meaningful ways to enchant a world increasingly seen as "disenchanted."[47]

Together, these Christian leaders, including Sheen, Pike, and Wicks, provided fashionable religion with a respected liberal and individual theological apparatus for thinking about Christianity at midcentury. Fashion magazines also featured other award-winning writers, esteemed artists, and figures of the past, which provided the "sacred moments" from other times, places, and contexts sought by spiritual seekers.

For example, Pulitzer Prize–winning poet, writer, and Catholic, Phyllis McGinley looked to the past to offer readers spiritual reassurance and joy in the present. *Vogue* published two of her articles, "A Little Grace" and "The Wit of Saints," that recount McGinley's relationship with the saints. She describes her practice as "saint watching"—a spiritual pursuit she began when imitation of these "men and women larger than life" proved impossible. Here it is worth noting that McGinley shifts herself away from the daunting goal of Christian perfection and moves into the position of interested and inspired observer. Instead of seeking spiritual heights or intense religious devotion, McGinley invited readers to join her on a quest to "chip away the plaster and release the merry human being" inside the saint. Implicitly embracing Wicks' model of separating "essence" from form, McGinley's articles highlight the humanity—the heart, humor, and ordinariness—to be found in even the most perfect saint. "They lost their tempers, got hungry, scolded God, were egotistical or testy or impatient, made mistakes and regretted them. Still they went on doggedly blundering toward heaven."[48] They also wrote songs, loved their friends, and told jokes.[49] Laughter, for McGinley, was a must and she vaguely recalled that the Catholic canonization process "demands proof of joy in the candidate."[50] McGinley found "gaiety" and joy in the jokes of Teresa of Avila and the billiard playing of Ignatius. Such a discovery reassured McGinley and readers that "there is truly laughter in holy places."[51] Consequently, McGinley and others began to accustom readers to this spiritual practice in fashionable religion—extracting Christian elements and ideas from their original contexts and viewing the past as a place for finding "authentic" Christianity. These elements could then be consumed as part of the diet available to hungry spiritual omnivores seeking more robust religious selves.

A 1960 article entitled "The Wisdom of the Desert" also exemplified this decontextualized and individualized way of viewing Christianity, past and present. Prior to a page full of quotes from various Desert Fathers, those third-century Christian ascetics who sought God in the desert landscape, prefatory remarks provided readers with a proper interpretive lens. This preface advised readers that they did not and should not flee the world, as did these great men of faith. It assured readers that an extreme religious commitment was neither desired nor necessary. As with McGinley's position of "saint-watching," the role of observer was preferred. Readers should distill the "essence"—the underlying lesson—that guided the ascetics' departure: a faith characterized by love and freedom. An "uncompromising" love of God and others drove these men to the desert. Refusing to be "passively ruled by a decadent society," "they sought a way to God that was uncharted and freely chosen." As the original seekers, the Desert Fathers rejected things "lofty," "esoteric," and "theoretical," and instead "distilled a practical and unassuming wisdom that is at once primitive and timeless."[52] Such men—"human," "ordinary," and "simple"—encouraged readers to see the Christian past as a vast resource for present day inspiration, which could, in turn, help them construct their own spiritual paths not bound by the dictates of others. In the list of extracted "wisdom," the first quote from the Desert Fathers emphasized the importance of this individual spirituality: "Each man should act according to his own spiritual way."[53]

Religiously oriented articles in fashion magazines embraced the language of reassurance and individualism that dominated the religious landscape. In response to the anxiety and despair that characterized midcentury life, fashionable religion offered people joy and laughter, simple faith and spiritual freedom. Featuring acclaimed religious leaders and writers infused fashionable religion with a sense of sophistication and cutting-edge relevance. It also encouraged people to see fashionable religion as something that they could extract from the past and experience through observation (rather than participation). It accustomed readers to seeing religion in more hybrid ways by blending elements of different religious traditions, particularly elements of liberal Protestant theology with Catholic history. In the next section, we will see how readers could acquire these ways of seeing and apprehending fashionable religion—what Bowen described as "Christmas vision"—through a particular understanding of the holiday.

Cultivating Christmas Vision

After World War II, the nostalgia for and popularity of Christmas increased.[54] Christmas movies from the 1940s and 1950s, including *It's a Wonderful Life*, *Miracle on 34th Street*, and *How the Grinch Stole Christmas*, and new Christmas carols, ranging from "Let It Snow, Let It Snow, Let It Snow" to "I'll Be Home for Christmas," emphasized the specialness of the holiday, its public presence, and the centrality of children.[55] Yet, even as Christmas occupied an increasingly dominant position in mid-twentieth-century American culture, no one vision of this holiday existed. Jewish rabbis debated its observance and Catholic confraternities urged the faithful to "Put Christ Back into Christmas" as early as 1949.[56] Within this context, fashion magazines articulated their own fashionable vision of Christmas.

Most of the religion-focused articles published in fashion magazines appeared in the months of November and December. *Vogue*, for example, regularly featured Christmas-themed articles from the late 1940s through the late 1980s. For readers struggling with the "mental abyss" or seeking "sacred moments" to enhance their sense of self, Christmas features provided the promise of reassurance and transcendence. In the twentieth century, "Christmas," as one scholar notes, "ha[d] come to function as the last widely celebrated public recognition of the miraculous."[57] Fashion magazine articles, as seen in Bowen's "The Light in the Dark," acknowledged this theme. They also emphasized the joy of faith, as with McGinley's saint-watching, and the possibility of religious experience. Attaining these "sacred moments," though, necessitated that readers cultivate a way of seeing Christianity through various art forms, such as stories, poems, and images, deemed sophisticated.[58] This, in turn, accustomed reader-viewers to seeing Christianity in the visual works and literary words of artists, as well as in other times and places. As such, it again emphasized the individual's spiritual experience and the cultivation of her spiritual imagination. This blending of spiritual experiences with artistic forms wove together Christian ideas of the supernatural with the demands of modernity. Such a combination produced a "different sort of vision"—a religion of eyes, ears, and heart that a variety of seekers could embrace.

Articles ranging from short stories to poems to artwork to photoessays emphasized the emotional, visual, and spiritual impact of this special holiday. Featuring color photographs of Christmas art, including Nativity scenes, rare crèche sets, and children's drawings, these articles reinforced a particular way of seeing Christianity—literally. Articles included "for the first time in colour" a range of works by influential artists, such as Giovanni Bellini, known as the Father of the Venetian Renaissance, and French painter Georges de La Tour, and, by doing so, schooled readers in the history of art and a particular vision of Christmas.[59] The inclusion of these lauded artistic creations celebrating the birth of Jesus emphasized the potential of art to generate spiritual experience and then offered reader-viewers a way to experience it—on their own and in the pages of a magazine.

For example, a short story entitled "Christmas Night" describes a Christmas service in a tiny Swedish village in evocative detail. On this snowy night the birch trees trembled, bells rang, candles burned, and people sang. In the little church, decorated with "century-old masterpieces of art," the people found themselves "spellbound" by the holiday experience.[60] The story holds out the promise to readers that they, too, could have such a magical and meaningful Christmas. The article implies that by reading about the faith of rural Swedish folk, modern people could partake in this experience of simple and "authentic" Christianity found in another time and place.

In addition, the story emphasizes how a sensory context filled with amazing art enhanced people's experience of Christmas. Such art surrounded the people in the Swedish village church, and *Vogue* made it available to readers. A color print of "The Presentation at the Temple" by Bellini and a full-page image of Matisse's charcoal sketch of "Madonna and Child" ("never reproduced before") accompanied the "Christmas Night" story.[61] Bellini's painting, representative of the Italian Renaissance, and Matisse's drawing, symbolic of Modern Art, not only educated the reader-viewer about important artists and styles but also emphasized art's enduring relevance to the holiday. This encouraged reader-viewers to cultivate the spiritual power of art, without having to become a saint, ascetic, or a Swedish peasant. This helped reader-viewers see how they could have similar "sacred moments" by reading stories and looking at art.

This article and others encouraged reader-viewers to discover "real" Christianity in the art and experiences of other times, places, and people.[62] The "reality" or "authenticity" attributed to the celebration described in "Christmas Night" rested on its associations with simplicity and rural living. Other articles also emphasized this sense of simplicity through stories featuring children—an increasingly central focus on the holiday.[63] These articles wrapped Christmas and children together in ways that urged readers to acknowledge their unique gifts—joy, simplicity, and freedom. Children's drawings of manger scenes and magi with gifts conveyed youthful excitement. For example, describing her drawing of the three kings, one young artist remarked, "It's the most joyful thing I can think of." "Untouched by education," "unspoiled," in their play and in their art, children "may come on that divine accident in which new visual discoveries are made."[64] Free from artistic and religious constraints, children embodied joy, represented creative potential, and symbolized hope. As another Christmastime article explained: "In the innocence and grace, and in the sense of joy and mystery that children express, the promise of the future resides."[65] Such articles fostered the idea that readers would discover the joys of faith and life by nurturing their own childlike sensibilities and creative potential. Like children, they should not be constrained by dated rules or unthinking conformity, but rather embrace lives characterized by freedom, joy, and laughter.

At the same time, though, these articles tempered childish enthusiasm and emotion with discipline and class. The same article that featured exuberant children's drawings and extolled their simple joys also emphasized the need for control through photographs. These full-page black and white photos showed aristocratic children—the children of Mr. and Mrs. John Jacob Astor, the Marquess and Marchioness of Anglesey, and Mr. and Mrs. Douglas Auchincloss—embodying different Christmas traits, "waiting, hoping, listening." For example, "Waiting," pictured the Astor children, Michael and Stella, wearing their pajamas and bathrobes. In the image, they each hold a lit candle in one hand and a teddy bear in the other. They gaze directly at the camera and their expressions are serious, but their body positions convey anticipation. Perched at the bottom of the stairs, Michael's body leans forward and his little sister Stella sits half on and half off the first step. Poised to run to the tree, to open presents, to experience the magic of Christmas, they wait. This photograph along with the others encouraged readers to cultivate and experience the emotions represented, but, at the same time, the photographed children are serious, posed, and frozen in time, which connoted a sense that readers should exercise some discipline and control over their emotions.[66]

This simultaneous fostering and disciplining of religious experience and emotion through art forms also appeared in other Christmas articles, particularly those featuring the infant Jesus. These vibrant images and their accompanying text framed art as a sophisticated and appropriate way for people to see Jesus and apprehend the feeling of the holiday. They focused on the visual and the emotional, rather than the religious or theological. For example, one article contrasted the "rigid, stern," and "blank" expressions typical of Byzantine art with a unique Nativity

Figure 1.1. "Waiting," a Christmastime photograph of Michael and Stella Astor by Toni Frissell that appeared in "Christmas: The Children's Miracle," *Vogue* 122 (December 1953): 78; Toni Frissell/ *Vogue* © Condé Nast.

example in which "human feelings appeared" on the faces of a Byzantine Mary, Jesus, and the angels surrounding them. Little more is said, but its December publication, along with a color foldout feature that yielded a two-page close-up of the fresco, encouraged a response simultaneously artistic and spiritual.[67] Fashion magazines avoided alienating readers with theological specificity. Instead, they encouraged readers to view religious art as a sophisticated spiritual tool that they could use to cultivate their own spiritual interpretations.

Monk, writer, and activist Thomas Merton had embraced this spiritual imagination and *Vogue* shared it with people by publishing his 1944 poem, "Holy Child's Song," in December of 1970. Written in the voice of the Christ Child, Merton's poem shared the infant and infinite Jesus's inner thoughts. Lines, such as "Incarnate joys dance in the bright rays of My childish voice!" and "I sit in this crib, and laugh like fire," paint a picture of unbounded laughter and love. The verses urge ancient shepherds and modern readers to come and "adore My joy."[68] As with other examples, fashion magazines celebrated the joy provided by Christianity, but at the same time connected these emotions to an acclaimed religious figure and an art form, poetry.

Jesus constituted part of this visual religion, but in these articles the power of Christmas loosed Jesus from the bonds of churches and doctrine. "The Land of Jesus," published in December 1963, invited readers to ponder the example of Jesus through art and draw their own conclusions. Characterizing Jesus as a "wandering preacher," who shared "his prophetic love—love, the real Christmas word," the article illustrated the life of Jesus. Bible verses, famous religious art, and a landscape photograph of its assumed location accompany each central life moment— Nativity, Baptism, Sermon on the Mount, and Transfiguration. Rather than telling readers about the life of Jesus and getting into potentially controversial theological debates about the Virgin birth or the status of Jesus' miracles, this textual and visual approach invited them into his life and encouraged them to cultivate their own interpretations.[69] The caption to a photograph of the Jordan River, for example, pondered the possibilities: "John the Baptist, perhaps dressed as a Bedouin, may have performed the great Baptism" in such a location. The accompanying image, a drawing of "The Baptism of Christ" by Peter Paul Rubens housed at the Louvre, also prompted the reader-viewer to consider the magnitude of this moment. The images and text accompanying the Sermon on the Mount also emphasized the spiritual imagination. A reproduction of Claude Lorrain's drawing, "The Sermon on the Mount," and an excerpt from the Beatitudes in Matthew 5 appeared alongside a photograph of the Sea of Galilee. The caption reads: "When Jesus stood on the Mount of Beatitudes in the country now known as Israel, He looked down at the people gathered by the trees near the shores of the sea of Galilee. What He may have seen can be seen on the facing page."[70] This spiritual imagining encouraged readers to think about religion as a visual, emotional, and individual activity that they could customize and experience on their own terms.

Whether in the 1940s or 1960s, fashion magazines constructed a fashionable religion that helped readers cultivate "a different sort" of Christmas vision. This way of seeing the tradition fostered feelings of religious mystery, awe, and wonder typically associated with children and simple folk. Such experiences of Christmas ranged from the extraordinary, "I felt I was standing under the star of Bethlehem,"[71] to the mundane, but no less profound, remembering "that there is goodness in the world, in life."[72] In fashion magazines, cultivating "Christmas vision"—or ways of seeing—came through the poetry of acclaimed religious figures, the paintings of famous artists, and the stories of award-winning writers.[73] These mediating forms simultaneously emphasized religious experience, yet distanced readers from unsophisticated modes of religious observance by shifting reader-viewers from participants *in* to observers *of* religious life.[74] These texts and images removed religious figures and traditions, such as Jesus and Christmas, from theological debates and traditional settings, which accustomed reader-viewers to seeing Christianity in decontextualized forms and encouraged them to cultivate their spiritual imaginations and a seeker mentality.

Experiencing a Different Kind of Church

Fashion magazines' emphasis on the spiritual power of art and the importance of individual religious experience extended beyond Christmas to include the church. Church building and attendance boomed in the 1950s, but the religion-oriented articles and the accompanying images that appeared in fashion magazines advocated an alternative vision of the church space and the experiences it offered. Rather than being characterized by a particular denominational identity or routinized attendance, church, these articles suggested, should be a visual experience—an architectural wonder or at least a place filled with awe-inspiring religious art. Through the use of color photographs, the emphasis on seeing and looking at "miraculous" churches, and the fostering of a cosmopolitan ethos, numerous fashion magazine articles emphasized that fashionable religion encouraged the experience of new "spiritual vistas" and "sacred moments." They also substituted religious observation for participation and encouraged the practice of looking to other places and times for spiritual inspiration.

Three articles from *Vogue* provided the basis for this preferred way of seeing and experiencing church—"Church Art: New Promise and Past Glory" (1948), "Matisse Designs a New Church" (1949), and "Church Full of Joy" (1951). "Church Art," as with the many of the articles already discussed, was written by an aristocratic aesthete. Edward Sackville-West was a British Baron, writer, and music critic who chronicled the history of church art for *Vogue*. He recounted the beauty of Byzantine mosaics that gave way to Gothic stained glass and how "Christian man was moved to show his love and reverence for the divine essence by encrusting its images with all he possessed of the most precious—gold, silver and gems."[75] Sackville-West then lamented how this rich heritage and spiritual resource was lost as Protestantism emerged. "The sacred edifice was drained of colour. Pictures and images disappeared, windows were filled with plain glass, and music was virtually reduced to what could be managed by the untrained voices of the congregation."[76] Sackville-West concluded that "religion, deprived of eyes and ears, went into a long doze."[77] Protestantism's rise meant that the rich visual history of Christianity was lost.

Yet, Sackville-West assured readers that significant changes were occurring, and that recent works of religious art could awaken their religious senses, including that of Anglo-Irish sculptor Henry Moore, English composer Benjamin Britten, and English artist Graham Sutherland. The works of these artists embodied the virtues of modern art, such as experimentation in technique and color, as well as the use of symbolism and the move from representation to abstraction. Through their embrace of modernism, they captured the "timeless truth" of religion in the present moment.[78] Color photographs of their religious art fostered *Vogue*'s didactic, cosmopolitan vision and engaged readers' senses. These color images not only introduced people to the artists in question but also provided a way for them to experience the art itself. Sackville-West urged readers to reclaim the spiritual power of art, while the magazine's inclusion of images offered a way to do so. "There is nothing derogatory in this," he reassured readers, "until the Reformation no one thought of looking upon religious art as a sign of spiritual weakness."[79] Sackville-West privileged a way of seeing Christianity that encouraged readers to embrace their senses and emotions, but, at the same time, constrained and elevated them by rooting them in the sophistication accorded to modern religious art.[80]

Less than a year later *Vogue* referenced Sackville-West's article and produced another on artist Henri Matisse's designs for the Chapelle du Rosaire in Vence, France. The chapel represented Sackville-West's vision of what could happen when artistic genius combined with modern art. The article distanced itself from more conservative Catholic interpretations by explaining the "well-known nonconformist" Matisse's circuitous route to chapel design. Matisse became involved, not because of a particular devotion to Catholicism, but because his former nurse, now a nun, asked for his input on the design. Having learned of this connection, Father Couturier, a Dominican monk and "the single most important vitalizer in modern French Church art" encouraged Matisse to take over the design process.[81] He agreed and the result, the article promised, would be "a church unlike any they have ever seen." Matisse decreed that it would be a "church full of gaiety—a place which will make people happy."[82] The different kind of church espoused in fashion magazines did not revolve around sermons and doctrines, but rather experiencing modern artistic expression and the resulting happiness that it produced.

This way of seeing was reinforced two years later, in 1951, when *Vogue* published a follow-up piece on this Matisse-designed "Church Full of Joy." The article simultaneously educated readers and stimulated their senses by including, "for the first time in colour," photographs of Matisse's artistic-spiritual achievement. Floor-to-ceiling stained-glass windows illuminated and reflected off the white-dominated interior where Matisse's Stations of the Cross and Madonna and Child, drawn in black and white, awaited worshippers.[83] Captions to the photographs, such as "The purer the colours, the stronger they act on the deepest feelings," reinforced the spiritual power of art. So, too, did the article text as it reminded readers that this church and others are both "House of God and Gate to Heaven."[84] Through the photographs and the captioning of them, the article emphasized that seeing such artistic creations

Figure 1.2. A photograph of the stained-glass windows designed by Henri Matisse similar to the ones featured in "Church Full of Joy," *Vogue* 118 (December 1951): 128–33; Hackenberg Photo Cologne/Alamy Stock Photo.

and architectural wonders could provide readers with a sophisticated spiritual experience.

Informed by strands in Catholicism that emphasized God's presence in material creation and those in liberal Protestantism that "emphasized the immanence of God in . . . human nature," this article and others celebrated the spiritual power of art and humanity's artistic achievements.[85] More specifically, they emphasized how religious architecture and art could express the inexpressible, the grandeur of the divine. Not everyone possessed such artistic gifts and the articles highlighted the individual genius of artists. For example, in describing Matisse's design process, the article noted: "Nothing mattered but the passionate exaltation of shapes which the genius of one man has carried to the utmost point of their spiritual power."[86] The celebration of the artist and his work framed them as gifts from God that provided people with spiritual inspiration. The articles urged people to consider how church art and architecture could counter anxieties and despair by providing joy, deep feelings, and awe. Including full-page color photographs of this religious artistry offered readers a way to access these spiritual experiences and emotions. These three early articles established a way of seeing Christianity as a visual experience of art and architecture accessible through a fashion magazine, rather than by visiting a church or touring a museum.[87]

This way of seeing Christianity shaped subsequent articles on churches and religious art that appeared in *Vogue*, as well as *Harper's Bazaar*. Over the next two decades, titles alone celebrated artistic genius and its religious potential: "Miracles of Faith," "Miraculous Churches of Khizi," and "Celebrations of Genius."[88] The accompanying text and photographs cemented this understanding. "Miracles of Faith," published in December 1967, informed readers that such miracles "are not easily come by. Sometimes they are the outward jut by geniuses who show thus an inner closeness to God."[89] Connecting artistic genius to a divine source, the article then cited liberal Protestant theologian Paul Tillich's definition of religion as "the state of being grasped by an ultimate concern." This "ultimate concern" grasped particular artists and architects, such as Giotto and Le Corbusier, to produce "miracles" of church art and architecture.[90]

Full-page color photographs of these miraculous churches invited readers to become spiritual tourists and visually visit and experience these sacred sites. "Miracles of Faith," for example, included photographs of "The White Chapel by Le Corbusier," "The Holy White City of Suzdal" featuring the "wondrous Cathedral of the Nativity of the Virgin, its five blue cupolas starred in gold," along with images of the churches at Kideksha, Bogolubovo, and Paraportiani. These photographs reinforced the power of religious architecture, but they also fostered the tenets of fashionable religion.[91] The photographs, void of people and focused on the buildings, positioned viewers as spiritual pilgrims journeying to sacred places. It offered them the potential to experience these miracles on their own terms and cultivate their spiritual imaginations.[92] The captions surrounding these beautiful photographs enhanced their spiritual potential. Phrases, such as "the power of faith," "three marvels," "unique beauty," along with anecdotes about a church's provenance emphasized the religious power of art.[93] And similar to Matisse's vision of a "church filled with joy," the article proclaimed that these "miracles had joy. A flaming faith in goodness. In Jehovah. In the Lord."[94]

Figure 1.3. The Church of Panagia Paraportiani on
the Greek Island of Mykonos. An almost identical
color photograph appeared in "Miracles of Faith,"
Vogue 150 (December 1967): 190; Ian Crowson/Alamy
Stock Photo.

Finding spiritual joy, happiness, or pleasure occurred through learning to appreciate religious art, architecture, and sometimes the ruins of
such wonders.[95] *Harper's Bazaar*, for example, published "The Pleasure
of Ruins," in time for Christmas 1964. Written by Canadian photographer Roloff Beny, the article combines Beny's photographs of beautiful,
yet haunting ruins with his ruminations on English writer and Catholic
convert Rose Macaulay's *The Pleasure of Ruins*. The pages featuring
Beny's photographed ruins juxtapose a variety of religions, time periods,
and geographies with little other than the categories of "religion" and
"ruin" connecting them. The sites include Sans Souci Palace in Haiti,
a Medusa mask from the Temple of Apollo, and a "serene, recumbent,

Buddha" in Polonnaruwa, Ceylon. According to Beny, "the mystery of their vanished glory fills the observer with awe," and he tries to fathom why we are so moved by ruins. His answer acknowledges that part of it is our "mystical pleasure in the destruction of all things mortal and the eternity of God."⁹⁶ Beny, as with Sackville-West and that of the chapel at Vence, emphasizes the individual's positive experience of religion through artistic genius. Such an experience does not depend on being Catholic or Protestant but rather on being able to connect the visual and the artistic, his photographs, to a larger religious principle or "timeless truth."

In these articles, religion most often means or assumes Christianity. However, Beny incorporates classical religion and Buddhism into his story. This inclusion, in a small way, acknowledges the increasing religious diversity that Americans encountered in the 1960s. It highlights the religious sites and traditions of other cultures and fosters a sense of tolerance and respect. In another way, though, the juxtaposition of these photographs combined with the lack of contextual information and the text's focus on the broader theme of ruins sets up an implied Christian "seeker" or "spiritual omnivore" perspective. Beny's photographs, for example, feature religious ruins and symbols, most notably from Buddhism, but his article does not discuss these specific religious traditions or locations. Further, two of his photographs include symbols of religious devotion—a priestly figure wearing a cassock and walking with his head down traveling along a dirt road in front of the ruins of Sans Souci Palace, while a monk, identified by his distinct robes, shaved head, and devotional posture, ponders the larger-than-life statue of the "recumbent Buddha." Devoid of specific context, these symbolic figures represent spirituality, rather than specific religious traditions. They emphasize a universal sense of religion and sacred space that offered any virtual visitor a spiritual experience filled with mystery and awe.⁹⁷ In this way, the authors and artists featured in fashion magazines encouraged readers to view the art, architecture, symbols, and ruins of Christianity and other religious traditions as resources through which they could produce spiritual experiences.

Other articles worked in a similar way. "The House of Shiva," a brief one-page article appearing in *Harper's Bazaar* in 1955, moved from a specific description to the universal idea. After explaining the "strange aspects" of a Hindu temple's exterior that "crawls with detail," the text guided the assumed Christian reader into the temple's more serene, simple, and silent interior. "What remains and what is constant, the reality behind the myriad shapes of the world, behind its dazzle of incidents and happenings, is God's true self." De-emphasizing context, the article implies that a connoisseur of fashionable religion can distinguish between the distinct form and its "eternal essence." By cultivating this particular way of seeing, the reader can then incorporate its spiritual power into her ever-evolving and expanding sense of self.[98]

For readers familiar with Christianity, yet questioning its relevance in a tumultuous era, fashion magazines encouraged people to seek and claim a different kind of church. They constructed a way of seeing the tradition that was not about church attendance, a strict moral code, or contextual knowledge. This way of seeing Christianity aligned with Wuthnow's characterization of spiritual seekers searching for "sacred moments that reinforce their conviction that the divine exists," and exploring "new spiritual vistas."[99] At the same time, though, this fashionable religion was distinct in that it emphasized the spiritual power of modern architecture and art created by geniuses grasped by "ultimate concern." Fashion magazines fused together the supernatural and the modern and made these religious wonders available to individuals through color photographs. As a result, fashion magazines provided individuals with spiritual experiences, such as joy, mystery, and transcendence.

Participating in Processions and Pilgrimages

Fashion magazines also provided the emerging "spiritual omnivores" of the mid-twentieth century with a feast in the form of Catholic processions and pilgrimages. Given its heritage as a patron and collector of religious art, as well as its support of religious art as a devotional aid, Catholicism often functioned as a visual repository for this fashionable religion. It provided numerous forms through which people could see and experience the "eternal essence" of the Christian message. Yet, these articles and images did not encourage people to become Catholics. Rather, Catholicism in these articles functioned "as a locus of authentic supernatural experience" available to a wide variety of spiritual seekers.[100] In fashion magazines articles and images, Catholic symbols and practices functioned as extractable elements that communicated the supernatural and religious experience both textually and visually. In contrast to the perceived "Puritan" austerity of Protestantism, Catholicism offered the implied Christian reader of fashion magazines a repository of fashionable means to experience spiritual "wonder," mystery, and awe without the demands of becoming Catholic or being a religious conservative.[101]

Articles on and images of Catholic religious processions and pilgrimages constructed ways of seeing Christianity that wove together spiritual experience and sophisticated sensibilities. Firsthand accounts and close-up photographs invited readers to join in these powerful spiritual experiences. The articles included tales of Easter processions, a visit to Lourdes, and the power of saints, which reinforced the artistry and power of religious rituals. The spiritual power recounted in these stories could not be contained. The literal spilling of Christianity out onto the streets in Marian processions or in the grotto where the young Bernadette saw "our Lady" underscored how divine power continually escaped church walls and transcended theological boundaries. As Catholic convert Kathryn Hulme recounted in her pilgrimage to Lourdes: "Its tremendous effect would have been the same had I been Hindu, Protestant, Jew, Mohammedan, or uncategorized pagan."[102]

At the same time, though, these images and stories provided readers with a sense of sophisticated distance from the accounts. The photographers' lens allowed viewers to see and experience the power of a religious procession on their own terms and in their own ways. Similarly, famous writers Herbert Kubly and Kathryn Hulme functioned as conduits to apprehend the power of religious pilgrimage from a safe distance. This combination of proximity and distance allowed reader-viewers to embrace the wonder and awe of religious experience, but, at the same time, not be beholden to Catholic theology and tradition and its "unsophisticated" implications, such as naïve belief in miracles or unquestioning faith in the Church. This simultaneous embrace and containment of religious experience allowed modern reader-viewers to experiment with more flexible and ambiguous religious positions. They did not have to choose between liberal rationalism and conservative experience. They could combine elements of both.[103]

One can see this combination in the writing of Herbert Kubly published in April of 1956. Author of *An American in Italy*, a National Book Award winner, Kubly's article "Procession of Mysteries" promoted his upcoming title, *Easter in Sicily*. In this article, Midwestern Protestant Kubly conveyed his struggle to understand the Sicilian celebration of Holy Week. From the first, the scent of wisteria and the sight of religious foods—"Easter hams and cheeses, cakes in the traditional shape of doves, and a harvest of chocolate eggs gilded with gold and silver"—overwhelmed Kubly's senses. Feeling uncertain, Kubly located an insider informant, Gerardo Tuerretta, who became his ritual guide, just as Kubly guided his readers.[104] Informed by Gerardo, Kubly learned and then described how the Madonna travels the streets of the town for over twenty hours seeking her son, Jesus, who has been arrested. The procession peaks at midnight when the Madonna faces a dilemma—to keep searching the streets for her lost son or to return to the church.[105]

Kubly recounted how the procession features two Madonnas, from different churches, as well as statue groups that depict the Passion of Christ and the life of Mary, made by local guilds. Devotees in "bright scarlet robes" "carried flaming torches," and "a black-robed guard of some twenty men," as well as a band, accompanied each group of statues through the streets.[106] Kubly's vivid account included his meeting one of the Madonnas. "Suddenly at a corner we came face to face with the Madonna of the People. She was in a glass shadow box, covered with beads, brooches, watches, and rings, and she rode on a catafalque covered with arum lilies and carnations and illuminated by fifty candles each one metre high."[107] Throughout the article, Kubly detailed the sensory nature of this religious experience—aromatic flowers, loud music, dancing people, and searching Madonnas—and its power. "The combined effect of all this over the city was one of excruciating melancholy."

Even when the procession was out of sight, Kubly explained you "never stopped hearing it" and at one point the Protestant Kubly could not resist its lure—"the bands wailed on. I went into the streets and followed the sounds."[108] Kubly then watched the final hours of the procession—the statues dancing on the backs of their carriers, Mary's guards in their robes covered with "wax and grime"—until Mary stood on the precipice of the church trying to decide whether to continue her search or return to the church. Kubly tried to apply rationality and logic to the procession, as he writes, "It was a fantasy for a child. There could be no doubt in anyone's mind that she would enter as she had entered for three hundred years." Yet, the procession overwhelmed Kubly's logic and he concluded: "But reason had no part in this and I felt myself caught in an inexplicable and overwhelming suspense."[109]

Kubly's story brings readers into the sensory world of this Marian procession. As with Christmas vision and a different kind of church, this fashionable religion emphasizes religious symbols, the senses, and spiritual experiences. Through vivid description, Kubly invites readers to join his quest for "authentic supernatural experience" and to partake in its wonder.[110] At the same time, his account positions readers as participant-observers, rather than participants. They experience the event through Kubly's overwhelmed and doubting Protestant lens. This assumes and generates a sense of distance alongside the proximity invoked by his prose. This detachment allows readers to maintain their modern and sophisticated commitments, but at the same time access the experiential and supernatural dimension of religion.

A similar combination appears again in a multipage article, "River of Light," by Kathryn Hulme, author of *The Nun's Story* of movie fame. In this firsthand account of her pilgrimage to Lourdes, the site where a young Bernadette is said to have seen an apparition of the Virgin Mary in 1858, Hulme introduces the reader to her excitement and anxiety. Being new to the faith, Hulme tried to prepare for this event by reading books and talking with friends. At the same time, she wondered if Lourdes could overcome the skepticism of her "former Protestant eyes" and "measure up" to her high expectations.[111] Upon arrival, Hulme described her initial dismay as she "might have been riding through the souks of an Oriental bazaar. Plaster images, which my ex-Protestant eyes shied away from were everywhere."[112] Yet, once Hulme joined the procession the shops faded away and she became, like the others around her, a devout pilgrim. As she recounted her movement through the sacred site, Hulme noted the overwhelming silence of the thousands around her, saw the "silk banners fluttering," and "smelled the burning candles."[113] Like Kubly, Hulme utilized rich detail and sensory descriptions. Overcome, Hulme explained her compulsive need to document her experience by taking photographs. "Only the testimony of a photograph, afterwards, would assure me that what I was seeing on that May afternoon in Lourdes had not been dreamed."[114] As Hulme struggled to describe her experience (like Kubly), she took pictures and returned to the once-disdained souvenir shops to "feverishly" buy mementos: "I had become part of it, whatever 'it' was. It had no name, but its claim was total."[115] And this was only Hulme's first day at Lourdes.

Each day Hulme processed and described her emotional journey— the unceasing prayers of thousands of pilgrims, the site of thousands of candles being lit and becoming a river of light, the strong belief in and hope for healing. Hulme noted: "My understanding gave out long before my feet and voice. I participated in everything, photographed and probed into every corner of that extraordinary spot that seems to lie outside of Time, outside our portentous age which, despite its latent power, is still explainable to those eclectics who read the equations of thermonuclear physics."[116] What these eclectics and Hulme could not explain, though, was the "electric expectancy" of Lourdes and its miracles. "It created an atmosphere difficult to breathe in, as if invisible lightning bolts were playing through it, rarefying it with huge and soundless discharges."[117] Hulme realized, like Kubly, that rationality and logic could not make sense of the power of Lourdes. Articles such as these assured readers that moments of enchantment and places "outside of Time" continued to exist and offer respite from an increasingly rational world characterized by anxiety, mass production, and despair. As with Kubly, Hulme's account delighted the reader with its sensory and supernatural wonder. At the same time, though, its emphasis on her "ex-Protestant eyes" acknowledged mainline Protestant doubts about such events and their material forms and encouraged readers to maintain a certain level of skepticism.

Yet, rather than forcing readers to choose a side in a zero-sum game, such as rejection of or belief in the supernatural power of religious rituals, the accounts by Kubly and Hulme enabled spiritual seekers to consider the both/and option of being an enlightened participant-observer. This perspective allowed "spiritual omnivores" to delight in the rituals seen and experienced, but not be fully immersed in or controlled by them. Reading about Holy Week in Sicily or a pilgrimage to Lourdes in fashion magazines allowed for the possibility of spiritual experience, but without the accompanying religious and theological commitments. Neither story suggests that readers become Catholic. Such actions are unnecessary when acclaimed writers can describe it for and to you. This promoted a way of seeing Christianity that aligned the experiential and supernatural dimensions of the tradition with the demands of a sophisticated and modern mainline Protestantism.[118]

Photographs of religious processions and saints accompanied by brief explanatory text also highlighted the sensory power of these religious symbols, along with an enlightened participant-observer position. For example, the caption to "Holy Week in Seville" stated that "all Seville is bright with beeswax candles, heavy with the scent of roses, orange blossoms, and carnations strewn at the Virgin's feet." The text invites the reader into this spiritual experience, yet the close-up photograph of the men carrying a Marian float juxtaposes the supernatural with the natural. Men carry the float and animate it.[119] In "The Angels of Campobasso" the photographs of children dressed as angels and flying through the air perched on poles arrests the reader-viewer's attention. The procession images highlight the beautiful costumes, the centrality of children, the pageantry of the event, as well as the crowds. It captures a powerful expression of religious faith and devotion. The text, though, explains and contains this ritual. The children "do not, it is true, actually fly, but they perch like birds on iron frames" and it also explains that parents purchase their children's position in the scene through an auction. The text carefully grounds this expression of the supernatural in the natural world of iron frames and economic exchange.[120]

"The Healing Saints," accompanied by photographs of Saints Lucia and Gilles, emphasizes the miraculous effects of such religious figures and their symbols. The brief text notes that Saint Lucia "has been the guardian saint of clear eyes and perfect vision ever since her own lovely eyes roused the passions of the Roman proconsul who ordered her martyrdom when she refused to become his mistress." It provides a similar historical account of the miraculous gifts accorded to Saint Gilles. The text also explains that people leave "gold and silver plated gifts representing the parts of the body their intercession has restored to health."[121] The photographs show the saints adorned with and surrounded by numerous ex-votos made of precious metals. The photo-essay highlights the wonder of supernatural healings, but by focusing on the saints, rather than stories and images of those healed, the article leaves conclusions about miraculous cures up to the reader herself.

Figure 1.4. Cecil Beaton's photograph of porters resting beneath a Marian float featured in "Holy Week in Seville," *Vogue* 119 (April 15, 1952): 80; Cecil Beaton/*Vogue* © Condé Nast.

These photographs of Catholic processions and symbols and their accompanying text afford the reader-viewer the pleasure of possibility. Through evocative stories and beautiful photographs, as with the redefining of church and Christmas, this fashionable religion offered individuals supernatural moments of mystery, awe, and joy. These articles invited readers to experience wonder and to feast on the religious experiences and symbols offered. By visualizing religion in this way, fashion magazines mediated a Christianity focused on the senses and emotions. Yet, sophisticated forms, the words and photographs of well-known artists, mediated these experiences and constructed a way of seeing Christianity that offered the comfort of distance and questioning. By being a participant-observer, rather than a devotee, readers could privilege their own interpretations and align these interpretations with their modern and sophisticated views, theological and otherwise. This created space for emerging spiritual seekers to avoid theological absolutes and instead ask questions (Does God work in the world? If so, what does this looks like?) and embrace a variety of possible answers.

Conclusion

Articles and images invited reader-viewers to experience the joy of Christmas, the artistic wonder of churches, and the spiritual power of pilgrimages. Yet, they did so in ways that, as Elizabeth Bowen wrote, merged the supernatural and the natural.[122] Fashion magazines combined the delight of spiritual experience with the logical demands of modernity, which contributed to the larger societal conversation about and practice of religion. They acknowledged the darkness, the anxieties that characterized mid-twentieth-century life, as well as the scientific and technological advances that encouraged increasingly rational and disenchanted ways of envisioning the world. Yet, they assured readers that when they cultivated Christmas eyes, the world would look and feel different.

This emphasis on the visual and spiritual emerged clearly in December of 1968, when *Vogue* published "The Ecstasy of the Eye." Like Bowen's different "sort of vision," this article emphasized the "eyes of the mystic" and extolled this organ's spiritual power. Chastising the Puritans who denounced it, the article assured readers that "Heaven draws near us, in this visual universe" and produces experiences of spiritual "ecstasy."[123] Opening your eyes to the "spiritual vistas" shown in fashion magazines and existing throughout the world offered seeking individuals "sacred moments" through which they could cultivate a fashionably religious self.[124]

This way of seeing Christianity assured modern religious people that they did not have to forgo spiritual experiences. Fashion magazines mediating these religious experiences through sophisticated forms, modern art, amazing photographs, and award-winning writing provided readers with a fashionable religion. This fashionable religion transcended theological and institutional distinctiveness and privileged the visual and the symbolic. It fostered the uncoupling of religion from institutions and religious symbols from their contexts. It offered people seeking reassurance tangible spiritual resources that promised enchanting experiences. Such literary and visual experiences demanded little historical or theological knowledge. Rather, they appealed to the sensual and emotional dimensions of people's lives even as they offered the comfort and sophistication of distance. They did not expect readers to become Catholic, embrace particular doctrines, or to be "grasped by ultimate concern." Instead, they provided "sacred moments" and spiritual food for hungry religious seekers, and thus helped shift the American religious mood from one of dwelling to seeking.

Award-winning British writer Rumer Godden's "The Feast of Christmas" published in December of 1955 captures this combination of sophistication and spirituality that runs through fashion magazine articles on religion. Godden's fictional story chronicles a young woman contemplating the meaning of a special Christmas gift—"a Bible and a bottle of champagne." The young woman concludes that this surprising and thoughtful present represents the "the two sides of Christmas." Champagne, a special form of wine, symbolizes the celebratory and feast-like dimensions of the holiday, while the Bible reminds the recipient and readers of the "reason" for such festivities. "A feast is not just a thing of the body; it is of the heart and mind, the soul, as well." Godden's story, accompanied by full-page photographs of aristocratic children, weaves together the spiritual and the sensual in a modern way. The young woman is no teetotaler and the gift-giver sees no tension between the sacred text and the spirits. Godden's story illustrates fashionable religion's "both/and" perspective—that spiritual seekers could embrace supernatural experiences and modern life.[125] They could have their Bible and champagne too.

2

Making Over Christianity

In an Easter campaign from 1956, an advertisement for Kayser gloves playfully merged the world of fashion and Christianity. It showcased three different pairs of gloves available in "white and Easter colors." Rather than generic renderings or photographs of the product, though, the gloves appear in the various hand positions described in and accompanied by the rhyme that many Christian children learn at an early age: "Here's the church, here's the steeple, look inside and see all the people."[1] Featuring the rhyme, though, does more than show off the gloves being sold. It highlights the imagined readers' familiarity with Christianity, while putting a whimsical twist on a traditional religious gesture. Further, the rhyme itself instructs readers to "look" and "see" the people in the church. It focuses attention not on God or theology, but on "seeing" church-going people and what they wear as an important dimension of the Easter celebration.

This advertisement and others that appeared in fashion magazines from the mid-1940s through the 1960s used religion to sell products. This is not surprising as religion has long been a part of advertising in general and sales constitute advertising's purpose, yet religion's appearance in fashion advertising also signals something different. As seen in chapter 1, articles in fashion magazines, such as *Vogue* and *Harper's Bazaar*, constructed a fashionable way of seeing Christianity; however, these articles did not explicitly connect the tradition with fashion. Christianity appeared as a topic in, but separate from, fashion. Fashion magazines published articles on what elite Christian ministers and aesthetes were saying about religion, not fashion.

During that same time period, though, theological concepts and religious symbols, particularly those associated with Christianity, appeared in fashion magazine advertisements. Numerous, different fashion advertisements ranging from gloves to makeup to silverware featured Christian language, concepts, and gestures. This inclusion simultaneously

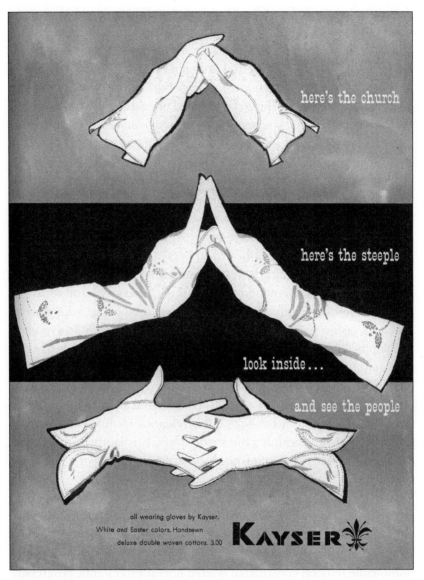

Figure 2.1. Christian rhyme and gestures illustrated in a Kayser glove advertisement, *Vogue* 127 (March 1, 1956): 45.

demonstrated the *de facto* Christian character of the fashion industry and how fashion advertisements constructed a particular way of seeing Christianity.[2] The made-over Christianity examined in this chapter incorporates many of the ideas addressed in chapter 1—religious individualism, universal religious sentiment, sensory experience and spiritual transcendence, and a decontextualized, fragmented utilization of Christianity. At the same time, though, one important distinction emerged. In combining religious language and imagery with the products and aims of fashion, these advertisements replaced the voices of spiritual elites with that of fashion. Advertising tableaux framed fashion as a mediator of Christianity and spiritual experience. This, in turn, sacralized the act of consumption and highlighted the spiritual power of material objects.[3] In tracing how God got on a dress, fashion advertising's visualization and materialization of Christianity constituted an important step in the movement of religious symbols from the textual and visual discourse surrounding fashion to its material embodiment in fashion accessories and attire.

By combining religious symbols, cues, and language with various products, fashion advertisements made over Christianity into a modern and sophisticated consumer-oriented enterprise. This is not to say that Christianity wasn't popular, dominant, or consumerist already. Numerous scholars have documented precisely this point.[4] Rather, this chapter focuses on how fashion advertising mediated a particular vision of Christianity—a vision that helped this religious tradition maintain its dominant status. Examining this made-over Christianity helps scholars better understand the religious changes occurring in the latter half of the twentieth century.

Advertisements played a central role in giving Christianity a new and stylish look. They emphasized the importance of wearing fashionable clothes to church, infused fashion-related products with supernatural potential, and tempted readers with the ability to change their lives. The fashionable religion constructed offered liberal Protestants, progressive Catholics, and spiritual seekers the promise of "sacred moments" and the spiritual power of personal transformation without the demands of theological dogma or conservative morality.[5] Rather, Christian dwellers could become spiritual seekers who controlled and managed their own religious lives through consumption and display, in addition to or instead of church-going.

To highlight the characteristics and mechanisms of this fashionable religion, this chapter analyzes four dominant ways that fashion advertising combined Christianity and fashion. The first section examines how Christianity formed part of the assumed backdrop of fashion advertising tableaux, while also framing the church as a space to exhibit one's sense of style. The second section shows how fashion advertising combined elements of the Christian supernatural—miracles, angels, and religious experience—with modern ideas that assured consumers of the faith's flexibility and freedom from dogma. In a similar way, the third section addresses how fashion advertising provided consumers with a chic Christian heroine, Eve, that condoned their consumption and encouraged their cultivation of beauty. And the last examines how fashion advertisements incorporated notions of magic in ways that challenged Christianity but could also be aligned with it. Together, these four patterns created a way of seeing Christianity that acknowledged its importance in everyday life but also provided alternative and modern ways of engaging with it.

Even more than the articles analyzed in chapter 1, this chapter shows how fashion advertising utilized Christianity and its heritage as a repertoire of visual, material, and linguistic elements that could be extracted from their institutional and theological contexts. This does not mean that religious symbols simply "lost" their "aura" or "spiritual" meanings, but rather they accumulated new meanings on top of and alongside older ones.[6] The effectiveness of fashion advertising depended on readers' knowledge of the Christian imaginary being invoked. Fashion advertising, in a sense, sought to preserve the older, traditional meanings of the Christian sacred even as they altered and expanded those meanings. Through this reprocessing—the de- and recontextualization of Christianity—fashion advertisements aligned Christianity with modern and sophisticated sensibilities that could appeal to a wide base of Christian and seeking consumers.[7]

Sunday Best Style

While Christian revivals and Cold War politics dominate narratives of American religion at midcentury, fashion histories highlight the global fashion industry's struggle to resume its prewar prominence. Many designers and fashion houses ceased operating during the war, while others were severely impacted by the rationing of supplies. After the war, European fashion houses went back to work dominating the couture industry, but they also established *prêt-à-porter* lines to compete with American ready-to-wear designers.[8] In 1947, designer Christian Dior helped fashion reclaim its revered status when he revolutionized design with his "New Look." This silhouette dramatized a woman's waist and shortened skirt lengths. Yet, other designers quickly copied and tamed his revolutionary silhouettes. Fashion scholars characterize much of the 1950s in terms of conformity, as seen in fashion textbooks with chapter titles that read "Fashion Conformity Prevails" and "Femininity and Conformity."[9] And one scholar noted: "The decade after World War II is often considered a time of conformity and conservative fashion. Women's overall looks were polished and mature, with a trend for matching accessories."[10] While scholars label these trends "conformist," they still represented "fashions" that were aligned with the religious revivals occurring in 1950s America.

Within this context, many fashion advertisements, as with articles, communicated the close connection between Christianity and fashion. They acknowledged in subtle ways how Christianity dominated American religious life. This midcentury trend reflected historical patterns in the advertising industry. According to Jackson Lears, in *Fables of Abundance*, Protestantism permeated early twentieth-century advertising agencies, as most staffers were liberal Protestants, "many the sons of Presbyterian or Congregationalist ministers."[11] Thus, Christianity infused many advertising campaigns. In the early twentieth century, for instance, advertising taught consumers "parables" about the importance of the first impression and that democracy meant "equal access to consumer products."[12] More explicitly religious ideas appeared in advertising through visual cues. In his examination of advertising from 1920 through 1940, Roland Marchand explains, "no advertiser would have dared to present his product under the headline 'God endorses.' But, a well-placed, radiant beam of light from a mysterious heavenly source might create a virtual halo around the advertised object without provoking the reader into outrage at the advertiser's presumption."[13] Other ads featured "adoring throngs" gathered around a product of "heroic proportions" or basking "in the presence" of the latest innovation, such as the newest vacuum cleaner or refrigerator.[14] To prevent controversy, advertisers avoided the inclusion of specific Christian figures (Jesus, Mary, apostles, saints, and ministers), and instead relied on symbolism and visual cues to connote a product's supposedly sacred significance and power.[15]

Neither Lears's nor Marchand's study focuses specifically on fashion or religion in advertising; however, their work and that of other scholars highlights the centrality of Christianity in advertising. While fashion advertisements do not directly reflect the realities of religious life, they still, as Marchand explains, "communicate . . . broader assumptions about social values" and often "reinforce and intensify existing patterns and conceptions."[16] Fashion advertising, then, can provide us with important insights into the societal conversation about religion in the middle of the twentieth century.[17]

While not all of these advertising techniques were unique to fashion, their appearance in fashion magazines alongside articles and photographs on various religious topics facilitated a particular way of seeing Christianity as fashionable.[18] Advertising included illustrations and photographs of churches, which acted as a metonym for Christianity and made visible the religious norm in American life. Its presence was so naturalized and recognizable in these scenes that the accompanying ad copy rarely mentions this sacred site. At the same time, these advertisements made over the church in different ways that highlighted its sophisticated and modern status, whether as a setting for one's Sunday best, or as a site for weddings and holidays.

In advertisements for products, ranging from makeup to textiles to perfume, churches appeared as part of quaint American scenes recalling idyllic visions of a simpler time and place. For example, a brightly colored illustrated Christmas scene for Avon cosmetics in 1946 featured a couple attired in Victorian-era dress. In the foreground, the elaborately dressed man in ice skates pushes his equally bedecked lady riding in a sleigh across the page. A village sits in the background with houses gently billowing smoke out their chimneys. The image evokes small town American life and draws the viewer's eye to the steepled church, situated in the center and framed by the gap between the Victorian man's body and the sleigh.[19] Similarly, in 1951, William Winkler, a company that made textiles, included a church in its advertisement. Squares and

Figure 2.2. Church backdrop in the illustration of an Avon cosmetics advertisement, *Vogue* 108 (November 1, 1946): 27.

rectangles of different bright printed fabrics fill the foreground and form fabric fields that surround a picturesque village complete with cozy little houses and a bright red barn with a white church in the center.[20] The churches' presence goes unmentioned in the ad copy, but their inclusion connoted the virtues—American-ness, integrity, goodness—advertisers hoped consumers would transfer to the products being sold.

Churches also appeared as a way to emphasize the sense of class associated with various products. The Maine-based Winthrop Mills, for instance, featured photographs and illustrations with large churches in their ad campaigns. Coming from "the land of white-spired churches," the copy promises that Winthrop's textiles are "pure," "native," and "part of [the region's] tradition of rugged integrity."[21] Other times church architecture suggested college campuses and the alignment of particular goods with the sophistication of higher education.[22] In these marketing devices, the appearance of the church with little, if any, reference to its presence highlighted Christianity's taken-for-granted status in American religious life, while simultaneously aligning it with fashion norms.

Advertisements not only reflected Christianity's assumed position within the fashion industry and American life but also fostered a way of seeing church and church-goers as stylish and modern. For example, a 1947 ad for Etta Gaynes Designs showed two women walking hand in hand down a path. Perhaps foreshadowing the "polished and mature" look combined with "matching accessories" attributed to the 1950s, the illustrated women wear skirts and jackets with coordinated hats and carry stylish handbags. In many ways, the ad seems unremarkable, but one additional element reveals the message conveyed by this advertisement. These stylish, sophisticated women appear to be leaving church

Figure 2.3. Church featured in an Etta Gaynes advertisement, *Vogue* 109 (March 15, 1947): 122; courtesy of Benjamin Gaynes and the Etta Gaynes Estate.

as the pathway leads the viewer's eye to the steepled building in the background.[23]

The advertisement for Kayser gloves urged readers to "see the people," and this Etta Gaynes ad along with numerous others emphasized the importance of looking your "Sunday Best." This notion highlighted the importance of seeing and being seen at church by presenting yourself in the best possible way through purchasing the right clothes, shoes, and makeup. Some ads showed this by including beautifully dressed moms with little boys in miniature suits set amid church pews or dads escorting their young daughters clad in Easter dresses.[24] In the spring of 1957 Du-Pont advertisements made this connection between religion and fashion explicit. One tableau featured two young girls in elaborate dresses and promised that "[n]ylon keeps them at their Sunday Best." Suggestive of Easter, the beautiful dresses worn by these young girls would look fabulous all day because DuPont's nylon kept its shape and did not wrinkle. While church and Easter are not explicitly mentioned in these ads, the language of "Sunday Best," as well as the settings—stained-glass windows, white lilies, and a large set of double doors—established the alliance of modern fashion and Christian context.[25]

Others, such as ads for "Sunday School Dresses" made out of Celanese acetate, and Saks Fifth Avenue's "Sunday Silk" dress, encouraged readers to purchase products that would help them cultivate a stylish way of being Christian.[26] In promoting its "Sunday-Best Pink" makeup, Jaquet cosmetics, for example, asked readers if they wanted "to look like an angel with a dash of sheer sophistication?"[27] Through visual cues and the language of "Sunday," these advertisements acknowledged Christianity's dominance in consumers' lives, while simultaneously creating a way of seeing the church as a space for exhibiting sophisticated fashion and a sense of style.

No religious symbols or particular design styles, however, distinguished these "Sunday" products or clothes as identifiably Christian. Unlike the appearance of a lone dress embellished with the signs of the zodiac in 1945 or the proliferation of evangelical T-shirts emblazoned with Bible verses and mottos that emerged in the late 1970s, according to fashion advertisements in the 1950s and 1960s, sophisticated church-going attire meant fashionable and quality garments that did not

Figure 2.4. "Sunday Best" Easter attire highlighted in a DuPont advertisement, *Vogue* 129 (April 1, 1957): 98.

announce one's religious identity or level of devotion.[28] This style provided many Christians with a way to look religious that was seemingly invisible and neutral. At the same time, though, the quality and style of the garments pictured implied the unsophisticated spiritual and cultural status of other religious people who wore less fashionable attire or styles broadcasting their faith. Thus, this "invisible" Christian style occupied the norm, which cast other forms of religious dress as "unsophisticated," meaning backward, primitive, and problematic.

Some advertisements dropped references to "Sunday Best," but implied a connection between church and sophisticated style through other visual cues. For example, an ad for Henri Bendel, an exclusive

The new season spreads its graceful wings...

in accompaniment, spread of accordion-skirt in a daytime Bendel Original

designed for immediate wear.

Of wool in navy, black, yarn-dyed grey and beige, $135...silk in navy or black, $145.

Henri Bendel
IO WEST 57
NEW YORK 19 NY

Figure 2.5. Stained-glass motif suggestive of a church context that appeared in an Henri Bendel advertisement, *Vogue* 109 (March 15, 1947): 4; used with permission.

New York City retailer, depicts a beautiful young woman wearing a hat, gloves, and a stylish dark dress. The description includes the words "graceful," "daytime," and "for immediate wear," but does not mention religion. This daytime outfit could be worn many places, but the stained-glass backdrop connotes an artistically inspired church context to the reader, as does the model's upturned, almost worshipful, gaze. This ad and others highlighted the alliance of Christianity with fashionable attire. They also emphasized the artistic wonders of church spaces, as seen in chapter 1, and the potential consumer's need for equally inspired and stylish church-going finery.[29]

The church as a place to display beautiful fashion and experience artistic genius emerged most clearly in advertisements for wedding gowns and gifts. Advertisements featured women adorned in bridal gowns posed in front of stained-glass windows, church altars, and church exteriors. These images highlighted the gowns' fashionable design and the quality of the fabrics used, while the church backdrop exhibited an equally impressive artistry.[30] Advertisements for wedding gifts also featured brides and churches in ways that highlighted sophistication and class. For instance, in a Gorham silver ad, the groom is literally cropped out of the illustration as light shines on the pink-cheeked blonde bride. She wears a veil and flowers in her hair and the requisite pearl necklace. The lighting draws your attention to her face and her expression, one of beauty and quiet absorption in the moment. The stained-glass windows in the background further establish the artistry of the space and the sanctity of this moment, as does the ad copy, which proclaims "to love . . . and to cherish."[31] The silver appears in a separate illustration at the bottom of this full-page ad, while the copy emphasizes its "exquisite workmanship," which will enhance the "graciousness" of the new bride's home. For those interested, the silver could be purchased in a "Modern Way"—one place setting at a time. Similarly, an ad for Oneida sterling features a church wedding scene complete with stained-glass windows and gothic archways, along with a bride, groom, and minister. In this tableau, the silverware of "heroic proportions," three on each side, acts as wedding attendants and a focusing device drawing the eye toward the couple. The description reinforces the grandeur of the church, the wedding finery, and the silver, as it highlights Oneida's distinguished work and the sterling's heirloom qualities.[32]

These advertisements acknowledged the centrality of Christianity in American life. They highlighted the church's place in family-oriented moments and reflected dimensions of the dwelling spirituality of the time.[33] Fashion advertisements, though, shaped, as well as reflected, dominant religious trends. They affirmed and amplified the existing alliance between faith and fashion, Christianity and commerce. They directed the reader's gaze to church-goers and the need for them to be stylish. They also helped construct a distinct Christian style that wove

Figure 2.6. Church wedding illustration featured in a Gorham
silver advertisement, *Vogue* 111 (April 15, 1948): 14.

together inspired clothing design and artistic church spaces. This fashionable religion focused on the individual and her cultivation of a sophisticated life through accumulating particular goods, attendance at the right churches, and wearing the latest styles.

The implications of this fashionable religion can be seen in advertisements from the late 1950s and 1960s that portrayed female consumers as sophisticated religious tourists or "spiritual omnivores." In these tableaux models pose in front of beautiful churches depicted as tourist sites. For example, a 1957 advertisement for "fine art fabrics," pictures two women in brightly patterned and elegant sundresses with spaghetti straps. Their hair is pulled back, their makeup perfect, and they carry jaunty white umbrellas. The image conveys sartorial sophistication for a sunny day. The white church in the background, the Church of San José in Puerto Rico, contrasts with the vibrancy of the colorful dresses, but it also introduces and glamorizes religious tourism. The picture of the beautiful church combined with a brief caption that identifies it and tells readers that it is "the second oldest in the western hemisphere," which suggests its worthiness and desirability as a cosmopolitan religious site.[34]

An ad for designer sunglasses in 1963 conveys a similar message. Three women, each wearing a different sunglass design (though "The Internationale" is featured), stand on a sidewalk by the Seine while the Cathedral of Notre Dame dominates the background. The description urges potential consumers to "wear them up the avenue or around the world and carry a world of sophistication with you wherever you go." The ad implies an equivalence between the sophisticated and stylish product and the equally inspired religious site.[35] Stylishly clad women also appear in front of other Christian landmarks, such as the Basilica of the Assumption in Baltimore and Saint Mark's Basilica in Venice.[36] These advertisements amplified the fashionable religion conveyed in fashion magazine articles through photographs and descriptive text, which invited readers to be participant-observers of religious rituals and miraculous churches. Advertisements in fashion magazines extended this logic. They showed consumer-readers what to wear, where to visit, and how to be seen and photographed at these cosmopolitan church sites. Unlike Kathryn Hulme's initial concern about religious material-ism at Lourdes, these ads urged the emerging spiritual seeker to accu-mulate the right look and products for their spiritual pilgrimage. These historic and architectural wonders still offered individuals sacred mo-ments and spiritual food, but these religious experiences were divorced from the context of worship and theology.[37] Fashionable religion pro-vided spiritual seekers with a way to combine Christian concepts with cosmopolitan experiences and the latest styles.

These various advertisements, ranging from little girls in Easter dresses to models posed in front of the Cathedral of Notre Dame, em-phasized Christianity's dominant religious status in American life at midcentury. Christian symbols, gestures, and language appeared in an assumed and often taken-for-granted manner. At the same time, though, these fashion advertisements constructed a particular way of seeing Christianity that reinforced and expanded the fashionable reli-gion seen in chapter 1.[38] While articles discussed religious topics, such as miraculous churches and Marian processions, advertisements fused faith and fashion. By analyzing this fusion, we can see how sophisticated forms of high art, award-winning writing, and amazing architecture mediated Christianity, but so too did fashion and its products. These advertisements emphasized the importance of seeing and being seen, of creating a chic Christian style.

Sophisticated Supernatural Products

Christianity provided the backdrop for numerous advertisements; however, others moved Christian symbols from the background to the foreground and made religion more central to the grandiose claims being made about products. No specific Christian symbols or imagery characterized the garments associated with "Sunday Best" Christianity, yet fashion advertising emphasized Christian ways of seeing, purchasing, and experiencing fashion products. As Lears writes, "The desire to endow objects with symbolic, perhaps even spiritual, significance persisted in a variety of forms."[39] Fashion advertisements used Christian language, symbols, and visual cues to extol the amazing qualities of their wares. In 1959, English journalist and writer Marghanita Laski affirmed this trend. She argued that advertising used the language and symbols of the sacred to "rouse in us 'passion of awe,'" and "trigger in us certain feelings that we value, those feelings that I.A. Richards calls life-enhancing."[40] These linguistic and visual choices demonstrated the dominance of the Christian imaginary in fashion advertising.

Advertisements emphasizing the Christian supernatural and its abundant benevolence through the language of *heavenly* and *miracle* demonstrate this pattern. Products, ranging from makeup to shoes to lingerie, proclaimed their spiritual connections. Coty promoted its "Miracle Make-up" and Lenthéric named its signature perfume "Miracle."[41] Others touted their celestial characteristics, such as "a heavenly fragrance," "heavenly new make-up," and "heavenly Macshore wash 'n' wear Dacron."[42] Such claims seem grandiose and exaggerated, but they also do more than sell products. They assume a consumer at least familiar with, if not a part of, Christianity and assure her that such godly generosity demonstrates the alignment of faith and fashion.

For instance, advertisers often combined visual clichés, such as radiant beams of light on women's upturned faces, with the language of *miracle* to emphasize how fashion products could produce a supernatural Christian experience.[43] Lenthéric's "Miracle" perfume features a woman wearing a wimple-like scarf over her head gazing upward as the light shines on her face. The wimple suggests a religious mystic or even a Catholic nun, but, at the same time, it hides her hair and thus highlights her flawless face. She appears the image of beauty and religious devotion, a depiction that emphasizes the transformative power and supernatural benevolence of the product.[44] DuBarry's "Royal Nectar" cream makes its supernatural claims even more explicit through text, rather than imagery. The ad copy proclaims: "This new age-defying liquid works so miraculously, so quickly . . . that your friends will notice the astonishing difference in your appearance in less than a week!"[45] Miraculous products produce miraculous results.

The use of grandiose religious claims and Christian imagery in these advertisements, however, does not mean that fashion magazine readers, predominantly women, simply accepted advertising claims in a literal and facile way. "Reading," as Janice Radway reminds us, "is not eating."[46] Rather, the combination of the Christian supernatural and fashion-related products suggests a sophisticated consumer familiar with what historian James Cook calls "the arts of deception." Cook's research focuses on nineteenth-century tricksters and humbug, such as P. T. Barnum's Feejee Mermaid exhibit. Cook argues that middle-class audiences gained pleasure through a combination of "illusionism and realism" (the dialectical movement back and forth between fact and fiction). "There was," he writes, "no reason to choose between illusionism and realism. The public was amused even when it was conscious of being deceived."[47]

Twentieth-century fashion advertising functioned similarly. It provided potential consumers with a combination of supernatural promises alongside technological developments and tangible products. This fusion of Christianity and commerce offered spiritual seekers a sophisticated option—one based on playing with the power of possibility. Advertisements used Christian concepts, such as miracles and angels, in ways that acknowledged their potential power and reality. At the same time, though, by decontextualizing these concepts and using the rhetoric of consumption, science, and technology, these advertisements added new meanings and provided alternative explanations that made room for doubt, skepticism, and questioning. Unlike fundamentalists who insisted on belief in the miracles of Jesus as a required tenet of Christian faith,[48] fashion advertisements challenged this zero-sum game. Ads created a space in which spiritual seekers could entertain the efficacy of supernatural experiences and miraculous products through purchasing goods, rather than committing to a particular theology or religious position.

Fashion advertising's reprocessing, its decontextualization and redefinition, of "miracles" illustrates this idea. Fashion miracles did not eliminate the possibility of divine intervention, but they also did not depend upon it. Rather, fashion miracles came from sophisticated sources, such as human genius, scientific advances, and proper consumption. For example, "Royal Jelly" ("the youth and beauty diet of the Queen Bee") constituted the "miraculous" element in "Royal Nectar,"[49] while the secret ingredients that comprised "Miracle" perfume enhanced its power and set it apart from other fragrances. This redefinition of miracle combined the enchanting possibilities of the Christian supernatural with the logic of modernity. Modern miracles relied on Christian notions but merged them with the language of science, human inspiration, and technological innovation. Created by this fusion, modern miracles provided consumers with access to supernatural products that could do seemingly impossible things.

As with the celebrated artists discussed in chapter 1, such as Matisse and Michelangelo, advertisements framed miracles as the product of human genius and technological advances.[50] For example, in the 1950s, textile companies marketed new synthetic fabrics, such as nylon, polyester, and acrylic that introduced miraculous possibilities—washability, stretchability, wrinkle resistance, new textures, and more.[51] Carter's called its washable nylon tricot featuring "golden twinkle" a "miracle for moderns," while Peck and Peck's "miracle of the age" was a new suit of "man-made" and worsted fibers that "defies wrinkles, packs and unpacks—without losing its crisp, clustered pleats."[52] These ads infused products with supernatural potential, yet grounded them in the natural world of human creation.

Over time, the technological and scientific genius of these modern fashion miracles became even clearer. From 1959 through the mid-1960s, Germaine Monteil ads proclaimed, "miracles don't just happen; they are caused." The company's text-heavy advertisements explained that their Bio-Miracle cream had a human and scientific basis; however, they dubbed their discovery of a catalyst for cell regeneration a "scientific miracle" and placed the text on a field of fluffy clouds. Ads explained, "every woman knows what this means: a skin that lies sweet and sleek against the bone; her good looks, whatever their degree, un-marred; and maturity without tears." They also informed readers that "most scientific miracles aren't true miracles," a claim that goes unexplained, but at the same time assured readers that Bio-Miracle cream was indeed a "scientific miracle."

Similarly, Helena Rubinstein's "Tree of Life" cream and emulsion promised potential buyers a miraculous transformation—"a new beauty treatment from the miracle of birth." Due to their "scientific genius," the company discovered and trademarked "placene"—"the very same biological elements that nature feeds the unborn baby," and "the very source of human life itself!" Your skin will be reborn—a miracle indeed.[53] The ad fuses religious ideas about the miracle of life and the conservative Christian discourse of being "born again" with human ingenuity and technological possibility. As these advertisements combined the discourses of science, fashion, and religion, they provided a way for reader-consumers to "believe" in miracles, but not be deluded by "blind" or "irrational" faith.[54] Human genius and science provided a sophisticated way to participate in the possibility of the miraculous.[55]

In addition to the miraculous results experienced as a result of human scientific achievement, fashion advertisements provided reader-consumers with access to the supernatural through the use of angels. These divine intermediaries helped make fashion accessible as numerous tableaux show angels delivering *heavenly* products. For example, a "Heavenly Blue" shoe advertisement included gift-giving angels to make this point. In a full-page ad, three blue high-heeled shoes appear to be drifting down from heaven accompanied by cherubs. A heavenly gift bestowed by supernatural beings.[56] Four years later, in 1951, you can see this combination again. In this ad, two descending cherubs each deliver a glove being sold as "angel-suede nylon gloves by Wear Right." The ad copy reinforces this religious association: "Heavenly to wear . . . heavenly to wash."[57] As with miracles, gift-giving angels emphasized the alliance of Christianity and fashion and the power of these products.

Ad copy and visual clichés touted the supernatural possibilities of these angelic products. Marketing for makeup, such as Dorothy Gray's "Angel Cake" and Pond's "Angel Face," utilized the Christian concepts of

Figure 2.7. Angelic and heavenly associations emphasized in an Avon cosmetics advertisement, *Vogue* 107 (April 1, 1946): 41.

heaven and *angels* along with visual cues to highlight the divine origins and supernatural power of these products.[58] "Heavenlight" face powder by Avon, for instance, promised its female consumers an "angel-like look" as its product was "milled to heavenly lightness." The illustration reinforced these supernatural connections and the promised transformation. Light shines on the woman's upturned face reinforcing the product's heavenly source and its worldly efficacy; however, as with miracles, this ad allows for the supernatural but also grounds this transformation in the science of the product and the act of consumption.[59]

Advertisements promised consumers the beauty of angels, but they also created some distance from these traditional Christian conceptions. In Christian history, angels are spiritual beings created by God that deliver messages, minister to humanity, and help lead people toward Christian perfection. Purity, perfection, and beauty often characterize them.[60] However, rather than being bound by notions of Christian perfection, fashion advertisements offered a sophisticated and edgy possibility more aligned with the interests of spiritual seekers.[61] Advertisements invoked this edginess by introducing different kinds of angels and the possibility of being transformed without having to become a "goody-goody." For example, an ad from 1951 showed the transformation of the female consumer into an angelic being through the wearing of "Seventh Heaven" nylons. In the illustration, she has wings and sits on a floating cloud suggesting a heavenly source and supernatural element, but there are no radiant beams of light or adoring gazes in this illustration. Further, the bolded ad copy insists that the wearer is "no angel." She has merely discovered "heavenly stockings."[62] The ad emphasizes the supernatural power of its product even as it pushes back against the Christian notions of perfection and purity associated with angels. It uses a powerful and familiar symbol to suggest a more sophisticated Christian consumer and interpretation.

Four years later, Angelique perfume, hoping to show the versatility of its fragrances, asked women: "What kind of angel are you?" The company developed different perfumes for various types of angels and occasions, including "gay innocents," "the sophisticate," "for exciting mystery," and "for provocative elegance."[63] While not denying that women could become angels, Angelique pointed out that not all angels are innocent or perfect. The illustrated figures wearing low-cut, strapless gowns, as well as their associations with different colors (white with innocent, black with sophistication) reinforced the different transformative possibilities. Thus, fashion advertising invoked Christian concepts, but in doing so redefined them in ways that made over Christianity into a more playful, permissive, and stylish faith that could transform your life through the purchasing of products, instead of or in addition to more traditional forms religious devotion.

While fashion advertising redefined miracles as modern and angels as naughty, advertisements also reconceptualized sacred moments in more fashionable ways. To sell fashion products, advertisements utilized the

Figure 2.8. "I'm No Angel" illustration by Henry Bennett for a
Seventh Heaven nylon advertisement, *Vogue* 118 (October 15, 1951):
62; courtesy of the Bennett Estate.

Christian imagery of praise and devotion, such as faces turned upward in
reverence, radiant beams lighting forms and silhouettes, or heads bowed
and hands clasped in prayer. These visual clichés emphasized how fashion mediated religious experience. They implied that simply putting on a
particular garment or trying a fashion product could provide consumer-
seekers with new spiritual vistas. Yet, the ads also introduced a playful
interpretive possibility: What or whom is being worshiped? By blurring
the referent, the ads suggested that stylish women could and should simultaneously worship fashion and God.

For example, a 1945 ad for Skinner's Satin showcased this sophisticated form of spirituality. Set amid a dramatic dark background, the light streams down from above and spotlights a woman wearing a beautiful satin gown, gloves, and cape in vibrant shades of blue and pink. Her hands are clasped as if in prayer and her upturned gaze suggests religious rapture or at least praise and adoration. The lit candles and the brief description "Satin—Fashion's Worldly Celestial" reinforces the supernatural tone. The advertisement emphasizes the power of satin, not churches or clergy, to provide reader-consumers with access to sacred moments, while also showing the devotion due to the G/god of fashion.[64]

Bates Fabrics also showed its female model gazing upward with her white-gloved hands clasped in prayer and the light shining on her face. These visual cues connote religious worship of and devotion to the divine. According to the ad, plaid fabric is the source of this sacred moment. The tableau emphasizes the possibility, power, and desirability of this religious experience. Yet, the beauty of the model, her fashionable attire, and the ad copy, "in praise of plaid," also demonstrates that this display of religious devotion encompasses the sartorial, as well as the spiritual.[65] Hansen promoted its gloves through a similar scene. The illustration shows a woman kneeling with her hands in prayer on the surface in front of her. Her closed eyes and averted gaze suggest the spiritual power of the scene. She is almost overcome by the light shining from above, which simultaneously highlights her elbow-length golden-yellow gloves and introduces the possibility of her dual devotion.[66]

Rather than criticizing fashion as a form of self-indulgent consumption, these advertisements infused products with supernatural qualities and established purchasing fashion products as a way to access religious experience.[67] Through Christian language, symbols, and gestures, fashion advertisements emphasized religious awe and enchantment, but framed these supernatural moments through the lens of fashion, consumption, and display. For consumers, this demonstrated how faith and fashion, Christianity and commerce went together and could provide "spiritual omnivores" with an unparalleled feast of supernaturally charged products. Further, for spiritual seekers shifting away from the dwelling mentality, the nondescript backgrounds in these ads reinforced the idea that a church context is not necessary for such powerful

Figure 2.9A. Model "praising" plaid in advertisement for Bates Fabrics, *Vogue* 112 (October 1, 1948): back cover; courtesy of Maine Heritage Weavers/Bates Mill Store.

spiritual moments. Rather, the ads imply that spiritual experiences could be accessed when one focuses on the self, makes the right fashion purchases, and displays them to others.

Whether modern miracles, naughty angels, or stylish religious devotion, these advertisements depicted Christianity and fashion as allies. This not only enhanced the claims being made about these items but also reassured consumers that purchasing such goods aligned with and even enhanced Christian values. Wrinkle-free garments, stockings that fit well, and cosmetics that restored youth were but a few of the many miracles available. At the same time, by decontextualizing Christian concepts and fusing them with ideas about science and consumption, fashion advertisements helped make over Christianity. This fashionable religion emphasized the supernatural and the symbolic, the visual and the sensual, but did so in sophisticated and modern ways. It merged ideas about piety with a playful permissiveness and infused Christianity with stylish potential.

A Chic Christian Heroine

In addition to framing the church as a place to exhibit fashionable styles and redefining familiar Christian concepts in modern ways, fashion advertising extolled the virtues of a controversial biblical heroine: Eve. Advertisers in the 1920s and 1930s sought to avoid controversy and therefore stayed away from using overt Christian figures in their marketing ideas[68]; however, by the 1940s something had clearly changed. Fashion advertising violated this general rule in playful and provocative ways. In 1944, for example, a Chen Yu lipstick ad turned Matthew 7:16 from "By their fruit you shall know them," into "By your lips they shall know you."[69] A biblical discussion of one's spiritual gifts became a campaign for the wearing of a specific lipstick. Other ads from subsequent decades mentioned biblical women, such as Salome and Delilah, known more for their sexual exploits than saintly personas.[70] These references assumed that participants knew the reputation of the figures in question, but at the same time, they eschewed biblical literalism and employed a playful and transgressive hermeneutic—one that offered consumers a sense of humor, as well as a world of temptation and pleasure in which they, like these biblical rogues, should indulge.

Eve became the face and embodiment of this transgressive and playful Christianity. Eve or references to her through the symbolic apple appeared more frequently in fashion advertisements than any other biblical figure from the 1940s through the 1960s. Campaigns for handkerchiefs, hosiery, perfume, and makeup drew upon Eve to sell their products. Her story provided fashion advertisers with a rich repertoire of concepts and symbols that invoked the Christian past and its heritage, but then utilized it in different and provocative ways. As the "first woman" she represented unparalleled beauty and proximity to the divine, but as the "first sinner" she also symbolized temptation and desire. Eve connoted the irresistible temptation of fashion products, women's sexual power over men, and the promise of transformation. By directly invoking and reinterpreting an iconic religious figure, fashion advertisements simultaneously upheld the supernatural power of their products and constructed Christianity as edgy by celebrating the sins of its female progenitor. This, in turn, ensured the cutting-edge character of fashionable religion.

Throughout this chapter we have seen how fashion advertisements assumed and reinforced an alliance between fashion and Christianity. The use of Eve adds another layer of complexity to this relationship. Highlighting Eve's transgressions does not mean that fashion advertising jettisoned Christianity or that Christianity suddenly became the enemy of fashion, but rather that fashion advertising began to more explicitly "break [the] rules" and "exceed [the] boundaries" traditionally associated with Christianity and fashion advertising.[71] Specifically, the sexual purity, honest character, and moral goodness (the rules and boundaries) associated with Christianity became a foil that highlighted the sexuality, trickery, and naughtiness cultivated by the fashion industry. This reframing continued to rely on and use the concept of Christianity. As Chris Jenks explains, "the transgression is a component of the rule" as it is a "dynamic force in cultural reproduction—it prevents stagnation by breaking the rule and it assures stability by reaffirming the rule."[72] Thus, even as fashion advertising pushed the boundaries of Christianity, it remained a vital part of the fashion story.

Eve's story contains tremendous symbolic power as she represents innocence and guilt, perfection and flaws, beauty and sexuality, duty and desire. Her status as an iconic symbol capable of producing multiple meanings made her an ideal resource for fashion and other realms of popular culture. In *Approaching Eden: Adam and Eve in Popular Culture*, Theresa Sanders documents how Adam and Eve permeated the American landscape, and they "appear[ed] in sources as diverse as Louis Armstrong's 1925 recording of 'Adam and Eve Had the Blues'; advertisements for faucets, cars, and condoms; a ballet in the 1960 movie *Can-Can*; *Mother Goose and Grimm* comic strips; computer logos; Japanese anime; songs by Elvis Presley," and more.[73] The widespread use of this mythical duo in popular culture highlighted Christianity's dominance in the US and the ways in which religion has long been a resource for popular culture.

Eve's narrative of sin and transgression, which seemed to directly reference clothing, made it particularly apt for use in fashion advertising. As Gloria Guiness wrote in *Harper's Bazaar*, "It was Eve that started it all."[74] Eve was the mother of fashion. Tempted by the serpent to eat the forbidden fruit (symbolized by the apple), she disobeyed God and persuaded Adam to do likewise. This "original sin" prompted the couple's realization of their nakedness, and hence the need for clothing. It was a rich narrative that fashion ads used both visually and rhetorically.

Through depictions of Eve, apples, and serpents, alongside the language of seduction and temptation, fashion advertising developed visual clichés that highlighted Eve's beauty and seductive power. In turn, this decontextualization and reinterpretation of the Eve story, similar to miraculous makeup and praiseworthy plaids, sacralized fashion products and their consumption. In the biblical account, Eve only had an apple to enhance her feminine wiles; however, the fashion industry offered women numerous tempting products to do the same. Fashion advertising assured reader-consumers that through the consumption of fashion products modern women could become Eve. They could be beautiful, sexy, and powerful, but still Christian.

The association of Eve, fashion, and temptation emerged as early as 1944 in an ad for handkerchiefs. The illustration included a serpent coiled around a tree wearing a top hat and holding a kerchief in its mouth. Next to the tree and serpent stands Eve wearing gloves, stockings, and high heels. A strategically placed leaf covers her lower body, but her breasts are bare and she looks up at the serpent in rapt attention. The accompanying rhyme updates the Eve story and frames it within a fashion context.

> The snake said to Eve in his sly little way "I tempted with apples back in My Day But now that these 'Kerchiefs by Kimball' are handy I find that as Tempters they surely are dandy."[75]

Recasting the consumer as Eve, the forbidden fruit as a kerchief, and the Kimball Company as the serpent, the ad encouraged women to indulge their desires. The rewards were worth the risk as material objects, whether apples or kerchiefs, would improve their lives.

Framing fashion as an irresistible temptation that women should indulge in, just as Eve did, appeared frequently in the 1950s and 1960s. Lenthéric, who created Miracle perfume, also produced makeup that used the language and visual imagery associated with Eve. In an illustrated ad for "Pippin Red" "sta-put" lipstick, a bright red apple and the word "tempting" in the ad copy invoked these meanings, as did their "Adam's Rib" perfume and "Apple of Eden" lipstick. In an advertisement for the latter, an illustrated tree, garden setting, and Eve connoted Eden, while the lipstick, "a primeval red for the uninhibited," came in a "Jewel of Eden" case that featured a serpent curled around the top of the lipstick tube.[76] The ad emphasizes Eve's associations with sexuality through its use of "uninhibited" and the color red, while the serpent on the lipstick tube serves as a tangible reminder to consumers of their edgy status and the supernatural power of fashion products.

While some advertisements included detailed illustrations of the Eve and Eden scenario, many others assumed readers' familiarity with the story and simply used the language of "temptation" or "Eve" and the visual cliché of the apple as shorthand for these ideas. For example, Revlon "double-dare[d]" women to partake of their "Fatal Apple" makeup and promised women the "look of Eve" in their ad copy, while the photograph featured a beautiful model and a bright shiny red apple.[77] Nina Ricci's "Fille d'Eve" perfume came in an apple-shaped bottle and beckoned "daughters of Eve" to try "the most tempting perfume this side of Paradise!"[78] As fashion advertising decontextualized aspects of Christianity, the apple symbolized temptation and often became the only visual cue to connote Eve. An advertisement for Formfit bras, photographed in black and white, foregrounded the model attired in the company's undergarments. Caught in motion, the model's pose highlights not only the product but also a sense of anticipation, as she is about to take a bite out of a bright red apple—the only color used in the tableau.[79] Dorothy Gray's "Apple on a Stick" lipstick, Shapemaker stockings, "Oh la la" perfume, and many others incorporated apples to highlight the lure of their products.[80] Other ads conveyed the same idea by using the symbol of the serpent, and occasionally the devil himself.[81] These advertisements used Eve to highlight fashion as a temptation, a sinful indulgence that would yield earthly rewards.

Eve-related products tempted, but more than that, they promised women the power of choice and personal transformation. This emphasis invoked long-standing Arminian theological ideas about free-will and self-transformation and thus, the possibility of "complete personal change through collaboration with cosmic forces."[82] Supernatural products promised consumers amazing transformational possibilities that reinforced the alliance between faith and fashion. "A postmillennial faith in progress combined with a perfectionist quest for transfigured selfhood to shape new images of health and beauty."[83] They assured spiritual seekers that spiritual (and physical) change was possible and provided them with the tools to achieve it.

Eve symbolized the "original" woman but also "every" woman. She represented the "purely feminine," as one ad stated.[84] And through fashion products, women could realize their "Eve" identity. One ad literally painted a picture of the biblical scene with Eve standing in a garden setting, her nakedness hidden by the limb of an apple tree and an "Eve petticoat" (the product being sold). A snake also lurked in the tree, but Adam is nowhere to be seen, and Eve occupies center stage. Beautiful and equipped with the power of choice, she represents female potential—an example of what women could buy and therefore be. By wearing this petticoat, the ad suggests that women can access Eve's femininity as the serpent whispers: "Come, pretty girl. Be Eve. You can, you know, in Trafedda."[85] Similarly, the words "for the many faces of Eve" dominate a two-page advertisement from Maybelline in 1961. The line plays on the biblical reference and the title of the movie "The Three Faces of Eve" (1957). The close-up of the model in beautifully done makeup on the right page shows her facing the camera and in profile—her many faces. The text on the left page provides the framework for interpretation. In large letters, it simply states: "You are Eve . . ." It then adds that you are "the eternal woman" with "a hundred faces to beguile and fascinate." By using Maybelline makeup, the eternal woman, you, can be a "siren," a "queen," "shy," or whatever you desire.[86]

The promised transformation and accompanying powers of "being Eve" depended upon making a purchase, and ads highlighted how fortunate female consumers were. They had significantly more options than Eve. For instance, alongside an illustration of Eve with an apple, the copy

Figure 2.9B. Vladimir Bobri illustration of Eve featured in a Hanes advertisement, *Vogue* 127 (March 15, 1956): 29; courtesy of Hanes Brand International and the Vladimir Bobri Estate.

for a Hanes hosiery ad lamented "Poor Girl! [Eve] She never knew the temptation of seamless stockings by Hanes."[87] Another proclaimed: "Eve . . . had only an apple, but you . . . have Intoxication perfume by D'Orsay."[88] Through these various products, advertisements assured consumers that Christianity endorsed the fashion enterprise and that fashion products would enhance their lives in diverse ways.

Eve in fashion added a strand of playful naughtiness to the fashionable religion constructed through these advertisements. She helped make over Christianity into a more modern and edgy religion that was not bound by strict notions of sin, frugality, or sexuality. For instance, in the early 1960s, Catalina, a prominent swimsuit company, launched an entire campaign focused on Eve, entitled "part of the art of Eve." Each ad featured a woman posed provocatively in a garden-like setting wearing one of Catalina's swimsuits.[89] The campaign suggested that any woman could be beautiful and wield sexual power in the right swimwear.

An Aziza campaign for eye makeup in the 1960s also made these connections clear. The ads that ran in 1965 and 1966 featured a close-up of a woman's face surrounded by leafy greenery, which simultaneously drew the viewer's gaze to the model's eyes and connoted the Garden of Eden setting. The ad copy reinforced this interpretation. It not only used the language of innocence and temptation, but the bolded copy reads: "If Eve had worn Aziza, she wouldn't have needed an apple."[90] Similarly, in the mid-1960s, Lady Manhattan, which sold women's clothes, consistently placed an image of a green snake coiled around a red apple in the corner of the page accompanied by the line "Here's how the first woman did it," suggesting that Eve's power came from her yielding to temptation and eating the apple. Lady Manhattan then provided women with a modern way to "be Eve" and proclaimed: "Here's how the first lady does it" alongside a large picture of a model in the advertised attire. The text completes the interpretive loop: "Eve's always first in the heart of her Adam because she knows a beguiling fashion when she sees it."[91] Eve simply had an apple and look what she accomplished. Lady Manhattan wanted a woman to imagine what she could do with the power of fashion at her disposal.

Fashion advertising's reconceptualization of Eve as a chic and edgy Christian heroine invoked the biblical text and Christianity, while simultaneously distancing this made-over Christianity from literal interpretations of the Bible, theological preoccupations with original sin, and institutional religion. This fashionable religion embraced moral imperfections, spending money, and feminine wiles. It focused on the individual, her choices, and her appearance. This personalization obscured (or attempted to) how this vision of female empowerment remained limited to the realm of beauty, the discipline of the body, and sexual relationships with men. At the same time, though, this fashionable religion emphasized the ways that Christianity revolved around appearances, symbols, and objects. This, in turn, highlighted how the seeker-consumer should think about Christianity in terms of the visual and the material.

This shift aligned with changes occurring in the American religious landscape. If revivalism and conformity characterized religion in the 1950s, then rebellion and experimentation described the 1960s. Events in this decade encouraged spiritual experimentation as people criticized institutional Christianity, joined new religious movements, and sought alternative spiritual paths. As Americans became spiritual seekers crafting temporary spiritual worlds through borrowing and blending, the fashionable religion seen in fashion magazines provided individually oriented spiritual seekers with numerous visual sights and material products designed to transform their spiritual bodies.[92]

Modern Christian Magic

While most fashion advertisements from the 1940s through the 1960s utilized the Christian imaginary, some employed other spiritual systems, such as magic, that allowed the spiritual seeker to reap their benefits.[93] As seen in chapter 1, referencing other religions tapped into liberal Christian ideas about religious tolerance and diversity, as well as representing dimensions of the "universal religious sentiment" that spiritual seekers could and should appreciate.[94] Robert Wuthnow writes, "white, middle-class Americans may believe that African Americans have always understood spirituality better than they have and that Asian religions are also better because they were never seduced by Western positivism."[95] According to this logic, those peoples and religious forms deemed "foreign" and "primitive" had access to more "authentic" forms of religiosity that tapped into raw supernatural power. This is certainly the case with conceptions of magic.

Historically, scholars have defined magic in contrast to Christianity and Western understandings of religion. Labeling magic as "superstition," a childish spiritual formation that enlightened people have outgrown, some early scholars deemed magic to be primitive, an early phase in the evolution of religion proper. This perspective emphasized how religion supposedly focuses on the spirit and mind, while magic concerns the body and the material world. Religion revolved around selflessness and devotion to others, but magic promoted the self—casting spells and performing rituals to achieve personal desires.[96]

While this interpretive framework established Western religions as enlightened and superior, the act of excising and assigning magic to "primitive" Others constructed "magic" as something to be "miraculously rediscovered and hailed as a new life-source."[97] By "discovering" and invoking these magical forces, advertisers highlighted the supernatural possibilities of their products. At the same time, fashion advertising made magic modern. The practice and efficacy of this modern magic did not depend on any specific cultural knowledge; it could be created and wielded by the fashion industry and its consumers. Rather than relying on "superstition," products worked through science and technology. Rather than requiring exotic rituals or paraphernalia, modernized magic demanded the purchasing of fashion products, and instead of an unpredictable supernatural force, fashion magic promised a controllable and efficacious system.

Stripped of any cultural specificity, modern fashion magic offered consumers tempting short-cuts to their desires that challenged elements of Christianity but could also be incorporated into it. For example, fashion advertising's emphasis on "magic tricks" along with the accompanying visual cues questioned Christianity's emphasis on hard work, discipline, and honesty. Christianity celebrated the possibilities of personal transformation, but such changes depended upon earnest and often challenging spiritual work, not tricks. However, by incorporating magic, these ads constructed a fashionable religion that provided all the power of a supernatural system, without all the effort. Not "born" with beautiful lashes? No worries, Maybelline's "magic mascara" makes it look as if you were.[98] Other advertisements lauded their ability to fool others. One ad proclaimed its product to be the "greatest make-up trick since lip rouge became lipstick." Promoting "lidstick" eye shadow (like lipstick for the eyes), the advertising tableau promised women the power of illusion: "Say you're sexy with Sapphire. Make believe you're modest with Mauve."[99] In tension with Christian discourses that emphasized the alignment of one's internal state and their outward appearance, these fashion advertisements promoted the magical possibilities of deception, illusion, and trickery. While these claims transgressed long-standing Christian ideas, the practice of fashion magic was not necessarily antithetical to Christianity. Magic tricks were made efficacious through buying and using particular fashion products that could be incorporated into the life of a Christian, a seeker, and those not affiliated with a specific religion. Magic did not demand a particular allegiance, an individual could simply use it, and it promised to work.

Like modern miracles, fashion magic offered "real" results for everyday life through innovative products that provided devotees with previously unattainable ends. New textiles, new technologies, and new designs provided patrons with increasingly impressive possibilities. These innovations transformed ordinary items into powerful sacred objects.[100] In 1946, Rosewood Fabrics advertised its "fabric magic," a new rayon blend. With its "delicate texture" and versatility, "perfect for afternoon or evenings," the fabric promised to empower its wearer with "fashion witchery."[101] Almost a decade later, Perma-Lift sold "Magic Gold" girdles and brassieres. In the ad, a Tinker Bell–like fairy offered women four undergarments (three girdles and one bra) to achieve enchanting results. The ability to "make you all you dreamed to be" without using any boning that could "break the spell." The imagined consumer could achieve her dream figure without the pain of bone stays. The gold thread added an elegant touch that transformed these undergarments from ordinary to extraordinary. They promised the magical ability to reshape your figure and therefore your life. You did not need different beliefs, punishing corsets, or more exercise, but rather the right foundational garments upon which to build your style.

Magical products that provided short-cuts to amazing personal transformations constituted a recurring theme. Relax-A-cizor advised women to "try magic," if they wanted "smaller hips." Promising "the magic of size-reducing exercise—without a whit of the wearisome work!" The ad copy explained that women simply needed to place the beauty pads on their "figure problem" areas, sit down, watch television, and let the machine do its work. By doing so, reader-consumers could look like the beautiful woman in the campaign dressed up as a magician in one ad and a witch in another.[102] Similarly, Jaquet cosmetics deliberately addressed the difference between real beauty and the illusion of it as it outlined the powerful effects of its "white magic" foundation. In addition to detailed instructions for its use, the advertisement assured consumers that they too could successfully employ "make-up tricks" to hide blemishes and shadows under the eyes. Blurring the lines between reality and trickery, "white magic" could transform a woman's face from sleep-deprived to dewy-eyed in seconds.[103] These advertisements invoked the concept of magic through innovative products that promised consumers enchanting results.

The results of this consumable and controllable fashion magic ranged from longer lashes to smaller waists to "fashion witchery." While numerous advertisements emphasized the possibility of "becoming Eve," others proclaimed that with the right tools, women could become "fashion witch[es]" and wield their own magical powers. This emphasized the rebellious and edgy element of fashionable religion and tapped into a range of wider cultural conceptions about witches. Television's *Bewitched* (1964 to 1972) emphasized the ease of protagonist's Samantha's magical powers in contrast to the hard-working and rule-abiding ethic embodied in her husband Darren. Disney movies, such as *Snow White* (1937) and *Sleeping Beauty* (1959), demonstrated the danger of witches and their powers, while *The Wizard of Oz* (1939) depicted witches of both the good and bad persuasion. Magic, regularly assumed to be the province of women, circumvented the regular order of things—hard work, ordinary objects, and future outcomes—by providing access to supernatural powers that could change their lives.

Often advertisements vividly depicted this transformation. A 1959 Max Factor ad, for example, showed a strong woman conjuring magic in front of a fire. The woman's direct gaze, unflinching proximity to the fire, and upraised arm position highlight her strength and witchlike status. Her red gown and perfectly done hair along with her actively pouring the ingredients (red and gold) into the fire demonstrate her elegance, as well as her power. In control, standing fearlessly before the blazing fire, she blends red and gold into one entity through the flames that she seemingly controls. The ad copy, "Cast a magic spell!" and the name "Goldfire" attempt to capture this exotic and new blend of red and gold that provided consumers with "bewitching new magic for your eyes." This advertisement for lipstick and eye shadow emphasized the supernatural, yet practical power women could gain and wield through the right makeup selections.[104]

Other ads also vividly depicted the power and enigma of the fashion witch. In 1960, Tussy's two-page advertisement for its "lidstick" eye

Figure 2.9C. "Bewitching" woman creating the "magical" Goldfire
Glow for Max Factor lipstick; illustration from Max Factor
advertisement, *Vogue* 134 (October 1, 1959): 58.

shadow included an illustration of six "magical" women. They wear black
veils over their hair and lower faces, which simultaneously highlights
their mysterious nature, as well as their eyes, which sport the various
colors of eye shadow being sold. The addition of stars and a black sky-
like background reinforce the connotations of supernatural power.[105]
Max Factor's "eye shadow magic," basic black, featured a similar illustration. A mysterious woman shrouded in black except for her eyes, which
are revealed by a masklike shape.[106] Women using such magical products, it seems, could do or be anything because as Pola Cosmetics stated
in its 1969 advertisements, its products possessed "the magic" of "making things happen."[107] By appealing to magical language and imagery,

fashion advertisers offered women the ability to challenge biology and transform their bodies through fashion products.[108]

Fashion advertisings' use of magic confined women's empowerment to the realms of commerce, beauty, and men. Magical products not only made women's lives easier and enhanced their beauty, they also granted them the ability to "bewitch" men. "Sheer witchery," described nylons that promised to "keep your audience spellbound," while Menace perfume proclaimed "deliberate witchery" and Magie perfume provided "Magic for the Women Men Remember."[109] An ad for Black Magic perfume, for instance, featured a close-up of a beautiful woman's face surrounded by a spiderweb. Her eyes gaze downward and direct the viewer's attention to the perfume's name in large script and an image of the perfume bottle imprinted with a smoking cauldron. These visual cues reinforce the product's promise: "bewitchery." Then, in the bottom right corner, one sees that this fashion witch has indeed caught a man through this magical potion.[110]

Yet, as with Eve and the other advertisements examined in this chapter, this particular conceptualization of magic contributed to a way of seeing religion as fashionable and avant-garde, which could appeal to emerging spiritual seekers. Fashion magic affirmed that supernatural power existed and could be accessed without having to delve into religious conservatism or primitivism. Further, personal transformation was possible without undue sacrifice and toil. Rather than the hard work required by some forms of institutional religion, the fashionable religion constructed through fashion magazines promised shortcuts and tricks to personal change. Modern fashion magic, as with Eve, miracles, and "Sunday Best" style, framed religion as a decontextualized, individualized, and sensual experience focused on visual and material forms.

Further, the ads suggested that these magical elements could be incorporated into and help make over Christianity. Advertisements' use of magic often appeared alongside language and visual clichés proclaiming heavenly miracles and divine gifts.[111] By mixing Christian symbols and concepts with that of magic, fashion advertising suggested that Christianity need not be so hard. In keeping with the rise of seeker-oriented spirituality and changes in the American religious landscape, a made-over Christianity offered people sacred moments and personal transformations that did not require sustained attention or hard work. Through modern miracles and magic tricks, fashionable religion placed the individual in control of her spiritual life—a spiritual life increasingly focused on her personal body, individual taste, and fashion products.

Conclusion

Fashion magazine advertisements from the mid-1940s through the 1960s reinforced the alliance between Christianity and commerce. As seen at the beginning of this chapter, a Kayser glove advertisement instructed consumers to "look" at church-goers in their Easter finery. In this ad and numerous others, we can look and see how advertising combined fashion and Christianity. It established fashion as a mediator of Christianity and framed the consumption and experience of fashion in the linguistic and visual rhetoric of Christianity. These advertising strategies not only enhanced their claims about fashion products but also, as the Kayser ad implied, emphasized the importance of looking and seeing religion at both an individual and conceptual level.

Fashion advertising's selective use of the Christian imaginary to sell products and highlight their potential reinforced many of the ways of seeing addressed in chapter 1.[112] Advertisements also focused on the individual spiritual journey, promised supernatural and sensory experiences, and decontextualized Christian concepts and symbols. "Sunday Best" styles, miraculous makeup, and praiseworthy plaids made over Christianity into a religious tradition that offered seekers spiritual possibilities that looked sophisticated and modern. Incorporating a rebellious heroine, Eve, and a "primitive" spiritual system, magic, also introduced a transgressive element into the chic Christianity being displayed. Not bound by church, defined by theology, or constrained by either literalism or rationalism, this fashionable religion promised adherent-consumers results—symbols, products, and experiences that would transform their lives.

Unlike chapter 1, though, in which religion remained a separate and parallel discourse to that of fashion, this chapter highlights how advertising combined these discourses. In doing so, advertisements emphasized the alliance between Christianity and fashion—the *de facto* status of Christianity in the world of fashion. At the same time, by mediating elements of the Christian heritage, fashion altered the appearance of it. Through words and symbols, illustrations and packaging, advertisements shaped fashionable religion into a decontextualized, individualized, and sensual force accessible through visual and material forms. This vision of a symbolic, material, and individual Christianity made available through fashion products represents an important development in examining how God got on a dress. This made-over Christianity accustomed seeker-consumers to the idea of seeing, purchasing, and displaying religion. This, in turn, focused attention on the "sacred objects" or "relics" of Christianity and encouraged jewelers and fashion designers to push these trends further. As we will see in chapter 3, they did so by incorporating religious symbols and inspirations into their jewelry designs.

3

Accessorizing the Cross

In 2002, tabloid and news headlines reported the religious furor erupting over celebrities wearing cross necklaces. According to numerous articles that circulated on the web, supermodel Naomi Campbell, actresses Jennifer Aniston and Catherine Zeta-Jones, and power couple Victoria and David Beckham "were all criticized," by the Vatican, "for turning jewel-encrusted crosses into 'the mania of the moment.'" The protesters explained that "the crucifix was a sacred symbol and described the fashion as 'incomprehensible.'" Bill Hunter, a leader of Churches of Christ who supported the Vatican's critique, explained his position. "Anybody who has faith in Jesus can express that by wearing a cross and if they don't believe then that piece of jewelry becomes meaningless to the person." He continued, "For Christians, the cross is at the centre of our faith and is a major part of our belief system."[1] The cross criticisms came from the "Vatican News Agency," Fides, which was equated directly with Pope John Paul II and a papal condemnation. A *NY Post* article proclaimed, "Pope's Cross Words," while another included a picture of Pope John Paul II (wearing a cross) accompanied by a caption, which read: "The Vatican under the Pope . . . has criticized celebrities for wearing crucifixes."[2] Whether the Pope approved or not, much of the coverage linked this controversy to an earlier one involving Madonna.

In 1984, the Michigan-born Madonna Louise Ciccone took the music world by storm with the performance of her new single, "Like a Virgin," at the first MTV Video Music Awards. Attired in a lingerie-style wedding dress along with a custom "Boy Toy" belt buckle and numerous necklaces, including a variety of cross pendants, Madonna sang the lyrics of her suggestive song as she made her way down a giant wedding cake and, as one observer described it, "eliminated any long-standing associations between 'white' and 'purity' and forever made the phrases 'wedding dress' and 'writhing' seem perfectly appropriate together in the same sentence." It was an iconic moment in both music and fashion history.[3] As James Wolcott wrote in *Vanity Fair* about the Virgin Tour: "Madonna has been vilified . . . as if she were an invitation to a gang bang and a threat to the nation's morals."[4] Her sexuality, her music, and her style were controversial, but she was wildly popular. Madonna's subsequent appearance with Rosanna Arquette in *Desperately Seeking Susan* (1985) cemented her look (rubber bracelets, cross necklaces, and lace gloves) in the fashion timeline—a feat aided by the advent of MTV in 1981, which helped make rock stars into fashion icons almost instantaneously. The retail power of female pop stars was such that in 1985 "the Associated Merchandising Corporation . . . recommended that its member department stores open FTV, or fashion television, boutiques. Macy's has featured shops named Madonnaland and Girls Just Want to Have Fun."[5] Thus, the cross emerged as a *de rigueur* accessory in the fashion landscape of the 1980s.

In these instances, controversy accompanied the wearing of the cross, but the media focus on controversy obscures the historical process by which the cross became a popular fashion accessory. As we have seen in chapters 1 and 2, from the 1940s through the 1960s, fashion articles and advertisements constructed a way of seeing Christianity that provided liberal Protestants, progressive Catholics, and spiritual seekers with a sophisticated and modern way to be religious.[6] This fashionable religion focused on the appearance, beauty, and display of Christianity, whether through photographs of churches, reproductions of high art, or the marketing of an angelic appearance. These sophisticated forms emphasized the supernatural and the sensual, the visual and the material, the symbolic and the individual, but did so in ways that distanced potential practitioners from the backwardness associated with religious fundamentalism and religious "primitivism."

The characteristics of this fashionable religion set the stage for additional combinations of religion and fashion. Fashion magazines primed reader-consumers to see the Christian heritage in bits and pieces— decontextualized concepts and visual symbols—and to view fashion products as powerful supernaturally charged sacred objects. Given fashion's way of seeing the tradition and the industry's demand for constant novelty, it makes sense that Christianity's dominant symbol, the cross, and the jewelry form, historically infused with spiritual meanings, emerged as one of the earliest and most popular instances of religion moving beyond the text and images of fashion magazines into fashion designs and accessories. God did not simply appear on a dress, but the visualization and materialization of Christianity in cross jewelry functioned as a crucial next step in understanding how this process occurred.

Through an examination of jewelry advertisements[7], photo shoots, and features in fashion magazines, as well as media coverage in newspapers, this chapter traces the cross in modern fashion history. Examining this history, though, does not mean dismissing cross jewelry as "simply" or "just" another fashion commodity—a symbol trivialized and corrupted by its reproduction throughout various forms of popular culture, its "authenticity" lost as it moves out of its traditional, ritualized context of the church.[8] Despite its repeated reproduction (or perhaps because of it), people in the past and the present find the symbol of the cross in jewelry form meaningful. Cross jewelry was not simply transformed from a devotional object into a fashionable accessory; rather, cross jewelry in fashion accumulated new meanings that were added to and layered on top of the old.[9] Put another way, the religious meanings ascribed to cross jewelry combined with fashion's emphasis on appearance, display, and beauty to produce an artifact for fashionable religion.

The first part of this chapter highlights the neglected genesis of the cross in modern fashion through the work of Gabrielle 'Coco' Chanel, which established the popularity of cross jewelry and the parameters for subsequent designs. The second part of the chapter analyzes how cross jewelry became a "fashion fad" by the late 1960s that, unlike the criticisms launched at celebrities, such as Madonna, generated little comment and controversy in either the secular or religious press. As an emblem of fashionable religion, these crosses combined the present with the past, and sophisticated style with supernatural potential. The third part of the chapter investigates the controversy that greeted cross jewelry as part of Madonna's wardrobe, but, its continued popularity in spite or because of this public debate. Chronicling this history highlights how the changing religious environment shaped responses to cross jewelry and challenged its status as a "summarizing symbol," an uncontested and respected representation of allegiance to Christianity, even as Christianity's makeover continued.[10]

The Cross and Coco Chanel

Fashion writer Georgina O'Hara Callahan points to the late 1980s as the time when "the cross or crucifix began to appear on runways as a jewelry accessory. By the 1990s it was a popular motif, in different forms and sizes, worn as a necklace, pin or brooch, and also as a shoe buckle."[11] However, long before Madonna's "Like a Virgin" performance or the Vatican's critique of the "mania of the moment," the cross was a vital part of the fashion industry. It appeared in fashion advertisements and photo shoots in the 1940s and 1950s and became even more prominent in the 1960s. Yet, this trend went largely unnoticed until 1969, when media sources declared cross jewelry a "fashion fad." From the 1940s until this declaration, the unremarkable appearance of the cross in fashion indicates that advertisers, designers, and consumers saw fashion and Christianity as allies. However, at the same time, these sources re-envisioned Christianity as a religion focused on appearances and display, practices made possible through the purchasing of fashion products.

The emergence of the cross in fashion occurred gradually and with little fanfare. In the 1940s and 1950s, cross jewelry appeared occasionally in advertisements and photo shoots, most often as an unremarked upon accessory. For example, in 1947, a full-page ad featuring a recently engaged Chicago socialite highlights her diamond ring and commitment to using Pond's cold cream, but the copy does not identify her elaborately jeweled cross necklace.[12] Similarly, *Vogue*'s two-page synopsis of Tennessee Williams' play "The Rose Tattoo" in 1951 includes a close-up of actress Maureen Stapleton wearing a bejeweled cross on a ribbon, but this accessory goes unmentioned.[13] Six months later, a short feature on "The Upkeep of Costume," includes more specificity. The text indicates that the model's necklace, a "silvered filigree and rhinestone cross on a rhinestone chain," is available for $35.[14] Yet, vagueness again characterized a 1955 feature on accessories. In this promotion, two jeweled cross pins appear, but the accompanying text describes one as a "singular flash of jewels" for $12, and the other boasts "fake diamonds, a 'pearl' in a black enamel pin" for $7.50. Neither caption names or refers to their cross shape.[15] The only other glimpses of the cross appear in smaller advertisements for charms that include Christmas trees, angels, Easter eggs, and Bibles with crosses on the front cover.[16]

During this time, however, one fashion designer, Gabrielle "Coco" Chanel, repeatedly included the cross as a part of her jewelry designs. Famous in fashion history for finding women's wear inspiration in men's wear, using jersey (a fabric previously used for undergarments) in her stylish attire, and designing simple silhouettes as seen in her "little black dress" of 1926, Chanel and her design house dominated fashion prior to World War II, and after fifteen years away, regained prominence in the late 1950s.[17] She launched Chanel No. 5 in 1921, "the first perfume to bear a couturier's name on the label," outfitted Jacqueline Kennedy in the 1960s, and famously said, "I don't like people talking about the Chanel fashion. Chanel—above all else, is a style. Fashion, you see, goes out of fashion. Style never."[18]

In addition to clothes and perfume, Chanel also designed and produced jewelry. Flaunting convention, Chanel wore "heaps of jewelry" with casual attire during the day, while wearing little or no jewelry in the evening. She also challenged the status of "real" and "fake" jewels, by designing and wearing costume jewelry.[19] Fashion historian Caroline Rennolds Milbank writes that "by inaugurating her faux jewels with pearls and crystals, Chanel was subversively referencing the two most ubiquitous totems of wealth: the string of natural pearls and the diamond rivière."[20] She challenged existing notions of luxury and fashion and made costume jewelry socially acceptable.

Chanel also helped make the cross an integral part of the modern fashion industry, a design choice that reflects her background and context. In France in 1895, after the death of his wife, Albert Chanel sent his daughters, including twelve-year-old Gabrielle, to an orphanage "run by the sisters of the Congregation of the Sacred Heart of Mary." Then, at the age of 17, she attended a convent school.[21] Chanel's unwillingness to discuss her childhood makes it difficult to assess her relationship to Catholicism and its influence on her work. Yet, fragments of this religious past resurface throughout her career and life. "To Marcel Haedrich [a French journalist] she confided that her suits had their origins in a tailored costume she wore during her teens," which suggest the residue of a Catholic school uniform.[22] Further, in describing one of her vacation homes, biographer Edmonde Charles-Roux notes how Chanel's friends "sensed a bit of the convent." In one account, "Chanel declared that she had advised her architect to visit a monastery where, as a child, 'she has spent marvelous vacations.' In truth, she had sent him to Aubazine, to that orphanage whose severe beauty continued, secretly, to haunt her."[23] In addition to her childhood, the environment of Western Europe remained steeped in Christianity. "The shared religious heritage of Western Europe," as sociologist Grace Davie reminds, influenced "a whole range of cultural values."[24] Catholicism shaped Chanel's childhood and inspired elements of her designs.

However, it did not define her life. Similar to Madonna in the 1980s, Chanel pushed boundaries and was a provocative figure—a prominent designer known for her flouting of convention and her famous lovers, including the Duke of Westminster, the Grand Duke Dmitri Pavlovich, and a Nazi officer. Yet unlike more recent controversies over cross jewelry, Chanel's incorporation of the cross into her fashion designs occurred with seemingly little debate. This difference in reception may reflect, in part, the different media worlds of the times. However, I suggest that these different responses also indicate something more.

Chanel's Catholic past, provocative persona, and designer status combined to make her cross jewelry simultaneously fashionable yet tasteful, traditional yet modern, respectful yet playful. This can be seen in one of the most famous Chanel jewelry design motifs. In the 1930s, she hired Fulco Santo Stefano della Cerda, Duke of Verdura, a Sicilian aristocrat, to design with and for her.[25] This collaboration produced one of the most iconic pieces of Chanel jewelry: enameled cuffs featuring Maltese crosses adorned with colorful gems. This cross became one of the hallmarks of Chanel's jewelry designs and numerous photographs show Chanel wearing the iconic cuffs.

A distinct variation on the cross shape and symbol, the Maltese iteration nevertheless drew upon the Christian past. In 1126 the Knights Hospitallers of Saint John adopted the Maltese cross as their symbol, identified by its eight points. Some accounts suggest that a tunic bearing the symbol protected the Knights from their enemy's weapons, while others emphasize that the eight points of the Maltese cross represent the Knight's eight obligations: "to live in truth, have faith, repent one's sins, give proof of humility, love justice, be merciful, be sincere and wholehearted, and to endure persecution."[26] The Maltese cross shape invoked ideas about Christian virtue and divine protection. The selection of this shape and its spiritual connotations aligned with the ways fashion

Figure 3.1. Chanel's original "Maltese Cross" cuffs
designed by Verdura; courtesy of Verdura.

magazine articles and advertisements emphasized the visual and the symbolic in Christianity, as well as the supernatural powers attributed to sacred objects and fashion products.

In addition, the Chanel-Verdura cuffs provided a fashionable and playful take on this traditional symbol that offered interpretive possibilities. Rather than Knights wearing starkly drawn crosses on their robes or shields, the cuffs sported a decontextualized Maltese cross adorned with numerous precious gems, connoting luxury and sophistication. These characteristics also identified it as a fashion item, rather than a devotional aid. At the same time, though, by preserving the basic outline of the Maltese cross and evoking the shape's exotic Maltese and Christian history, the cuffs connoted ideas about the object's potential spiritual power. As a result, the Chanel-Verdura cuffs provided consumers with a sophisticated way to simultaneously exhibit fashion and religion.

In his classic essay "The Work of Art in the Age of Mechanical Reproduction," Walter Benjamin laments arts' loss of "aura" through its replication, but he also highlights how the reproduction of an art object detaches it from tradition and "meet[s] the beholder . . . in his own particular situation."[27] In a similar way, the Chanel-Verdura cuff offered potential consumers proximity to and personalization of the meanings (spiritual and cosmopolitan) ascribed to the source—Malta and the Maltese cross. Consumers did not need to be spiritual pilgrims who visited Malta; rather, they could invoke Malta and any potential supernatural powers associated with its cross through purchasing a reproduction and wearing it. As discussed in chapter 2, the pleasure and possibility of such objects resided not in a zero-sum game based on Chanel's sincerity or the object's authenticity, but rather in a back-and-forth movement between "illusionism and realism."[28] Birgit Meyer explains, "As belief becomes thus vested in the image, it becomes hard to distinguish between belief and make-believe, miracles and special effects, or truth and illusion."[29] The Chanel-Verdura cuffs offered consumers this possibility—an object that could transform their sartorial and spiritual lives.

Fashion columns in the 1930s commented on Chanel's jewelry designs but said little about the inclusion of this religious symbol.[30] Yet, the cross remained a vital part of her design aesthetic, and Verdura designed numerous variations of the Maltese cuff. Many of these pieces were reproduced in the 1950s, when the House of Chanel reopened after the war.[31] So renowned are these cuffs, that in 1987, when Diana Vreeland, former fashion editor of *Harper's Bazaar* and former editor-in-chief of *Vogue*, auctioned off her jewelry at Sotheby's, including four of Chanel's cuffs, it made the *New York Times*.[32]

Chanel's jewelry designs also included styles of crosses that modernized another historic, "traditional," and "authentic" source. Chanel was inspired by the Byzantine period in Christian history, renowned in fashion for its rich artistic repository. "From the point of view of jewelry, no empire was ever richer in traditions than that of the Byzantines."[33] One historian notes, "The symbolism of Christianity pervades much Byzantine jewelry, and pendant crosses (some of which also served as reliquaries) were among the earliest and most popular pieces."[34] Chanel experienced this rich tradition of jewelry and religion on a visit to the

Tomb of Galla Placidia in Ravenna, Italy. The site, which dates to the fifth century CE, features numerous mosaics of biblical figures, saints, and Christ the Good Shepherd. It inspired Chanel.[35] According to Patrick Mauriès, in *Jewelry by Chanel*, the impact of this visit "can be seen especially clearly in the great number of crosses . . . which she designed using combinations of pearls and precious stones."[36]

In the 1950s, Chanel hired French jeweler Robert Goossens to work on Byzantine-inspired designs, which meant the use of gold, colored gemstones, and Christian symbols.[37] Given this inspiration, Goossens and Chanel designed numerous cross pendants and brooches, many of which were produced in 1954, when the House reopened. In comparison with the bright and shiny character of the Chanel-Verdura Maltese cross cuff, the Byzantine cross pendants and brooches evince a simpler aesthetic. They use gold and precious gems, but the settings and style reflect their Byzantine inspiration. In one design, from the 1960s, gold, pearl, turquoise, and tourmaline adorn the face of the cross, while a saint is engraved on the reverse. The turquoise stones are rough and uneven, and the gold has a similar, almost primitive, appearance, and the saint on the back adds another layer of simplicity and austerity to this grand piece.[38] Here, again, we see Chanel's jewelry offer a modern and sophisticated interpretation of a historic and traditional form. Her use of precious gems echoes the grandeur of the Byzantine style and highlights the wealth of the era and the consumer. At the same time, the simplicity of the settings and the inclusion of the saint recall ideas about devotion to and the protection of the divine.

Despite Chanel's evolving aesthetic, the cross remained a recognizable element of her jewelry designs that fashion journalists highlighted in the 1950s. For example, in a 1957 *New York Times* article, Phyllis Lee Levin described the latest fashion trend in "Spring Clothes Deserve Medals." She notes "that the spring suit lapel without a bold jewel will look forlorn." Levin attributes this trend to the work of Coco Chanel, "a kind of Queen Mother of costume jewelry." She explains, "In many cases, the outlines of her wonderful tangles of sapphires and emeralds followed the classic Maltese cross, star and medallion shapes."[39] More than twenty years later, fashion reporters continued to mention Chanel's influence in the realm of jewelry, especially her use of the Maltese cross.[40] For example, in 1988 fashion journalist Bernadine Morris characterized the details of designer Yves Saint Laurent's collection as "an unmistakable homage to Chanel," as the jewelry adorning his models included Maltese crosses.[41]

Fashion journalists and scholars of Chanel have noted this cross motif and emphasized the iconic status of the cuff bracelets, but few have commented on its significance as a religious symbol that was seemingly at home in the world of mid-twentieth-century fashion. While this silence is frustrating, it is also illuminating. In the 1950s, at the height of the Christian revivals in the United States, the cross as a fashion accessory drew little censure. In this context, the cross continued to function primarily, anthropologist Sherry Ortner would argue, as a "summarizing symbol." As such, the cross "sums up and stands in for a larger system; it represents many ideas, attitudes, and meanings all at the same time."[42] She explains that summarizing symbols discourage reflection and foster "a sort of all-or-nothing allegiance to the whole package." Fashionable cross jewelry, then, represented Christianity in an acceptable and sophisticated way.

At the same time, though, the emerging popularity of cross jewelry highlights how fashion increasingly constructed a way of seeing Christianity focused on symbols, appearance, and display, which was seemingly accepted. This reinforced and expanded the fashionable religion focused on art and emotion, the supernatural and the symbolic, as well as the individual and the material. As discussed in previous chapters, Western Christians and spiritual seekers often utilized a romantic worldview focused on the past. They viewed "primitive" peoples, distant locations, and earlier eras as more connected to religion and its power.[43] Chanel's designs utilized these ideas. Her inspirations drew on places (Malta) and time periods (the Byzantine era) seen as "antimodern" and thus conceptualized as "authentic" and "pure" sources for spiritual and artistic wonder. Her designs then captured, confined, and commodified these conceptions in a fashionable artifact. Beautifully crafted artistic renderings of a Christian symbol in designer jewelry embodied these notions and made them accessible to consumers—for a price. It also foreshadowed the shifting symbolic meaning of the cross—from a "summarizing" to an "elaborating" symbol, a symbol that helped people work through "complex and undifferentiated feelings and ideas."[44] Given its combination of a traditional form with modern style, Chanel's cross jewelry could be read as a "summarizing" symbol, even as wearers experienced and interpreted it as an "elaborating" one. And as cross jewelry became more popular, this trend continued.

The Cross as a Fashion Fad

Chanel's successful incorporation of the cross in fashion inspired other designers to follow her example and led to its increasing popularity. In the 1960s many others began designing, selling, and wearing cross jewelry. Pendants and brooches dominated, but rings, belts, and headpieces featuring cross designs also emerged as part of the style. The cross became a popular fashion accessory, which culminated in *Vogue* proclaiming the cross as fashionable in July 1969 and a *New York Times* article declaring "Ancient Symbol Becomes Fashion Fad" in November 1969.[45] *Vogue* explained, "No one knows how these things get started. Or why they catch on. But there it is. The cross has all at once—in Rome, in London, in Paris, and now in New York—become the thing one wants to wear."[46] Yet, a look through *Vogue*'s own pages shows how this trend emerged over the course of the decade. In the first half of the 1960s, fewer than five crosses appear each year in photo shoots, feature articles, and advertisements, but after 1965, the appearances increase each year, with more than ten cross items in both 1967 and 1968.

The trend started by Coco Chanel continued as Maltese and Byzantine crosses became increasingly common and commented upon.[47] An October 1963 *Vogue* article on the latest trend, "The Good Grey Jersey," a dress "every closet should have," encouraged women to accessorize with brown boots and a Maltese cross. The buying information for the cross shown on the model, handily available on a subsequent page, let readers know that it is a "gilt Maltese cross of fake rubies and rhinestones" ($25), while the chain is made of "more bogus rubies" ($5).[48] In the same year, in a short feature on "The Poet's Blouse," the dancing model wears said blouse with black tights and a Maltese cross necklace.[49] By 1966, the costume jewelry company Trifari was advertising Maltese cross pendants, which *Vogue* also sold in its "Shop Hound" section, a regular column that provided consumers with purchasing information on trendy items.[50] Even more indicative of its rising status, a Maltese cross appeared on the cover of *Vogue*'s October 1, 1967 issue. In this close-up

Figure 3.2. Jean Shrimpton wears Maltese Cross brooch featured on the cover of *Vogue* 150 (October 1, 1967); photograph by Richard Avedon, © The Richard Avedon Foundation and Condé Nast.

of English model and actress Jean Shrimpton, her long hair frames both her face and the "jewelled pin" that she wears. The description of the cover image never refers to the pin as a Maltese cross, but its shape is clear. The trend was established.[51]

Also following Chanel, the Byzantine cross emerged as a popular variation on the cross theme in the 1960s. For Chanel, Byzantine meant smaller but noticeable pendants featuring precious gems in intricate gold settings; however, the meaning of Byzantine ranged widely in 1960s crosses. Trifari, for instance, combined the Maltese cross shape with a Byzantine mosaic pattern, resulting in a colorful cross inset with blue and green stones that could be purchased for $17.50.[52] However, Byzantine looked very different in a *Vogue* photo shoot entitled "Turkey: Eastward to Eden." The name alone suggests the religious character of the

Figure 3.3. Model wearing Byzantine cross jewelry for "Turkey: Eastward to Eden," *Vogue* 148 (December 1966): 198; Henry Clarke/*Vogue* © Condé Nast.

landscape, an interpretation enhanced by the models sporting Byzantine cross jewelry. Standing on the "white-lime cliffs of Pamukkale," the model, wearing flowing long-sleeved "pajamas" of "chill-white crêpe," sports a "Byzantine cross." The simplicity of the backdrop and her casual attire contrast with the large gold cross, embellished with green stones. In this context, Byzantine means big and bejeweled.

A few pages later, in the same shoot, a model perches on a rooftop "two clear shouts from the domed and turreted rooftops of the Seraglio in Istanbul." Surrounded by "steeples," she appears with her arms outspread as if ready to take flight. The long "lacquer-red crêpe" dress by Dior looks beautiful in its simplicity—the only ornaments are the model's adorned sandals and an elaborate cross on a diamond-like chain. The caption does not define or describe the cross as Byzantine, but in the "fashion details" section, it is called a cross and made by the same company as the previous one.[53] Two years later, in 1968, *Vogue* explicitly promoted Byzantine cross jewelry in its "Vogue's Own Boutique" section, which provided details about the latest trends and where to purchase them. The brief entry, accompanied by a picture of a model wearing three different Byzantine cross necklaces, explains that they are "copied from the museum's collection, the chains, about $130; the crosses about $8.50. To be bought at The Metropolitan Museum of Art."[54] Inspired by Chanel and the exotic history of the empire, the Byzantine cross became a fashion statement.

The increasing popularity of cross jewelry in the 1960s encouraged diverse designers and outlets to meet consumer demand. Options ranged from famous jewelers, such as David Webb and Van Cleef & Arpels, selling diamond-decorated crosses to more accessible and affordable wares.[55] A Christmastime advertisement for Kay Jewelers, for example, used bright red bows and ornaments to highlight various pieces of jewelry. Amid gold pins, bracelets, and rings selling between $99 and $400, a more modest "cultured pearl cross" sold for $39.95.[56] Another cross, the "Crusader's Cross" from Jerusalem, was "inspired by a 13th century medieval treasure" and could be yours for $22.95, while the "Nature's Cross," was formed from the "incredible crystals" of Patrick County (most likely a reference to Croagh Patrick, a mountain and Catholic pilgrimage site in County Mayo, Ireland). "Unchanged from their original shape," these "natural crosses" could be yours for an affordable $4.50 and came "boxed with legend story."[57] The trend became more accessible as designers and manufacturers sold expensive jeweled crosses to actresses and wealthy socialites but also offered affordable versions for any and every woman.

The popularity of cross jewelry inspired some companies to produce other religiously themed jewelry, albeit with less success. For example, *Vogue*'s "Shop Hound" section endorsed a 14-karat gold Saint Christopher[58], while Johnston Jewelers promoted its "Eternal Tree of Life Brooch" crafted out of 14-karat gold and adorned with three diamonds and fruit made from seven "dangling jades."[59] Trifari, though, played up a different (and affordable) biblical theme—Noah's Ark. In the foreground of this full-page advertisement, a number of jeweled animal pins (two versions of each) appear on a ramp leading into an illustrated ark. The title "Trifari's Ark," underneath the ramp, provided the preferred

Figure 3.4. Noah's Ark–inspired illustration utilized in a Trifari advertisement, *Vogue* 148 (October 1, 1966): 149.

interpretation, but the text explained these pieces in fairy-tale, rather than biblical, terms. "Once upon a time," it proclaims, "Trifari discovered that there were no animals in the jewelry world lovable enough, sleek enough, chic enough, and which every fashionable girl could afford to have as her pet." The Trifari collection solved that dilemma and offered the "fashionable girl" the pet of her dreams for only $7.50.[60]

Experimentation also included, in a few instances, the cross moving onto the clothing and into the fashion designs. Whether intended or not, in a few dresses the color blocking of the fabric created the shape of a cross. In one, red strips of fabric on a field of white form a cross, while in another white stripes on blue fabric do the same.[61] In other designs, you cannot mistake the intentional use of the cross. The two issues of *Vogue* from September 1967 each showcase gold sequined dresses adorned with crosses. In the first the headline reads: "Spangled tennis dress—chained, crossed." In this case, the "large beaded formée cross" hangs from a gilded chain belt worn with the tennis dress. In the photograph, though, it appears as part of the dress, as it creates a unified and cohesive look.[62] On the bodice of the second gold dress, referred to as "This year's Crusader dress" by Chester Weinberg, the cross constitutes part of the design. A gold embroidered cross on a field of purple sequins rests on the bodice of the dress. The accompanying caption makes no more mention of the cross motif; instead it explains how to align your hairstyle with your eye makeup.[63]

Yet, cross jewelry, not dresses, and the cross shape, not Noah's Ark animals or trees of life, dominated in the 1960s. It appeared not only in jewelry advertisements or exotic photo shoots but also as a regular part of fashionable ensembles, socialite attire, and in advertisements for fabric, hosiery, and clothing labels.[64] And as the decade advanced, the cross became a more prominent and promoted accessory. 1968 saw "Vogue's Own Boutique" promoting Byzantine crosses inspired by the Met's jewelry collection, and Maltese crosses as adornments for outwear, as well as a bold necklace featuring not just one but multiple crosses by Kenneth Jay Lane.[65] By 1969, when the cross was deemed "fashionable," the jewelry appeared with diverse apparel ranging from short skirts and halter-tops to evening gowns and, of course, a Chanel suit.[66]

In her article proclaiming that "Ancient Symbol Becomes Fashion Fad" in 1969, journalist Marilyn Bender sought to document and explain this trend. In doing so, she acknowledged Chanel's influence as well as the current cultural context. "In the age of Aquarius, the cross is becoming a high fashion symbol," she wrote and then went on to describe how crosses "are being worn by mannequins, socialites and other stylish pace-setters." For example, Bender reported that Mrs. Harilaos Theodoracopulos, a former model, collected her cross necklaces in Greece, while model Ann Coleman found hers "here and there." The article includes pictures of both women wearing multiple crosses, emphasizing their exotic travels and illustrating the fashion trend.[67]

Throughout the article, Bender does not mention any controversy about this trend; however, she does probe fashion insiders about its meaning, and their answers highlight physical features of the cross. When asked "Why crosses?" Consuelo Crespi, editor of *Vogue Italia*, responded: "We've had medals and bells and gypsy chains. And the cross is a pretty classic form, isn't it?" Crespi emphasized the attractive and artistic qualities of the shape, while some liked the sounds it made—"the noise of it. It clanks." In addition to these sensory qualities, some explained that they had received such jewelry as a gift; others remarked that they donned it because "they don't wear diamonds now." The only hint of potential controversy occurred toward the end of the article. Bender concluded her piece by reporting that jewelry designer Bill Smith decided not to pursue a project featuring "a Star of David as a peace symbol." Smith explained his rationale: "I don't think it would sell because there's trouble between the Jews and the Arabs, and, besides, nobody would understand what I was trying to say."[68] Even as increasing diversity and questioning characterized American religious life in the 1960s, the Christian cross continued to function as a "summarizing symbol," unlike the Star of David. Smith acknowledged the potential for controversy and poor sales with the Star of David, but no such issue emerged in relationship to cross jewelry.

Bender, though, highlighted a few issues that illuminated the emerging seeker spirituality of the 1960s and helped explain the popularity of fashionable crosses. Specifically, while acknowledging Chanel's influence, Bender attributed this current trend to the emerging fashion power of youth and street styles—"to the youth and hippie cultures."[69] This insight points to changing dynamics within fashion *and* religion. Hippies challenged the conformity of '50s and early '60s fashions even as they questioned religious norms and critiqued religious institutions.[70] While some experimented with Buddhism or joined the Hare Krishnas, others reclaimed Jesus. The "Jesus People," who emerged out of the counterculture in the late 1960s, sought to create a Christian lifestyle. To do so, they embraced a range of things. Historian Larry Eskridge writes, "The enthusiasm they showed for buttons, bumper stickers, Bible covers, posters, crosses, and other 'Jesus Junque' was but one aspect of the Jesus People's friendliness toward popular culture."[71] During this time various subcultures, religious and nonreligious, utilized style, fashion, and popular culture items to express their religious identities.

Religious trends in the 1960s fostered the popularity of cross jewelry and helped protect this trend from critique. The increasing religious emphasis on individuals rather than institutions, feelings rather than faith commitments, and searching rather than settling created more ephemeral understandings of religion. Many today call this "spirituality." One of Bender's consultants describes this more fluid, spiritual environment. "You could also take it [the cross fashion trend] from the mystic standpoint. Remember the motorcycle people and their craze for Nazi crosses? Now everyone is involved in astrology and witches."[72] Another remarked, "It's just something in the wind. I don't feel it's religious unless it's a subliminal kind of thing."[73] In 1969, these people attempted to articulate and capture the changing religious ethos, and the "spiritual, but not religious" significance of the cross.

This sensibility can be seen in the cross collecting done by Theodoracopulos and Coleman. Bender simply notes these women's travels and their sophisticated souvenir shopping; yet, its inclusion highlights a modern impulse examined by scholars. Fashionable religion provided seekers with access to the religious sights and objects of other places, times, and religions, such as the spiritual electricity of Lourdes and the magic of makeup.[74] Anthropologist Brian Spooner argues that we need to consider "the possibility that the evolving constellation of social relations in our complex society generates a need for authenticity, which leads people to cast around for cultural material."[75] Such "authenticity" could be found in the cross jewelry collected while traveling, as seen in Bender's article.

The fashionable religion constructed by the modern fashion industry, in articles, advertisements, and now accessories, reinforced and amplified the emerging seeker spirituality of the time. Fashion magazine articles provided readers with access to wondrous works of religious art and spiritual destinations, while fashion advertisements encouraged women to wear stylish garb when traveling to these cosmopolitan sites. According to MacCannell and other scholars, "the tourist, in his desire for authentic experience, is the modern embodiment of the religious pilgrim."[76] In Bender's article we can see how Theodoracopulos and Coleman added another practice to this fashionable form of spiritual tourism—the purchasing of sacred objects and mementos.

These mementos not only indicated one's cultured status through international travel but also provided a modern and stylish way to search for and possibly obtain spiritual enchantment and wonder. People in the 1960s remained drawn to spiritual explanations and possibilities, such as "astrology and witches," even as they increasingly embraced scientific advances and events such as the Space Race.[77] It is a paradox that Patrick Allitt highlights in his history of American religion since 1945.[78] Within this context, cross jewelry highlighted the wearer's fashionable and sophisticated status while also containing the promise of supernatural potential. It provided spiritual seekers who did not like the material or theological characteristics of "Jesus Junque" with an artifact that embodied and represented their fashionable religion.

Invoking cross forms from other times and places in the Christian past, such as Maltese, Byzantine, "Crusader," and "Nature," highlighted the "authentic" and "pure" origins of these designs and, hence, their supernatural and experiential potential. Such jewelry made these possibilities simultaneously modern and accessible. They also drew on the Christian history associated with the cross. Early Christians ascribed sacred power to the "True Cross" of Jesus. By the fourth century, legends circulated about the arboreal origin of the cross, its discovery by Empress Helena, and its healing powers. Churches proclaimed to possess remains of the "True Cross," which were authenticated, in part, by their "wonder working" powers.[79] While later reproductions of the cross did not claim such a miraculous provenance, cross jewelry—and Christian jewelry, in general—retained its supernatural potential.

Historically, Christian jewelry not only communicated one's faith, but it also functioned as a protective device—as an amulet. Rings and brooches, for example, often featured religious inscriptions, such as the words "Ave Maria," "Jesus," or the names of the three kings, to ensure protection.[80] Further, decoration of the jewelry could transform the object into a talisman, which amplified the gifts of its wearer. For example, "In the Middle Ages gemstones were not chosen simply for colour or rarity, but also for the healing and spiritual properties attributed to them."[81] Marbodus, Bishop of Rennes, wrote one of the most influential books, *Liber Lapidum*, on the properties with which God had infused these gems.[82] For instance, sapphires not only protected wearers (amulets) but also made them "beloved of God and man" (talismans). As a result, they were often used in bishops' rings.[83] Infused with religious power, this elaborate jewelry adorned priests, monks, and friars, as well as kings and those with great wealth.[84] Religious jewelry functioned as adornment but also as a device that could protect the wearer and amplify the wearer's gifts—meanings that could be reclaimed by seekers in a spiritual marketplace.

Numerous advertisements in the 1960s fostered and enhanced this older religious interpretation of jewelry. By placing jewelry on statuary evocative of Asian, African, and classical religions, advertisers reinforced the association of jewelry with "primitive" supernatural powers. They sought to enhance its religious "aura."[85] This statuary encouraged reader-consumers to associate a kind of international cosmopolitanism and exoticism with the product in question, but it also suggested idolatry and a kind of animism—a spiritual power that infused the product through its close proximity.[86] For example, a full-page color advertisement for Bulgari jewelry from 1969 features a statue of what appears to be a Buddha, with "snail-shell curls," a "cranial bump," and in a meditative position, wearing an elaborate necklace of precious gems.[87] No copy, other than "Bulgari Roma," appears. The tableau associates the artistic qualities of the sculpture with that of the jewelry, which imbues the product with a sophisticated and high culture sensibility even as it reinforces a visual way of seeing religion based on decontextualized symbols and artifacts.

At the same time, the advertisement implies contagious magic—the idea that the supernatural power of this "idol" has been infused into this beautiful necklace through their proximity.[88] What matters are its potential religious connotations and magical powers, not its historical origins or its "real" identity as the bodhisattva of compassion, known as Avalokiteśvara or Guanyin.[89] A number of other ads imply a similar "magical" interpretation. Diamond clips, for instance, adorn a Buddha's head and ears in another jewelry ad, numerous necklaces encircle a Haniwa figure (a Japanese funerary object), and a vaguely illustrated "jade goddess" accompanies a Lady Coventry jewelry collection.[90] The frequent use of religious statuary socialized reader-consumers into seeing jewelry, Christian and otherwise, as filled with supernatural potential, and a few companies attempted to capitalize on these associations, as in a 1947 advertisement for "Hindu Temple Jewelry" and one for "Buddha pins" in 1961.[91]

However, cross jewelry, not renderings of Buddhas or Hindu gods, became popular in the 1960s. As the meaning of institutional Christianity was shifting in profound ways during this time, the proliferation of cross jewelry aligned with and amplified the increasingly individual-ized way people approached the spiritual marketplace. The symbolism of cross jewelry resonated with but was not bound by the Christian tradi-tion, yet at the same time, its recontextualization within modern fashion added new layers of meaning and highlighted old ones. In an Ameri-can religious context characterized by questioning and controversy, the materialization of Christianity in the form of fashionable cross jewelry offered people individualized, supernatural possibilities that differenti-ated them from the beliefs of Jesus People and the "superstitions" as-sociated with non-Christian religions. Further, these crosses exhibited craftsmanship and design, which made them more modern and exclu-sive than their devotional counterparts. Yet, these fashionable cross ac-cessories were not *only* fashion statements. Through their connections to "authentic" sources of inspiration, they also could potentially per-form religious functions, such as protecting the wearer and amplifying her gifts. Cross jewelry's embodiment of sophistication and spirituality, fashion and faith, made it the perfect spiritual object for fashionable religion and its adherents.

Fashionable cross jewelry offered a more modern and sophisticated way to "elaborate" on and experiment with Christian and religious identity.[92] It provided spiritual seekers with a familiar and potentially powerful religious symbol in a material form. It offered 1960s seekers an experience of Christianity that invoked but was not bound by con-ventional meaning. As such, cross jewelry exemplified and amplified a fashionable religion defined by visuality and materiality, art and beauty, individualism and emotion. Further, it could be accessed through a store, rather than a church. Thus, even as religion appeared more priva-tized and social institutions more secular, religion and religious symbols constituted part of the marketplace and hence public life.[93]

The Cross and Controversy

Cross jewelry continued to be popular in the early 1970s. It was featured in the "American Spring Collections" and the "New York Collections" described by *Vogue* in 1970. Big, bold, and often bejeweled, it made a fashion statement.[94] In an article entitled "Your Best Bets '71," one of the featured outfits included a chocolate-brown jumpsuit with an ankle-length coat and a cross choker.[95] Crosses were appropriate fashion accessories for all types of garments—from evening dresses to T-shirts, from outerwear to bathing suits.[96] They also remained a favorite with socialites and celebrities, such as Prince Juan de Borbón and Desi Arnaz, as well as actress Lois Chiles.[97]

Things changed, though, in the mid-70s. During these years, the frequency of cross jewelry in *Vogue* coverage dropped dramatically. In 1975, only two crosses appeared in *Vogue*—one a belt with a cross pendant, the other in a photograph of a ballerina.[98] In 1976, only one cross appeared—a Christmastime Tiffany's ad promoting Elsa Peretti's "diamond cross pendant" on a gold chain for $375.[99] A similar decline in coverage occurred in *Harper's Bazaar*.[100] Predicated on dynamism, innovation, and the need for consumers to continually purchase new products, fashions change. By 1976, the cross-jewelry fashion fad of 1969 had passed, only to reappear again in the 1980s.

Adding religious history onto the workings of the fashion cycle illuminates another important factor in this decline. Cross jewelry went out of fashion in 1976, the "year of the evangelical" as proclaimed by both *Newsweek* and Gallup.[101] In the 1970s and 1980s, the "Jesus Junque" of the 1960s had become a vibrant evangelical subculture that "redeemed" various cultural forms, such as television shows, romance novels, and women's jewelry, for the purpose of Christian evangelization.[102] Often characterized as "kitsch," in contrast to the more "sophisticated" forms of culture embraced by liberal Protestants, progressive Catholics, and spiritual seekers, these religious products emphasized the importance of a particular religious look, especially the alignment of interior identity with external appearance and display. As a result, they highlighted Christian people who "dwelled" in their religious identity, rather than spiritual tourists seeking "sacred moments."[103] By doing so they sought to control and define the meaning of Christian symbols, such as the cross.

In 1980, religion editor for the *Chicago Tribune* Bruce Buursma noticed this trend when he documented evangelicals' use of "witness jewelry" or "in more cynical circles, 'holy hardware.'" This jewelry provided evangelicals with a way of proclaiming their religious identity and evangelizing others by "wearing their professions of faith around their necks or on their lapels."[104] In advancing their faith through cross jewelry, evangelicals in some ways made it unfashionable. The rhetoric of conservative Christian retailers and consumers framed cross jewelry as a "summarizing" symbol that expressed and advanced their religious identity. Thus, they elevated the communication dimension of fashion, the idea that your external appearance reflected your internal spiritual state in an authentic and transparent way.[105] As a result, they sought to restrict the wearing of cross jewelry to those associated with a particular kind of religious belief and practice. This embrace of religious authority, Christian tradition, and evangelical identity helped frame cross jewelry as out of style and, thus, hindered its fashionable status.[106]

Yet, a few short years later, cross jewelry became fashionable again, according to newspaper fashion columns and fashion magazines.[107] Puzzled reporters tried to explain the trend.[108] For example, one reporter's informant pointed to the economic recession of the early 1980s: "When times are tough, people want religion," such as crucifix necklaces and "It's Fun Being a Christian" Frisbees. John Bass, then executive director of the Christian Booksellers Association, echoed this interpretation. "There is a return to religious belief and the economic downturn is a major reason," he explained, while "New Age designer" Lucy Isaacs stated, "Sales are up when bad things happen."[109] These interpretations highlight how cross jewelry continued to be spiritually significant even as the religious and economic landscape shifted.

In this environment, oversize, designer, and controversial characterized cross jewelry's reappearance and also helped explain its renewed popularity. As with previous iterations, the jewelry drew upon the past, on previous historical periods, referred to as "medieval" and "heraldic."[110] Size, though, was a central feature of this revitalized trend. One article described the style as "*huge* pins with fake diamonds, rubies, sapphires, emeralds, or pearls; *overscaled* heraldic crosses of crystal," while another, entitled "Bold Baubles," cited Chanel's influence and "the plethora of *oversized* baubles" that needed to be "as impressive as the clothes" being sold and worn.[111] *Vogue's* coverage of Paris fashions echoed this with reports that "jewelry—and more jewelry—is a focal point of all collections," which included "heaps of Byzantine medieval crosses."[112] In the 1980s, crosses were no longer subtle, unremarked upon accessories but rather large, visible, "heaping" "statement" pieces.[113] In addition, as seen in this coverage, cross jewelry constituted a central part of the collections of exclusive designers, including Yves Saint Laurent, Christian Lacroix, and Betsey Johnson.[114]

The exaggerated size and designer status of 1980s cross jewelry helped, at least conceptually, to differentiate it from "witness wear" and previous iterations of the form. These features also helped "reinvent" or "revitalize" its fashionable status.[115] Sociologist Erik Cohen explains, in his analysis of authenticity and tourism, that as "cultural products" of the host society become more banal, tourists want "more spectacular, exotic and titillating attractions."[116] Thus, making cross jewelry bigger, bolder, and more bejeweled helped infuse it with renewed fashionability, emphasized its aesthetic qualities, and challenged the limited interpretations placed on it by some evangelicals.

Popularity and revitalization of the cross also came through controversy. Evangelical Christians continued to claim and wear Christian symbols. For example, one Christian retailer credited Jerry Falwell, "who has sent out little 'Jesus First' lapel pins to his viewers," with "the broader acceptance of the products [Christian jewelry]." Perhaps, though, more credit for the popularity of cross jewelry could go to Falwell's foil, Madonna, who courted controversy. According to one industry insider, "the cross worn by Madonna in her music video 'Like a Prayer' and her short-lived television commercial for Pepsi-Cola had a noticeable impact."[117] Throughout the 1980s, cross jewelry, as well as rosaries, constituted part of Madonna's wardrobe, performances, and music videos. Falwell's "Moral Majority" and other conservative Christians found Madonna's wearing of these religious symbols trivializing and even blasphemous. Others, though, found her rebellious stance toward conservative religion and her juxtaposition of religious symbols with female sexuality fashionable, and sought to emulate her style.

The controversy, which included but also went beyond cross jewelry, culminated in 1989, with Madonna's "Like a Prayer." The video was voted "the second best music video of the 1980s" in a 2011 Billboard poll and named one of Fuse TV's ten "videos that rocked the world."[118] In it, Madonna again wears a lingerie-style outfit and a cross necklace, but the video also includes burning crosses, stigmata, an African American gospel choir, and "Madonna kissing a black Jesus figure." Concerned Christians, in the United States and Italy, "complained it was blasphemous."[119] "Some critics," wrote one reporter, "can't even agree over what happens on the video because it's layered with different dimensions of reality. Some contend that a black Jesus actually makes love to Madonna; others say no."[120] Others pointed out that the "black Jesus" was in fact Saint Martin de Porres, known for his commitment to social justice, which reinforced the antiracist message of the video.[121]

However, Pepsi's use of the song and hiring of Madonna in a multimillion-dollar ad campaign amplified the controversy and provided a way for conservative Catholics and evangelical Protestants to apply economic and social pressure. The American Family Association, with a membership of 380,000 at the time and led by Reverend Donald Wildmon accused Madonna of "blasphemous use of a crucifix" in the video.[122] Others, including Catholic priests, agreed with these charges and more, and all threatened to lead boycotts of Pepsi. As a result, Pepsi pulled the ads but was quick to explain that "consumers confused the commercial with a music video by the singer."[123] And Madonna's record company Warner Brothers, hoping to fend off a blasphemy lawsuit in Italy, did not air the video there.[124]

Madonna had entered the "culture wars" wearing a religious symbol that fundamentalists, evangelicals, and conservative Catholics wanted to own. Conservative Christians envisioned themselves and their belief system as under attack by corrosive and evil forces. According to James Davison Hunter, in the 1980s religious conflict occurred "around our most fundamental and cherished assumptions about how to order our lives—our own lives and our lives together in this society."[125] Rather than being divided or separated by denomination or tradition, alliances occurred across religious traditions on issues, such as abortion, education, and popular culture.[126]

For these conservative Christians, Madonna's cross wearing and music videos represented small parts of a larger battle being fought in popular culture. In addition to disdain for Madonna, the American Family Association's Wildmon and others feared the influence of heavy metal and rap music, especially The 2 Live Crew's 1989 rap album *As Nasty as They Wanna Be*, which included "over 200 uses of the word 'fuck,' over 100 uses of explicit terms for male and female genitalia, over 80 descriptions of oral sex, and the word 'bitch' was used over 150 times."[127] They also flexed their economic muscle by endorsing Christian retailing and enacting boycotts (or threatening to) of companies they believed endorsed positions detrimental to Christian values, including Pepsi, General Mills, Ralston Purina, and Domino's Pizza.[128] Others, not content with boycotts, took to the streets to protest the sexual and violent content of television and film, and protested the perceived blasphemy of Martin Scorsese's "The Last Temptation of Christ" (1988).[129] And Andres Serrano's "Piss Christ" (1987) and Robert Mapplethorpe's 1989 tour of photographs, which included many BDSM and other sexually explicit images, elicited controversies about federal funding for the arts and the nature of art itself.[130]

Within these global battles over culture, religion, and politics, Christian symbols emerged as central.[131] "Each side," Hunter explains, "struggle[d] to monopolize the symbols of legitimacy."[132] For conservative Christians, religious symbols, such as the cross, represented a specific vision of *the* tradition. They sought to define and defend the cross as a "summarizing symbol" that meant a particular kind of Christianity on a particular kind of body. Further, they policed its use and tried to delegitimize those who wore the cross, such as Madonna, for "inauthentic" purposes that problematized its ability to function as a clear communicator of Christian identity.

For liberal Protestants, spiritual seekers, and progressive Catholics, the Madonna controversy revitalized the power ascribed to the cross and they could wear it as a way to challenge fundamentalist views and articulate different visions or even criticisms of Christianity. Madonna, for example, used the cross as a way to work through her conflicted Catholicism. For her, it functioned as an "elaborating" symbol. She explained, "the theme of Catholicism runs rampant through my album. It's me struggling with the mystery and magic that surrounds it. My own Catholicism is in constant upheaval." She continues, "I renounced the traditional meaning of Catholicism in terms of how I would live my life, but I never stopped feeling the guilt and shame that are ingrained in you if you are brought up Catholic."[133] At the same time, Madonna also used the cross as a "summarizing symbol"—as a way to criticize the Moral Majority and cultivate her image as a cutting-edge artist. In an interview, Madonna stated that the "Like a Prayer" controversy was "a strong indication of how America is lurching backwards into bigotry." She explained, "I know the moral majority is up in arms against me but I consider that an achievement. I know I'm offending certain groups but I think that the people who understand what I'm doing are not offended because it's pro-life, it's pro-equality and it's pro-humanity."[134] Madonna's wearing of cross jewelry, then, provided her with a way to grapple with her Catholic past, while simultaneously provoking the Moral Majority. Fashionable consumers could do the same.

The modern fashion industry and celebrities, such as Madonna, made cross jewelry fashionable again by enlarging its size, associating it with designer status, and embroiling it in controversy. These events transformed it into a piece of jewelry that signaled sophistication, style, and rebellion. As such, it created, at least conceptually, a difference between the sophisticated wearers of fashionable designer crosses and the fundamentalist and evangelical Others clad in "witness wear." This, in turn, questioned cross jewelry's function as a "summarizing" symbol and fostered various ways of wearing the cross as an "elaborating" symbol—ironically, playfully, and/or sincerely.

One additional trend helped revitalize cross jewelry's fashionability, as well as its potential supernatural powers as a sacred object—the rise of the New Age movement. While evangelicals remained leery of jewelry's supernatural potential, spiritual seekers embraced it in the form of the cross and other spiritual symbols.[135] As one merchandiser for Barneys New York remarked, "Mysticism and healing are big business now."[136] In the 1960s, fashion advertisements emphasized the supernatural characteristics of jewelry, in the 1980s, the New Age movement did so.

The emergence of the New Age movement reinforced existing trends in seeker spirituality that focused on individual spiritual growth through a variety of spiritual means, ranging from astrology to crystals to crosses.[137] Fashion magazines acknowledged this diffuse spirituality in articles, such as "Crystal Power," published in *Vogue* 1988, which chronicled the burgeoning crystal movement, including "crystal consultants," "crystal healers," "crystal channelers," and "crystal cleaners." Numerous different crystal practices emerged, but they emphasized the spiritual power embedded in or accessed through objects deemed sacred.[138] Further, claims about crystals' efficacy often rested on older beliefs about the religious power of jewelry and gems. As author Lynn Snowden noted, "they [crystal practitioners] often bring up historical precedent, such as bishops wearing gemstones during the plague to ward off disease."[139] While crystals are not crosses (although crystal crosses did exist), the potential supernatural qualities attributed to both were often intermingled and fused together.

This can be seen in a 1989 article entitled "In Jewelry, Choices Sacred and Profane, Ancient and New Age." Here, reporter Deborah Hoffman investigates the popularity of crystal and cross pendants, along with astrological charms and African talismans. What these diverse accessories seem to share, besides their decontextualization, is their purported function as amulets.[140] As one man explained in Hoffman's article, "The sacred and profane mixed together bring me luck."[141] Another commentator remarked on this equivalence: "The cross seems to be this year's version of last year's New Age crystal pendants. That's fashion for you: The iconography goes from heathen magic to Christian orthodoxy in the twinkling of a season."[142] The supernatural associations with and attributions to these sacred objects helped revitalize cross jewelry by differentiating it from "witness wear," but still celebrated its religious potential. Such conceptions reinforced the fashionable religion constructed by the modern fashion industry that offered sacred moments of awe made possible through the consumption of fashion products.[143]

In the 1980s, the popularity of cross jewelry contributed to a fashionable religion that emphasized spirituality and style, possibility and play, which, in turn, distanced it from conservative religiosity. As discussed in chapter 2, similar to nineteenth-century humbug and twentieth-century advertisements, the meaning of cross jewelry was not a zero-sum game that forced wearers to choose between "religious" and "secular" interpretations; rather, this jewelry and fashionable religion offered the possibility of both. This fashionable religion amplified the trend toward seeker spirituality and encouraged people to wear and display decontextualized religious artifacts that could provide them with sources of "authentic" meaning while expressing their individual identities and personal tastes.

Conclusion

Fashion magazine articles about Christianity, advertisements using Christianity, and jewelry featuring Christian symbols demonstrate the ways that this religious tradition occupied an assumed and often taken-for-granted place in fashion. The popularity of the cross in the modern fashion industry affirms the dominant, and often implicit, Christian framework that shaped this realm both discursively and materially. While some advertisements emphasized transgressive themes through illustrations of Eve and Madonna introduced elements of controversy into cross-wearing, Christianity and its history remained the *de facto* resource for religious inspiration.

The history of cross jewelry in modern fashion highlights recurring and expanding dimensions of fashionable religion. Chanel inaugurated a fashion trend with her Maltese cross cuffs and Byzantine cross necklaces. Her work materialized Christianity in fashion by moving it from ad illustrations and article fodder into the designs of fashion. It also highlighted a way of seeing Christianity, and religion more broadly, as a romanticized force associated with distant historical time periods and "primitive" Others yet filled with sacred artifacts and relics that could be utilized in the present. These objects and the "authenticity" attributed to them could then be captured, controlled, and accessed through the purchasing of particular products. In the 1960s and again in the 1980s, the popularity of the cross jewelry positioned fashion consumers to see themselves as spiritual seekers, tourists, who controlled their spiritual lives through consumption and display. For them, religious artifacts became "elaborating" symbols that expressed personalized experiences and stories.

Material objects function as powerful creators and sustainers of a religious tradition. Marita Sturken argues that "cultural memory is produced through objects, images, and representations," while David Morgan adds that "visual culture can be a powerful part of the shared apparatus of memory."[144] Amid the religious shift from "dwelling" to "seeking" or from institutional religion to the religious, fashionable cross jewelry provided people with a fashion statement as well as a beautiful object that reflected their individual taste and a way to "hold on to" Christianity, as its meaning(s) and status were shifting.[145]

Fashion magazine articles and advertisements reprocessed elements of Christianity and accustomed reader-consumers to seeing it in bits and pieces.[146] The form of cross jewelry took this trend further. Experiencing Holy Week in Sicily through an article or having revitalized skin through a miraculous lotion emphasized the centrality of religious experiences in fashionable religion. Yet, even as articles and advertisements visualized these experiences, they were framed in individualized, privatized ways—reading a magazine on the couch or applying lotion in the bathroom. The emergence and popularity of cross jewelry maintained fashionable religion's focus on appearance and display, as well as the supernatural power of material objects, but pushed it further into the public eye. It established the fashionability of wearing Christian symbols in public as a sartorial statement. Unlike the seeming neutrality associated with church-going styles seen in chapter 2, in this chapter we see how the fashion industry emphasized style and display through its materialization of a Christian symbol in a fashion accessory. This shift is vital to understanding how God got on a dress.

This decontextualization and reconceptualization of cross jewelry, in turn, problematized notions that fashion functioned as a clear communicator of identity. Conceptually and rhetorically the divide between "witness wear" and "cool" cross jewelry was clear; however, in reality, how could you tell if the wearer of a cross pendant was an evangelical testifying to her faith, a fan of Madonna's style, or some combination of both? Take, for example, a case from the now defunct online fashion world of polyvore, where participants could curate fashionable outfits and share them with others. On her information page, polyvore member Chelsea-Walker-1 identified herself as religious, "I am a Christian," and created a few explicitly Christian-themed outfits. Most notable, perhaps, is "My Love for Jesus and Cheetah's in One Outfit," which included a cheetah print cross on a tank top, cross-embellished jeans, cut-off denim shorts and sneakers with cross appliques, and a cheetah print-cross phone case. Her outfit blends Christian identity and fashion choices. The continuing popularity of cross jewelry and cross-inspired fashions has made it increasingly difficult to discern intent and identity affiliation through apparel, which has and continues to upset many religious conservatives.

Disrupting ideas about fashion as a transparent communicator of identity has caused many industry observers and consumers to assume an antagonistic relationship between fashion and religion. Madonna's provocative use of the cross and the rise of the Moral Majority in the 1980s reinforced this perception. Within the context of the "culture wars," cross jewelry and the use of religious symbols in fashion became ways to "shock" and capture attention. Using decontextualized religious symbols in fashion functioned as a way to be innovative and avant-garde—a way to push fashion boundaries, challenge religious norms, cause media controversy, and stimulate sales. As a result, designers, celebrities, and others used cross jewelry to transgress, blur, and rebel against particular conceptualizations of Christianity. Yet, as documented here and in previous chapters, transgression is an act of "denial *and* affirmation."[147] Even as various people used Christian symbols to flout the Moral Majority or make critical statements about Christianity, their defiance acknowledged its power. The Christian imaginary remained a popular visual and material repository for fashion and offered consumers pious and playful interpretive possibilities that went beyond jewelry, as we will see in chapter 4.

4

Innovating Religious Dress

In 1993, journalist Henry Alford commented on the current fashion trends for *Vogue* in a piece entitled "Simply Divine." He reported, "Sink to your knees and start atoning for the acquisitive 1980s; designers are increasingly finding inspiration in the vestments of priests, nuns, rabbis, and monks." Alford described the style as "one of penitence and personal conviction," but simultaneously seemed humorously surprised at some of the designs. Why would anyone, he wondered, want to wear "voluminous black robes reminiscent of body bags without zippers" or "be mistaken for the grim reaper?" In attempting to understand this fascination with monks and nuns, Alford mentions the public's interest in things religious and the appeal of "the drama of spirituality," yet comes to no satisfactory or definitive conclusion.[1]

Why would fashion designers adapt the religious dress of Catholic priests, monks, and nuns for their designer garments? How does this trend fit into the broader trajectory of religion and fashion? And what are the implications of this trend for thinking about the history of religion in America? To answer these questions, this chapter first analyzes features of the fashion industry and religious history that fostered these designs. It then uses fashion magazines, newspaper articles, runway shows, and designer biographies to examine the emergence of and the public's response to Catholic-inspired designs in the 1950s and 1960s, followed by an investigation of its resurgent popularity in the late 1980s and early 1990s. Assembling the history of this trend illuminates another way that the fashion industry mediates Christianity and how it constructs a vision of fashionable religion.

In this chapter, I argue that structural features of the fashion industry and elements of the religious landscape in the 1950s and 1960s fostered the selection of Catholic religious dress as a source for inspiration. Within this context, fashion designers used the concept of Catholic religious dress in different ways to produce "innovative" designs. Examining the range and history of these religiously inspired designs illuminates how a designer's biography and aesthetic functioned as variables that viewer-consumers assessed in deeming these garments "authentic" and popular or problematic and controversial.

Further, the emergence and recurring popularity of designs influenced by Catholic religious dress reinforced and amplified the ways of seeing Christianity already established through magazine articles, fashion advertisements, and cross jewelry.[2] By drawing on additional Christian referents and creating entire garments and ensembles based on them, this ecclesiastical trend expanded fashion's use and materialization of religion. Rather than being an accessory to fashion through the content of fashion magazines or cross jewelry, religion, specifically Catholic religious dress, became part of fashion design and garments. This, in turn, increased fashion's claim to and use of religious symbols, concepts, and images. It de-emphasized the role of religious institutions, strict moral codes, and specific theological tenets in defining Christianity. Rather, fashionable religion offered mainline Protestants, spiritual seekers, and others a personalized way to access a diffuse and benevolent supernatural that wanted to help and enhance, but not control, their lives. One did not need to live the austere life of a monk or nun or even be Catholic to experience the transcendent or have "sacred moments."[3]

By analyzing this Catholic religious dress design trend, we can see the continuation and expansion of the modern fashion industry's mediation of Christianity. Chapter 1 focused on how religion-oriented articles in fashion magazines emphasized text and image, while positioning the readers as sophisticated participant-viewers. Chapter 2 analyzed how religious imagery and text became integrated into fashion through advertisements that promised readers the pleasure of possibility. Chapter 3 examined the materialization of religious imagery in cross jewelry that simultaneously connoted fashionable style and supernatural potential. A few cross-inspired garments appeared in the 1960s; however, designer dresses and clothing featuring religious symbols and images rarely appeared in magazines or on the runway. Designs inspired by Catholic religious dress, though, gained popularity in the 1950s and 1960s and periodically ever since. This form of mediation constitutes an important step in understanding how God got on a dress.

Creating Catholic Religious Style

In his article, Alford ponders why the "unfashionable" religious uniform of monks' robes, nuns' habits, and priests' cassocks have become runway ready and headline worthy. "Perhaps," he writes, "it is only to be expected that the current fascination with spirituality and New Age practice would trickle down into the world of fashion."[4] Alford's focus on the religious landscape of the early 1990s, though, overlooks the longer historical trajectory of this design trend, as well as the ways the structures and goals of the modern fashion industry shaped its emergence.[5] The modern fashion industry does not convey "traditional" religion or construct religion as a religious institution would and to expect it to do so would be misguided. Thus, to understand the incorporation of the Christian imaginary into fashion we need to examine fashion's structuring principles and how they mediate particular ways of seeing.[6]

First, the fashion industry prizes innovation. Even a casual watcher of *Project Runway* has heard host and supermodel Heidi Klum exclaim, "I have never seen that before!" She often employs this rationale to endorse a designer's work during the judging portion of the show. Novelty matters. Historically, the rhythm of the fashion seasons necessitated that designers produce *at least* two collections per year (traditionally fall/winter and spring/summer). Over time, the number has increased to include mini-collections, such as Resort or Pre-Fall. This schedule creates a relentless demand to produce unique apparel that pushes the boundaries of fashion. Further, given the close relationship between fashion and art, fashion observers and critics often assume that fashion, especially high fashion, should be avant-garde—experimental, unusual, and challenging of the status quo.[7]

Second, and as we have seen, fashion privileges the visual. The cut of the clothes, the look of the fabric, the use of a print, or the inclusion of an accessory all rely on our ability to see what has been fashioned. Designers create garments to be seen and arrest attention, while consumers purchase particular designs to display their personal sense of style—a look. In thinking about the ways fashion constructs and circulates ideas about religion, the heritage of Christianity has been dominant. Its imagery and symbols intertwine with the discourse and practice of fashion.[8]

Christianity's appearance in fashion magazine articles, advertisements, and accessories accustomed people to seeing bits and pieces of religion in fashion, even as it established a foundation for more far-reaching and expansive incorporations of it.

Third, fashion designers constitute the artists of the fashion world. In chapter 1, we saw how fashion magazines educated readers about religious art and celebrated the divinely inspired genius of artists. A similar valorization of fashion designers' processes and work exists. Sociologist Joanne Finkelstein explains, "The idea that designers are artists was a mid-nineteenth century French invention which enabled the dress designer to be deemed an original genius, much like the painter. The great couturiers thus gained reputations for being above commercial influences, and as having purely aesthetic visions unmodified by client demands or public responses."[9] Emphasizing the artistry and aesthetic gifts of fashion designers highlighted their seemingly divinely given talents, as well as their need to draw inspiration from various sources. This, in turn, helped legitimate their uses of religious imagery, symbols, and designs. It framed designers' choices, religious and otherwise, in terms of their artistic vision, personal biographies, and aesthetic sensibilities. Thus, Christianity and its history functioned as a repository of artistic inspiration that provided designers with novel, visual elements for their garments, which simultaneously reinforced discourses that valorized the artistry and purity of fashion designers.

Further, this vision of the fashion designer helped mitigate the increasingly fraught commercial environment of the modern fashion industry. While many famous fashion designers started their own brands or houses, they also struggled financially, and eventually became part of larger corporations. As of 2014, six fashion corporations own over forty brands, such as Dior, Alexander McQueen, Balenciaga, Saint Laurent Paris, and Jean Paul Gaultier.[10] Within this competitive, corporate environment, fashion designers provide the human face of fashion. Their artistic inspirations and creative intentions ostensibly elevate the fashion design over the commercial component, as well as personalize the industry and make it accessible. As a result, fashion houses emphasize, and people often want to know about, designers' lives and creative processes—what has influenced them as individuals and as artists.

These governing principles matter because they shape *how* and help explain *why* fashion began mediating religion in more material ways. Fashion's emphasis on innovation and experimentation, for example, means that designers must constantly seek out new or revisit old sources of inspiration to enliven their designs. In this quest-for-inspiration atmosphere, the Christian heritage offers a repository of ideas and images, styles and symbols that can be incorporated into fashion in ways that start a new trend or enliven an existing fad. Further, given the history of using Christianity as a resource for fashion in playful advertisements and cross jewelry, it makes sense that the fashion industry would return to the Christian imaginary in a more expansive way. The addition of *garments* inspired by Christianity alongside *accessories* inspired by it makes sense as part of this larger trajectory focused on inspiration and innovation. The use of Christianity in fashion designs occurred in a few instances prior to the 1950s[11], but in the 1960s and even more in the late 1980s, this became a more widespread trend.

While these principles explain fashion's increasing incorporation of Christianity, other historical and contextual factors clarify why designers turned to Catholic religious dress, rather than other elements in the Christian repertoire. Notably, by adapting forms of religious dress, rather than pictorial imagery, fashion designers avoided the potential controversy associated with placing religious figures on clothing. Just as advertising tended to avoid the overt use of religious figures (with the exception of Eve), so too, did designers until the late 1980s and early 1990s. Emphasizing abstraction and inspiration over literal representation also highlighted that fashion designers embraced the values of "modern" art in their designs.[12] Through their different takes on Catholic religious dress, designers played with meanings and possibilities that industry critics deemed innovative and thus fashionable.

Moreover, Catholicism provided a rich history of art and symbols familiar to fashion designers, many of whom were from or trained in France, Italy, and Spain. Catholicism's dominance in Western Europe's legacy of art and architecture not only influenced the aesthetics of numerous designers, it also embodied the meaning of high culture for many Americans. This association helped Catholicism retain its Western European heritage and cachet, which could be seen in American

Catholic churches. In her analysis of nineteenth-century American Catholic vestments, Katherine Haas highlights how many priests' vestments came from Europe and reinforced the connection between these locations. She also documents how this sacramental attire became more elaborately decorated over time and fostered the emergence of "devotional Catholicism" (as opposed to "plain piety"), which focused on a "new performative style."[13] Catholicism's use of religious symbols and religious dress, as well as its influence on art and architecture, helped create a repository of familiar religious looks. Given the fashionable status of Western Europe, garments invoking its history, art, and religion were seen as inspired, beautiful and "authentic" expressions of this high culture.

The expansion of fashion's power beyond Paris to other Catholic-dominated areas also helped foster this design trend. In the 1950s, Italy emerged as a prominent player on the fashion scene. Having had extensive training and a long history in fashion before World War II, Italian designers organized and exerted their influence more prominently in the postwar context. With three prominent fashion cities, Rome, Florence, and Milan, Italian designers rivaled those from Paris, London, and New York. When top Italian designers and boutiques invited American buyers to a group show in 1951, they, "challenged Paris."[14] Newspaper headlines and fashion columns in the 1950s, such as "Florence Fashions Add a Fancy Fillip," "Richness Prevails in Rome," and "Rome, Too, Dictates Styles," regularly spotlighted the fashion trends from Italy.[15] Rome's friendliness to filmmaking also helped establish its fashion leadership. As one source states: "The fifties were the golden age of Cinecittà studios, the Hollywood on the Tiber, where major American studios could produce films cheaply. The most important Italian haute-couture ateliers, especially those in Rome, became famous for dressing American actors and actresses both on and off the set."[16] By 1956, Italy led France and Great Britain in exporting clothing to the United States.[17]

Fashion columns also emphasized the artisanal qualities and "authenticity" of Italian fashions. "Opulent and original embroideries, novel use of unrelated fabrics," and "inspired by Renaissance paintings" constitute a few of the accolades bestowed upon Italian designs.[18] These qualities helped establish the artistry of Italian fashion, as well as its distinctiveness. Stories highlighting the personal lives and struggles of Italian designers encouraged reader-consumers to view Italian fashion as an "authentic" product rooted in Italian Catholic culture.[19] For example, a number of fashion features highlighted the work and background of the three Fontana sisters, who founded Sorelle Fontana in Rome. One article focused on lead designer Micol Fontana to underscore their "rags-to-riches" trajectory. "Born thirty-eight years ago in Parma of a family that for 200 years had been engaged in the needlecraft trade, she began sewing when only ten years of age and designing for her mother's customers when 15."[20] From these humble needlework beginnings, the three sisters established a fashion house in Rome that dressed Queen Narriman of Egypt, designed Margaret Truman's wedding dress, and was favored by Ava Garder.[21] Another reported that "with indomitable courage," these "little dressmakers" opened their fashion house and helped move Rome to the center of Italian fashion.[22] Highlighting the artistry and "authenticity" of European fashions and emphasizing the designers' biographies helped foster the creation, acceptance, and popularity of designs inspired by Italian Catholic heritage.[23]

Another factor fostering the incorporation of such designs was the familiarity of the Catholic imaginary. In the 1950s and 1960s, Americans and Europeans recognized figures of priests, monks, and nuns, or at least the stereotypical image of them. Most broadly, the Catholic heritage of Europe and the increasing presence and power of American Catholics accustomed people to the idea and look, if not the reality and nuances, of Catholic religious figures.[24] This general context and familiarity was reinforced through popular culture, including the articles, imagery, and advertisements that appeared in fashion magazines.[25] Yet, the public presence of Catholicism was not limited to fashion magazines. In *The Look of Catholics*, Anthony Burke Smith argues that in the United States "popular culture seemed to have gone Catholic crazy at midcentury." He highlights how the numerous Hollywood film offerings "indicated a[n] . . . infatuation with Roman Catholicism."[26] One can see this infatuation in *Vogue* as the fashion magazine ran stories on and advertisements for many of these movies, including *Little Boy Lost* (1953) and *The Nun's Story* (1959).[27]

Amanda Porterfield refers to this rise in Catholic visibility and popularity as "The Catholicity of American Spirituality."[28] Amid increasing religious pluralism and eclecticism, Protestantism and Catholicism increasingly intersected and shaped each other, especially in the mid-twentieth century. For Protestant converts to Catholicism, the tradition provided "an antidote for the rationalism" of Protestantism through its rich heritage of art and architecture.[29] Catholic religious dress evoked this aesthetic past and its supernatural "aura"; however, when recontextualized within the realm of fashion, ecclesiastically inspired designs offered a sense of distance that allowed potential viewer-consumers the power of sophisticated, spiritual possibilities. The fashionable religion being constructed celebrated these qualities and elements of Catholicism while offering spiritual seekers a way to incorporate them into their own private lives—all without having to become Catholic.

In addition to the "high culture" status of Western European Catholicism, its dominance in the fashion industry, and the popularity of Catholic religious in popular culture, the religious significance of these spiritual figures, Catholic priests, monks, and nuns, was also central to this emerging fashion trend. In her introduction to *Roman Catholicism in Fantastic Film*, Regina Hansen explains, "the imagery and ritual of Catholicism are as common and recognizable as they are supernaturally evocative, at least to Westerners."[30] Hansen emphasizes how the visual look of Catholicism functioned as a metonym for the supernatural. Other interpretations point out that religious dress itself "has mana" or supernatural power.[31] The modern fashion industry, as we have seen in previous chapters, utilized these ideas. They employed a romanticized notion that "antimodern" peoples and past historical epochs served as repositories for the supernatural and "authentic" religion.[32] Catholic priests, monks, and nuns embodied this notion. Their vows of poverty, chastity, and obedience conveyed the primacy of their spiritual lives, while their donning of religious apparel, whether plain brown tunics, black cassocks, or modest habits, visually symbolized their rejection of "worldly" ways.[33] Catholic religious dress, then, provided fashion designers with a semiotically rich sartorial source.

While Catholics, as Sally Dwyer-McNulty demonstrates, used the details and nuances of religious dress "to negotiate relations between religious authority and laity, men and women, adults and youth,"[34] fashion designers emphasized the stereotypical idea and look of Catholic priests, monks, and nuns. By adapting these recognizable religious uniforms, designers could play with both form and meaning, and thus create an innovative design. Such a feat depended upon a delicate balance of stability and change. Fashion designers had to alter the basic form of the religious garb to showcase their artistic genius and avoid accusations of "costumery" and "literalism." At the same time, though, they could not change the form so much that the "aura" of religious dress—its associations with "mana" and "authentic" religion—became unclear and lost its ability to enhance the designer's reputation as innovative and inspired.[35]

A 1947 advertisement for "Monk's Robes" demonstrates this idea of balance and foreshadows the emergence of this design trend. The garments feature solid fabric, high collars, and rope belts, which reference the idea of monastic dress. Further, the bowed head of one model and the clasped hands of the other reinforce this interpretation. At the same time, the ad copy proclaims that these designs, "right out of the middle ages," constitute the "latest invention for summer lounging" and introduce a new take on an old form. The robes could be worn in public or private, came in a variety of bright colors (coral reef, sandstone, riptide blue, and ocean aqua), had a shorter hem length (ending at the knee), and a female wearer. These qualities all provided this "old" look with a "new" life. Thus, while the juxtaposition of "middle ages" and "latest invention" seems jarring at first, it reveals how religious styles and symbols were seen as a way to innovate in fashion.[36]

Together the structuring features of the modern fashion industry combined with these various factors, from European sophistication to American popular culture to the spirituality accorded Catholic nuns, priests, and monks, to help establish the appeal and fashionability of Catholic religious dress at midcentury (and in subsequent decades). The religious uniform, the seeming antithesis of fashion, became part of it. This not only expanded the ways that fashion mediated religion but also reinforced fashionable religion's emphasis on the ability of visual and material mediations to provide consumers with personalized sacred moments that promised to enhance their lives.

From *Il Pretino* to "Mini-Medievals"

In the fall 1956–57 fashion season, we can see these various influences come together in the "Cardinal Line" designed by the Fontana sisters. Inspired by the dress of Catholic Cardinals, the collection featured dresses and redingotes in austere black, bold reds, and rich purple. The shapes of the garments, their button details, and accompanying accessories recalled their religious referents. The collection made headlines when actress Ava Gardner, at the height of her fame, was photographed around Rome wearing *il pretino*, or the little priest dress. The dress, inspired by the Roman-style cassock or soutane, was black with red buttons and featured a hint of white showing at the collar. However, unlike the typical priestly garment that flowed out from fitted shoulders, this priest dress accentuated Gardner's bombshell body. A pectoral cross and cardinal's hat (in black with a red tassel) topped off Gardner's sacerdotal style.

Newspapers briefly noted Fontana's "ecclesiastical" trend with dresses in "churchly reds"[37] and another described how the Fontana sisters had "adapted glorious ecclesiastical purples and reds—and the sweeping backward flow of a cardinal's robes—to the uses of fashion."[38] However, the *Daily Express (London)* focused on controversy as it proclaimed "Ava's Dress Shock." The brief copy highlights Gardner's penchant for trouble and the frowns she garnered "for strolling around Rome in a high-collared dress almost like a close-fitting priest's cassock." It continued, "The Vatican says this dress is a deliberate and distasteful copy of the garb worn by priests," and that it had "severely reprimanded" the Fontana sisters.[39]

While the Baptist-reared, North Carolinian Gardner may have garnered suspicion on the streets of Rome, the tabloid-like *Daily Express* exaggerated Vatican disapproval. The Fontana sisters of Rome, devout Catholics and favored designers of Gardner, designed the dress (and the broader collection) having gained permission from the Pope to do so. In an interview, Micol Fontana explained, "We are Catholic: Asked permission to the Vatican. They sent us a cardinal costume to be copied." Other coverage of the line reported that it was done "with the official permission of the Vatican."[40] Certainly the adaptation of male priests' attire for the purposes of fashion and the female body, seen particularly in the form-fitting silhouettes of the line[41], introduced an innovative fashion trend and raised the specter of controversy. However, the Fontana sisters' personal connection to Catholicism and their status in the fashion industry helped authorize their inspiration.

While the religious inspiration of the "Cardinal Line" did not dominate American fashion headlines, the Fontana sisters made their

Figure 4.1. Ava Gardner wearing *il pretino*; courtesy
of the Micol Fontana Foundation.

American presence known. In addition to having a base in New York,
they involved themselves in the American fashion scene. For example,
in October 1956, on the heels of this collection, Micol Fontana arrived in
Chicago for the "annual Fontana show," which strengthened her American consumer base. The fashion house also sponsored three scholar-
ships to American college students interested in fashion.[42] And, in an
effort to avoid fashion insularity, the Fontana sisters bought and sold
American fashions in their Fontana Boutique.[43] The fashion house also
stayed in the public eye when Anita Ekberg wore a version of *il pretino*
in Federico Fellini's *La Dolce Vita* in 1960, and again in 1962 when Zoe
Fontana Montanarini's daughter and the heir-apparent to the fashion
house became a nun.[44]

Il pretino and the "Cardinal Line" captured some of the changes
occurring in both religion and fashion at midcentury. Conformity

characterized religion and fashion in the 1950s and can be seen, to some extent, in the framing of *il pretino*. The emphasis on the Fontana's Catholicism and the Vatican's permission to design the line constructed the garment and larger line as "authentic" and faithful to tradition in a particular way. Yet, the line also signals something new and different in fashion's relationship to religion. A contingent of scholars argue that the "long sixties" began in 1956,[45] and we can see strong currents of the emerging '60s seeker spirituality in the "Cardinal Line." This collection framed Catholic religious dress, and the Christian imaginary, as an acceptable source for innovating and inspiring fashion design. In doing so, it reinforced a way of seeing Christianity in terms of the visual and the material world of fashion—decontextualized from its institutional Christian framework.[46] The resulting fashionable religion emphasized how these religiously inflected visual and material products offered individual access to the sacred aura of religious garb personalized through designers' inspirations and consumers' taste.

This way of seeing emerged from and reinforced larger trends occurring in the broader religious landscape in the 1960s. In the United States and Europe, church attendance, particularly among young adults declined. Many joined the counterculture, which challenged notions of traditional religious authority and reveled in "flouting conventions of decency in a way that [not only] shocked many respectable citizens, but also accustomed them to new ways of thinking."[47] People were also exposed to more diverse religions and celebrated pluralistic and ecumenical trends as sociologist Will Herberg famously articulated in *Protestant, Catholic, Jew*.[48] In the midst of this tumult, Protestant and Catholic institutions (most notably through Vatican II and its commitment to *aggiornamento*), attempted to reform and keep up with a changing world.[49] Alongside institutional changes, individuals cultivated more individualized, rather than collective, identities—the rising seeker mentality that Wuthnow documents.[50] These numerous factors produced "a mood of eclecticism which proclaimed the possibility, even the desirability, of mixing elements drawn from different traditions and belief-systems."[51] The various religious currents of the 1960s, including individualism, reform, "flouting convention," and "eclecticism," occurred not only at the level of everyday spiritual practice but also in terms of religious visual and material culture, which we can see in the fashions of the 1960s.

Alongside these religious trends, the modern fashion industry culti-vated its boundary-pushing status, and consumers increasingly concep-tualized their fashion choices as expressions of individual identity. "Now is the time of the individual," explained designer Geoffrey Beene, while another stated, "there has never been more individuality in fashion."[52] The stylish suits of Jacquelyn Kennedy began the decade, but mini-skirts and jeans dominated by its end. During this time, "street styles," such as those worn by mods, rockers, and hippies, not only expressed a par-ticular aesthetic and subculture but also began to influence fashion and increase the array of acceptable styles.[53] This disrupted the traditional "trickle-down theory," which suggested that fashionable styles began with the elite and eventually found their way to the masses.[54] As a re-sult, fashion houses and designers incorporated more diverse styles and pushed boundaries through "op art" designs, ethnic looks, space-age collections, and Catholic-inspired designs.[55] The conformity of the 1950s gave way to a cacophony of styles in the 1960s.

During this decade, fashion inspired by Catholic religious dress went from an interesting occasional design choice to a widespread fashion trend that met with diverse reactions. In reflecting on this trend, fash-ion columnist Evelyn Livingstone explained that in the past fashion had utilized "ecclesiastical bits and pieces," but in the 1960s this inspiration went further. The attire of Catholic priests, monks, and nuns, as well as "today's fashions" had been revolutionized.[56] Leading the fashion revo-lution on various fronts was the Vienna-born, California-based fashion designer Rudi Gernreich. He excelled as an award-winning fashion de-signer but also challenged some of the existing norms of the modern fashion industry by designing sportswear (rather than haute couture), advocating for reasonably priced clothes (his garment pricing generally ranged from $20 to $200), and embracing the taboo-breaking of the 60s.[57] He is perhaps best known for his infamous 1964 swimsuit design. The monokini (or topless suit) featured a high-waisted bottom with a strap that went around the neck but left the female wearer's breasts bare. Gernreich never intended to produce the suit, as he envisioned it to be a statement about the freedom and future of fashion, but he ended up selling three thousand of them and "his name became a symbol of con-troversy, nudity, and sensationalism."[58] His "no-bra bra," released the same year, used "two wispy cups of molded nylon," rather than layers of padding and structure, and reinforced his reputation as a designer delighting in nudity and sexuality.[59] In many ways, he became fashion's "enfant terrible, who shocked innumerable sensibilities."[60]

By 1966 and 1967, Gernreich's avant-garde status imbued his work with fashionable cachet, but at the same time, the modern fashion industry demands constant innovation. Designers cannot keep repeating the same looks or ideas, so innovation for Gernreich in these two years sometimes meant more "conservative" looks. For example, in 1966, he showcased how to wear a "modest" printed shirtwaist dress fashionably, and, as fashion reporter Bernadine Morris noted, "the dresses that got the most applause were the long ones that, oddly enough, bared nothing."[61] A few months later, Morris reiterated that Gernreich's dresses "covered a woman from her neck to her toes" and featured "big, puffy sleeves that looked demurely Victorian." She added that Gernreich, too, "dressed almost conservatively."[62] Gernreich had established himself as "cutting edge" through his more audacious designs, but he also kept innovating as demanded by the fashion system.

One design that did so appeared in the fall of 1967. Photographed on model Léon Bing, Gernreich's outfit suggests a kind of space-age nun, and some called her the "The Sister of the Immaculate Mascara," a reference to the design's inspiration and Bing's heavy eye makeup. Some described it as "a cross between the monk's and nun's habits."[63] In the photograph, Bing is covered from head to toe, which was in keeping with Gernreich's designing of a "total [head to toe] look."[64] Suggesting the nun's veil, Bing wears a two-layered headpiece, a tight-fitting white layer that surrounds her face while covering her head and neck and a black helmetlike piece over top. The nunlike look continues as the model sports a flowing black, sleeveless, tunic worn over a white dress featuring long, bell-shaped sleeves. The caption in one text notes that the outfit "is really just two simple, pretty dresses worn together"—a white shift and a black jumper.[65] Both dresses, though, unlike nuns' attire, end at midthigh, in keeping with the popular hemline of the day. While this may have raised the ire of those opposed to the mini- and microminiskirt, white tights cover Bing's legs and black socks with low-heeled black shoes completed the ensemble. Everything, except the model's hands and face, is covered. Media headlines, such as "From Nude to Nun Look: Gernreich's Fashions Run Gamut" and "Gernreich Unveils

Shockers Again," sensationalized Gernreich's space-age nun, but the content of the articles framed this design in terms of his avant-garde aesthetic.[66]

The coverage also shows that other designers found similar inspiration in the dress of Catholic monks, nuns, and priests. In 1966, Halston's "millinery collection" included an "interpretation" of a "nun's coif" in "jet-embroidered stiffened net," while another designed "a nun's bonnet of black lace" to go with a "matching dress."[67] American-born designer Geoffrey Beene's 1967 collection included "long black wool stylized cassocks with white Roman collars—and topped them with padre hats."[68] Alongside the rising popularity of cross jewelry, numerous designs turned to Catholic religious dress for fashion inspiration.

While these designs made headlines, more acclaim went to the work of Spaniard Cristóbal Balenciaga. Known for his dramatic silhouettes— his "deep knowledge of the sculptural possibilities of certain firm textiles, and on letting the textile determine the cut of the garments"— Balenciaga's designs often evoke images of priests, monks, and nuns.[69] In the 1960s, according to fashion journalist Bill Cunningham, his bridal gowns "can always be identified with the habits of nuns or monks as inspiration."[70] This was certainly true in 1967 when Balenciaga designed two such ensembles—a wedding dress and a dinner dress with cape. In keeping with his reputation for innovative silhouettes and masterful tailoring, *Vogue* described these designs as "marvels of form," "pure and calm," and "carved."[71] The full-page photographs of the two designs highlighted the deceptively simple, yet striking shapes, as well as Balenciaga's "mastery of execution."[72] The headpiece that accompanied the bridal gown as well as the gown's train called to mind a nun's habit, while the dinner dress and cape connoted a priest's garb. In the latter, the cape suggests the priest's mantle, while the dinner dress resembles a modified cassock. Unlike Gardner's fitted priest dress, Balenciaga padded the gown so that it stood away from the body and emphasized the lines of the garment. And, unlike Gernreich's futuristic nun, Balenciaga's design emphasized elegance of form and technical skill, which was even clearer when the design was seen from the back.

Balenciaga's ability to fuse a traditional religious uniform with modern lines and dramatic silhouettes made this look stand out as innovative and sophisticated. It was also framed as "authentic." Balenciaga had not designed dress-up costumes; rather, his more abstract designs connoted the rich artistic tradition of Western Europe and its Catholic heritage. In describing the dinner dress and cape, one source states, "The area of Spain from which Balenciaga came was densely populated by such figures clad in black—and the colour, layered effect, circular and tubular shapes relate closely to their garb. In other respects it is entirely modern."[73] Another historian writes, "He was profoundly impressed by two divergent aspects of the Catholic Church that dominated his boyhood town—both by the splendor of its ecclesiastical vestments and by its austere religious strictures and monkish clerical garments."[74] While these connections can be seen clearly in retrospect, as with the Fontana sisters, the fashion public of the time knew of Balenciaga's personal ties to Catholicism. This, in turn, enhanced the sense that his designs were authentic to his personal experience and hence his aesthetic, in the same way that Gernreich's nun-inspired outfit aligned with this avant-garde reputation. Despite their different aesthetics, these designs accustomed people to seeing elements of religion in the visual and material forms of fashion, while simultaneously interpreting religion in individual ways, including the consumer's personal taste, the designer's biography, and the designer's aesthetic sensibility.

In 1968, though, the popular media took more notice. Twelve years after *il pretino* and Micol Fontana's visit to Chicago, the London-born, Chicago-based designer Walter Holmes embraced the emerging ecclesiastical trend. Holmes did not achieve the historical acclaim of designers, such as Gernreich, Beene, and Balenciaga, but in the 1960s, he was relatively well known. A regular part of the Chicago fashion columns, Holmes designed the dresses for one of Dinah Shore's "TV spectacular[s]" and won the prestigious Gold Coast fashion award in 1966 (previous winners included Oleg Cassini and Bill Blass).[75] He was also commissioned to redesign the "stewardess' uniform" for Mexicana Airlines in 1967,[76] and tapped into the youth market through his relationship with the boutique, Paraphernalia. This boutique and others attracted young people through their reputation for "fashion novelty and experimentation," as well as their "space-age" interiors. Paraphernalia also had a party-place reputation as it stayed open late featuring "music and live models dancing on platforms."[77] When a branch of Paraphernalia opened in Chicago, Holmes was there for the launch party, along

with "uninhibited young American designer" Betsey Johnson and playboy Hugh Hefner.[78]

In the spring of 1968, Holmes designed two outfits that he called
"mini-medievals"—one inspired by nuns' habits and the other by monks'
robes—for Paraphernalia. The designs made both local and national
headlines.[79] A long-sleeved mini-dress with a scooped neck and "nun's
collar" that came in various colors, including gray, royal blue, and white,
constituted Holmes's interpretation of the nun's habit and sold for $29.
Optional accessories included the $6 nun's "hood," and "a silver chain
necklace with a tiny tinkling bell on the end for $5."[80] Holmes's monk-
inspired dress sold for the same price and was also mini in length. The
mini-dress came in off-white, beige, and brown, and featured midlength
wide sleeves and a "sort of authentic" knotted rope belt. According to
Holmes, "I copied it from a real monk's belt that I bought for research
purposes." A separate hood could be purchased to accompany this style,
as well.[81] Holmes's biggest and perhaps most controversial adaptation
was the garments' short length. Reporter Judy Klemesrud noted that
"without the hoods, the dresses look like most other minidresses around
town." Similar to Gernreich, Holmes's design took recognizable religious
styles—the nun's habit and the monk's robe—and transformed them to
create an innovative design and push the boundaries of fashion. And
it sold "to everyone from suburban housewives to Playboy Bunnies."[82]

Yet unlike Gernreich, who cultivated an avant-garde and *enfant terrible* persona, Holmes denied any such troublesome intention and emphasized his sincerity. "I had nothing sacrilegious in mind at all," and
in an interview with Klemesrud, Holmes explained, "After all the nudity and everything else, I felt strongly about the complete opposite—
propriety and prudence. I thought nuns and monks most aptly typified
it." Klemesrud's *New York Times* article also highlighted Holmes's religious background (Church of England) and his explanation that "he
thought they would be well received due to the recent modernization
of nuns' habits." Klemesrud bolstered Holmes's claim to sincerity in a
follow-up article, published a few months later, that detailed how the
Wisconsin-based Community of Our Lady hired him to update their
religious garb. The article further emphasized Holmes's authenticity by
noting that the Community was impressed by his "extensive research"
for the "mini-medievals."[83]

Figure 4.2. The "mini-medievals" designed by Walter Holmes; photograph by Michael Evans; courtesy of Zuma Press and the Evans Estate.

Whether sincere or not, his stated intentions and the framing of his work as authentic positioned Holmes as someone attuned to the Catholic culture of Chicago and Catholicism in general. In the 1960s, "the Chicago area with its 2,163,380 Catholics in Cook and Lake counties" constituted "the largest Catholic archdiocese in the United States" and seminary enrollments in the city reached an all-time high.[84] More broadly, the 1960s saw Catholic monks, nuns, and priests grappling with their forms of religious dress. As part of Vatican II, many within each of these groups slowly adopted reforms to "update" their distinctive attire.

In regard to nuns, "*Perfectae Caritatis* stated that 'the religious habit, an outward mark of consecration to God, should be simple and modest, poor and at the same time becoming.'"[85] Such changes encouraged manufacturers to expand the available options, and Jamieson's, the largest supplier of clothing to nuns, created a sixty-page booklet entitled "For the Nun in a Changing World," and held fashion shows to introduce the sartorial possibilities, from "traditionalist" to "semi-traditionalist."[86] According to fashion journalist Bill Cunningham in the late 1960s, Vatican II fostered these adaptations to the nun's habit and the incorporation of Catholic dress into fashion. He explained, "the door has been opened . . . especially since Pope Paul VI abolished hereditary papal court tiles, functionaries, and many of the costumes, to awaken in the public a preference for the 'efficacious, functional, and logical' over the 'nominal, decorative, and external.'" "It would be natural," he explained, "for fashion designers . . . to now pick up the papal discards as a new direction."[87] They did.

Despite the emphasis on Holmes's authenticity and the widespread reforms of Catholic religious dress, his designs produced controversy. Virginia Kay of the *Chicago Daily News* gave it "The Shockingly Bad Taste Award of the Year, Decade and Century," stating that she "looked up to nuns" as a young girl. Rev. Msgr. Joseph T. V. Snee declared them "blasphemous" and wished that people would imitate other "habits" of nuns, namely "modesty, purity, and chastity."[88] Pictures of the "mini-medievals" and headlines emphasizing the controversial outfits circulated throughout the country from national magazines and newspapers, such as *Newsweek* and the *Chicago Tribune*, to local newspapers, including the *Akron Beacon Journal* (Akron, Ohio), the *Battle Creek Enquirer* (Battle Creek, Michigan), and the *Arizona Republic* (Phoenix, Arizona).[89]

Holmes's "mini-medievals" caused controversy for a few reasons. The mini-length of the outfits and their consumption by the youthful, avant-garde Paraphernalia shopper caused some to reject Holmes's claims to spiritual sincerity and authenticity. The outfits' short length and optional hoods emphasized the contrast between religious and secular, pure and sexual,[90] which caused some to interpret them as "blasphemous" and antagonistic to Catholicism. For these interpreters, the "mini-medievals" undermined the sacrality and holiness associated with Catholic religious dress and challenged the authority these garments helped confer upon the Catholic Church and its leaders.

Critics and observers had some reasons to doubt Holmes's stated intentionality. Given his connections to the boutique, it is likely that he knew the typical Paraphernalia customer cultivated a rebellious persona at odds with the conservatism he expressed regarding his "mini-medieval" designs. Further, Holmes's decision, in 1969, to design the Playboy Bunny stewardess uniforms for Hugh Hefner's "big black bunny plane" shows that Holmes did not shy away from designs highlighting female sexuality.[91] He also did not back away from the notorious trend and designed a fall collection for Paraphernalia that again embraced the ecclesiastical theme, including a "black crepe mini-cardinal's dress with red moiré sash and black pontifical hat,"[92] and "a lace after-five dress that's a 1968 version of a choirboy's surplice."[93] Holmes's follow-up line did not gain the same kind of notoriety, but Chicago fashion columnist Evelyn Livingstone described the collection "as dramatic, contemporary simplicity rather than church pageantry" as long as you did *not* wear the padre hat.[94]

Another factor, though, accounts for the widespread controversy surrounding Holmes's designs. Gernreich's design was equally mini in length and few would confuse socialite Gloria Guiness, who owned Balenciaga's priest-inspired dress, with a Catholic religious leader, which suggests the need to look for additional explanations. Unlike the work of these other designers, the public could easily access and afford Holmes's garments. Not confined to the rarefied world of high fashion that emphasized the purity of designers' artistic visions, Holmes's commercialized "mini-medievals" opened up more discursive space for questions about his taste and that of his consumers. Further, the garments' accessibility and popularity foregrounded fashion's use of Christianity in a more public and, for some, more threatening way, as evidenced by the criticisms. In the "mini-medieval," Americans could literally see the religious landscape changing.

This controversy provides a glimpse into the different ways people responded to the rise of seeker spirituality. While some disapproved, as noted above, others reveled in the "mini-medieval's" fusion of sartorial and spiritual possibility. A Manhattan secretary reported that she wore "the nun's dress to work and attache[d] the coif for parties,"[95] while another consumer thought it "was cute," but qualified her remark by clarifying that she was not Catholic. Fashion writer Bill Cunningham described the experience of seeing the designs in New York: "The sights of the models dancing the frug under psychedelic lighting in mini-skirted monk's robes . . . was a shocker for the most sophisticated."[96] This sense of shock was precisely what delighted some wearers. For example, a twenty-two-year-old consumer called it "a real goof" and enjoyed the juxtaposition of ideas, stating, "When you take the hood off, it's like this total antithesis."[97] Part of the pleasure of wearing these garments was how they "produce[d] a pleasurable 'grinding' sensation of inappropriateness."[98] The "mini-medieval" was controversial for some and "a goof" for others, not because it no longer resonated with sacred meanings, but because it did—and did so in ways that looked new and were experienced differently.

The emergence of the ecclesiastical dress trend alongside the popularity of cross jewelry highlights how fashion increasingly mediated bits and pieces of Christianity in the 1960s. The convergence of these two trends fostered particular ways of seeing Christianity.[99] It accustomed people to extracting religious symbols, visual cues, and material forms from the Christian past and recontextualizing them within the fabric of their lives, which reinforced the emerging seeker-oriented spirituality of the time. Further, the emphasis on fashion designers' personas, whether their aesthetic vision or their personal ties to religion, framed the act of reprocessing as an expression of personal taste and inspiration. This personalization not only highlighted the status of designers as artists, but it encouraged fashion followers to adopt a similar individual and inspirational approach to religion.

As a result, the fashionable religion fostered by these forms of mediation emphasized the individual's experience of religion—its look and feel. While critics of the "mini-medieval" feared that its appearance was a harbinger of Christianity's eroding place in American society, sociologist Thomas Luckmann challenges this secularization framework. He writes about these broader changes in religious life in terms of "shrinking transcendence." The result, he argues, is that religion is increasingly privatized, and the scope of transcendence focuses on the individual and can be seen in "modern religious themes such as 'self-realization,' personal autonomy, and self-expression." He continues, "The dominant themes in the modern sacred cosmos bestow something like a sacred status upon the individual himself by articulating his autonomy."[100] Luckmann's insight captures how the emerging seeker spirituality of the 1960s focused on the development of the self. This self could be cultivated and enhanced through the consumption of cross jewelry and "mini-medievals." Designers' use of ecclesiastical inspirations invoked the idea of the Christian supernatural, the transcendent, thought to be embodied in the "antimodern" commitments of priests, monks, and nuns. Yet, one did not have to be a priest or even a Catholic to see and experience the beauty of Catholic-inspired design. One could simply buy the outfit. Similar to the way fashion magazines promoted spiritual tourism, these ecclesiastical designs promised "little" moments of transcendence by invoking the "aura" associated with Catholic religious dress, but they did so in ways that could be personalized as a "goof," "cute," or something else. In doing so, fashionable religion highlighted its "modern" and "sophisticated" status.

Not unexpectedly given the demands of the fashion cycle, this ecclesiastical trend faded in the 1970s. Glimpses of it appeared in a 1972 advertisement for the Chicago-based Stanley Korshak. The advertised dress's long length and style resembled a priest's cassock, while the white-cuffed sleeves, collar, and cornette-like hat connoted nun's attire.[101] A few years later, Yves Saint Laurent experimented with a "cassock shirt" and a dress and raincoat that resembled monks' attire.[102] The trend, though, reappeared, in the late 1980s and early 1990s when designers revitalized it and extended it to other religions.[103]

From "Dressing Ascetic" to "Penitential Chic"

In the 1980s, despite the religious battles being fought in the "culture wars,"[104] a number of fashion designers returned to and expanded upon the earlier Catholic religious dress trend. During this decade, increasing diversity in terms of inspiration and styles characterized fashion. For example, for the working woman a "conservative, tailored" look epitomized by the "power suit" dominated, while a "glamorous, feminine, and sexy" style was deemed appropriate for "leisure time," and the more casual and androgynous choice of jeans, T-shirts, and sneakers was expected for casual wear.[105] The diversification of available looks and the expectation that one should have an abundant wardrobe meant, "Americans went shopping in the 1980s."[106] Designer jeans, *Flashdance*-inspired off-the-shoulder styles, and stirrup pants became wardrobe staples.[107] And the haute couture industry made a comeback. "Although," as fashion historians note, "only a few women could afford couture, the European designers influenced many of the styles of the decade."[108] Fashion shifted toward "more expensive, ostentatious fashions, which reflected a more money-obsessed, image-conscious era."[109]

Despite the acceptance of more diverse styles, ecclesiastical trends did not merit much respect in the "image-conscious" fashion world of the early 1980s. In 1981, fashion columnist Nina Hyde commented that "when the designers start borrowing church fashions you know they are straining for ideas."[110] Deeming the trend trite and unfashionable, Hyde dismissed it and moved on to other, more innovative designs. However, as the decade advanced and fashion embraced more "ostentation" and "body-conscious" clothing, glimpses of garments inspired by Catholic religious appeared accompanied by the language of "simplicity" and "asceticism."[111] In 1987, fashion reporters and magazines acknowledged the religious inspiration for these styles, as they emphasized the shift in fashion focus. Bloomingdale's vice president, for instance, noted, "There is a whole school of intellectual fashion catering to those who are anti-fuss, antifrill, and even anti-accessories."[112] The clothes were described as "lean and dark," and another called them "Dark. Draped. The intellectual, 'other' side, now, of fashion." Six years after dismissing the trend, Nina Hyde labeled its 1987 version "avant-garde."[113]

Of the designers embracing this trend, such as Marc Audibet, Geoffrey Beene, Yohji Yamamoto, and Angelo Tarlazzi, the name Geoffrey Beene stands out.[114] Having designed cassock-inspired dresses notable for their "padre shape" in the 1960s, Beene, sometimes called the "godfather of American minimalism,"[115] returned to this Catholic religious inspiration in the late 1980s (with no mention of these earlier iterations). The media celebrated Beene and the designs for his Fall/Winter collection for 1987 as "elegant," "intellectual," and "simplicity" personified.[116] While not mentioning Beene in their brief one-page feature on "Dressing Ascetic," which highlighted the trend, *Vogue* included a ten-page photo shoot entitled "The World of Geoffrey Beene" in the very same September 1987 issue. The second page of the photo shoot makes his "ascetic" style clear. The image features two models wearing long black coats standing outside. One coat has a hood, while the other features a cowl. The cut of the coats, the serene setting, and the models' poses (one has her hands clasped in a prayerlike gesture, while the other looks contemplative), reinforce a religious interpretation. The description, "a stark, almost monastic simplicity," further emphasizes the religious inspiration of these looks and the entire collection. While other looks in the line appear less literally inspired by Catholic religious dress, some "ecclesiastical" elements appear. For example, the collection's black jumpsuits feature high collars that seem to be a subtle play on priests' collars, while other looks feature hoods, gloves, and lace, which showcased "the interplay of simplicity and sophistication." According to *Vogue*, Beene's combination of old and new, fashion and religion, resulted in clothing that was "modern" and "streamlined."[117]

In the late 1980s, fashion writers framed the use of monastic or "ascetic" inspiration in terms of a "simple" and "elegant" design aesthetic at odds with fashions characterized by ostentation, overt sexuality, and shock value. As we saw with the work of Rudi Gernreich and as one observer pointed out, when "clothes of major designers are exploding with color and heavily decorated fabrics," more subdued colors and designs stand out as surprising and avant-garde.[118] In this instance, the "simplicity" of "dressing ascetic" reflected not only the lines and colors of the garments but also the connotations associated with their religious referent. Even though the wearing of Catholic religious dress by priests, monks, and nuns was significantly diminished by the late 1980s, it continued to be recognizable and symbolize an "antimodern" devotion to spiritual and simple living. Designers invoked these religious ideas as a way to enhance the innovativeness of their garments and the promise they held for respite from a complicated world.

French designer Jean Paul Gaultier took a vastly different and more Gernreich-like approach to his nun-inspired Spring/Summer 1990 Collection. In the 1980s and early 1990s, Gaultier, like Gernreich, earned the label of fashion's *enfant terrible* for his daring designs, and news headlines, such as "Gaultier: Fashion Designed to Provoke," "Anarchy by Gaultier," and "Couture's Bad Boy," affirmed this characterization.[119] According to one fashion journalist "he delights in attacking what he calls a 'taboo mentality'" and "plunders the past and the world around him" for inspiration.[120] And another wrote, "Gaultier always likes to be naughty and offend people with his presentations, which have included models wearing padded ice-cream-cone-shaped bras and men wearing skirts." Most outside of fashion circles know him for designing Madonna's "cone bra" worn during the Blonde Ambition tour.[121] Given his provocative persona and taboo-breaking design aesthetic, it is not surprising that Gaultier took on the subject of religion in some of his notable collections.

Gaultier's Spring/Summer collection debuted in the fall of 1989 at a Paris show characterized by pageantry and spectacle. Fashion editor Nina Hyde remarked, "one goes to his shows not only for the clothes and the music, but [also] to see the unexpected way he presents them."[122] This was certainly the case in October of 1989. The show opened with "women in nun's habits spreading incense from swinging censers," which according to journalist Bernadine Morris, "provide[d] an unusual setting for fashion."[123] Dramatic lighting and religious music—Gregorian chants and church bells—heightened the spiritual mood. And rather than walking the runway, models ascended and descended into view on mechanized platforms, and often their gestures—clasped hands, bowed heads, outstretched arms—reinforced the religious framework of the performance. Throughout, Gaultier employed the sensual world of Catholicism, incense (smell), chants (sound), coifs (sight), to create a sense of mystery, awe, and wonder for his audience, and enhance the significance of his collection.[124]

As with other designers, Gaultier's show and his collection rested not on the complicated nuances of nuns' lives or the particularities of their habits, but on a particular stereotypical look and understanding of nuns. The first five models emerging from under the stage wore white coifs and garments in black and/or white with their hands together as if praying. Not all of the collection's garments kept with this "nunnish"[125] theme, but as Morris notes, "later hoods or chin bands made reference to the coifs." Throughout the show, Gaultier's use of the nuns' coif highlighted "aesthetic antipodes," the way opposites work together to create meaning.[126] The coifs emphasized the tenuous boundary between coverage and exposure, purity and sexuality, constraint and freedom. For example, some coifed models opened their leather jackets to reveal bathing-suit clad bodies and reveled in the act of exposure, while others

Figure 4.3. Gaultier's runway show featuring his nun-inspired collection; Pierre Vauthey/Getty Images.

wore visible garter belts with thigh-high hose, and still others suggested liberating women from repressive dress codes as models removed cage-like sculptural outerwear.[127] As one account noted, "They [the models] retained the sober, black head-dresses, *even when* their outfits featured bras over T-shirts or boxer shorts over men's suits."[128] And another reported stated that it "look[ed] as if it were inspired by the forbidden sexual fantasies of a repressed religious fanatic."[129] Morris concluded that "the staging was so riveting and the ecclesiastical overtones so outrageous that nobody talked much about the clothes."[130]

Unlike Beene's use of Catholic religious dress as a way to play with garment form and line, Gaultier used this visual code to provoke and transgress. "I was shocked," one fellow designer stated. "The story of the nuns was cattivo gusto, bad taste."[131] Others commented that Gaultier "uses fashion for its shock value,"[132] called it a "bizarre ecclesiastical theme,"[133] or remarked that he was "not at all afraid of what such sacrilege could mean for his afterlife prospects."[134] One article reported that, "When he was told that some in the audience were offended by the nuns' garb the models wore, Gaultier said, 'But I'm Catholic!'"[135] He also explained, in a manner reminiscent of Walter Holmes, "What I was saying was that we are coming into more serious times, quieter times."[136] As with other designers, Gaultier attempted to diminish any controversy by appealing to his personal experience as a Catholic, which attempted to frame his use of Catholic symbols and cues as "authentic."[137] He also emphasized his artistic intention, making a statement about religion and the future, as a way to establish the legitimacy of his work. Whether sincere or not, his rationale emphasizes a personalized way of seeing Christianity[138]—that individuals control what and how they use religious symbols based on their own experiences, stories, and aesthetics.

The personalized way of seeing fostered by fashionable religion promised interpretive possibilities that played with the perceived boundary between "sacred" and "profane." In his article, "From Friars to Fornicators: The Eroticization of Sacred Dress," William Keenan explains, "Part of the lure of the religious dress fetish lies in the *frisson* obtained when carnal and spiritual bodies juxtapose and commingle, when 'the lusts of the flesh' commune with 'the garments of God,' when the conventional morality of dress is overturned."[139] Such challenges to norms produce "a pleasurable grinding,"[140] a sense of edgy rebellion,[141] and the possibility of "questioning . . . the boundaries that separate categories."[142] The longstanding popularity of this transgressive pleasure can be seen in Maria Monk's salacious and best-selling account of sexual deviance among Catholic priests and nuns in *Awful Disclosures* (1836), and more recently in the rise of pornographic "nunsploitation" films, and in the number of "Halloween costume nuns" ("naughty" and "nice") that you can find doing a simple Google search.[143] While these acts of transgression question, alter, and add meanings to religious dress, they also, as Keenan insightfully argues, continue to "operate . . . at some level of religio-moral consciousness."[144] Put another way, the religious meanings attributed to these garments do not simply disappear as they are decontextualized and eroticized. Chris Jenks explains, as noted previously, "transgression is a deeply reflexive act of denial and affirmation."[145] Thus, even as ecclesiastically inspired designs, such as those by Gaultier, challenge dimensions of Christian theology and authority, they also reinforce particular understandings of the tradition and its spiritual exemplars. Consequently, amid the culture wars of the 1980s, discussed more fully in chapter 3, the "aura" of Catholic religious dress continued to resonate with designers, consumers, and critics.

Fashion designers' return to this ecclesiastical trend in the early 1990s highlighted the continuing salience of the garments' religious meanings. Even as the high-profile debates of the 1980s became more muted, religion continued to permeate American culture as people contemplated the implications of the millennium, debated involvement in the Gulf War, and grappled with episodes of religious violence—the Branch Davidian standoff in 1993, the Oklahoma City bombing in 1995, and the Heaven's Gate suicides in 1997. In this more fraught American and global environment, fashion historians explain: "Clothing design began to reflect a general interest in ecology and spirituality and many designers looked for inspiration to communities whose garments and bodily adornment were not shaped by international fashion trends. Authenticity became the new buzzword and subcultural style and ethnic clothing traditions entered fashion as major influences."[146] Amid these religious and fashion trends, designers once again returned to ecclesiastical dress as a symbol of simplicity and authenticity, rather than as a source of shock.

Six looks in Italian design house Krizia's 1991–92 Autumn/Winter Collection adapted priests' garments and resembled more contemporary versions of the Fontana sisters' *il pretino*. Black dresses in cassock-styles, with midthigh hems, jaunty white collars and cardinal hats walked the runway, as did cassock-inspired suits with purple buttons and piping accessorized with Maltese cross brooches on purple scarves.[147] And in 1993, when Henry Alford wrote his "Simply Divine" article for *Vogue*, the sheer number of designers utilizing this inspiration almost overwhelms—Christian Dior, Michael Kors, Calvin Klein, Donna Karan, Geoffrey Beene, Richard Tyler, Ralph Lauren, and more.[148] While much more could be said about the designs themselves, their general appearance bore more resemblance to the work of the Fontana sisters and Geoffrey Beene (who returned to this trend yet again), than Jean Paul Gaultier.

For example, head designer for fashion house Christian Dior, Italian designer Gianfranco Ferré, titled his show "The Keys to Heaven," set it to church organ music, and featured clothes that "could have come straight from the closet of a Vatican cardinal."[149] Fashion reporter Marylou Luther described the fashion scene: "Clerics appear in padre hats at Calvin Klein, preacher coats at Lauren, and nunlike evening gowns in black and white satin at Yeohlee."[150] The *Chicago Tribune's* Genevieve Buck came to a similar conclusion. "There are basically two looks, both lean and spare and both called 'monastic': One is loosely based on monks' robes, sometimes with a cord at the waist, sometimes hooded; the other is a multibuttoned long dress that resembles a priest's cassock."[151]

Unlike the "shock" that greeted Gaultier's adaptation of nun's habits, the words "simplicity" and "austerity" dominated the voluminous coverage of this 1993 fashion trend. Both fashion reporters and some designers emphasized that it was "penitential chic." Meaning that these simple and plain garments were a way "to denounce the evils of vanity, artifice, affectation" and "make up for the excesses of the 1980s."[152] Another reporter saw the trend as "penance" for "previous sins of excess, such as baubled bustiers, peekaboo laces and leather lingerie." She concluded, though, that "whatever the motivation, clerical is chic, monastic is modern."[153] And designer Michael Kors echoed this interpretation and saw his "stripping clothes down to utmost simplicity" as "an antidote to the excesses of the '80s."[154] These explanations associated religious dress with "simple" designs that garnered the label of "modern" and "innovative" by emphasizing their contrast with previous "ostentatious" fashion trends.

Within this context, some designers emphasized the religious roots of their inspiration, while others downplayed it. Richard Tyler, for example, told his personal story and explained, "It's the Catholic boy in me." He went on to tell how his mother made clothing for priests, that his sisters went to Catholic school, and that he still carried a crucifix. He concluded his story with the sentence: "It's my belief."[155] While not biographical, German designer Ane Kenssen named a very specific influence on her collection—"nuns' habits in Dusseldorf."[156] While Tyler rooted his inspiration in biographical details, and Kenssen cited a specific religious reference, others highlighted the aesthetics of shape and design. Designer Jennifer George, who "presented long dark coats with an ecclesiastic feel," explained that long coats with mandarin collars "tend to look like religious clothing."[157] She also mentioned that she was Jewish but did not celebrate the holidays or have a particular religious referent in mind (Jewish or Catholic) when she was designing the collection.[158]

While fashion designers framed their work in terms of personal inspiration and taste, which encouraged consumers to do likewise, fashion reporters pondered the meaning of fashion's puzzling religious turn. One simply stated, "I'm flummoxed by this one," while another asked, "So what's with all this monk business? This sudden reverence for severity and austerity?"[159] Some observers considered that this trend "represents some deep collective search for spiritual meaning,"[160] or a "deep thirst for spirituality after the unfettered materialism of the 1980s."[161] Calvin Klein, for example, stated "There is a sort of spiritual awareness creeping into clothes, mine and others. It has to do with beauty as a reflection of who you are inside."[162] Fashion historian Richard Martin rooted the trend in the "heightened awareness we all have that religion is surprisingly an issue in people's lives in the latter years of the 20th century,"[163] while another noted the "current fascination with spirituality and New Age practice."[164]

Most fashion reporters, though, found these explanations lacking and highlighted the structuring principles of fashion. Amy Spindler of the *New York Times* noted the friction between religion and fashion, while pointing out that the "industry's real religion is change."[165] Others agreed, explaining that the trend was more about "sagging sales" than "some sort of miraculous conversion of repentant designers."[166] This antagonistic framing of fashion and religion allowed reporters to highlight debate and controversy, which, in turn, helped sell papers. For example, Spindler's "Piety on Parade" linked the current trend to the controversy surrounding Madonna's wearing of cross jewelry and cited fears that the current ecclesiastical focus would "have the same profane effect."[167] Quotes from religious figures criticizing the trend reinforced this sense of antagonism. "I regret that the religious symbolism is being trivialized and secularized in this way," and "I think it's revolting to have sacred symbols be used as a little decoration. It's decadent."[168] Such interpretations emphasized the continuing public debate between orthodox and progressivists over religion and the use of religious symbols,[169] while reporters' framing of the issues amplified conceptions of religion as serious, unchanging, and traditional, in contrast to fashion's superficiality, dynamism, and innovativeness.

In the late 1980s and early 1990s, the media's focusing of attention on "dressing ascetic," its novelty, and its potential controversy necessarily entailed forgetting or obscuring other things.[170] Specifically, the media coverage of this trend neglected fashion history and previous incarnations of this trend. It is as if the trend appeared for the first time in 1993. There is no mention of Gernreich's nun outfit, the Fontana sisters' *il pretino*, or Holmes's "mini-medievals." The Catholic inspiration of Balenciaga's designs appears infrequently, while the earlier religious references of Geoffrey Beene's work go unmentioned. To include this history would seemingly diminish the innovative status of the current fashion season and acknowledge the long, intertwined history of religion and fashion. Thus, in an interesting way, even as designers decontextualized religious dress in their designs, fashion reporters, in turn, decontextualized this trend from the broader history of fashion, which bolstered designers' claims to innovative status.

The 1990s iteration of "ecclesiastical dress" highlights the modern fashion industry's continued and expanding use of Christianity and its past. As we have seen, in the 1950s and 1960s designers drew on the Christian imaginary in a more expansive way through the visual code of Catholic religious dress, and designers returned to this inspiration in the late 1980s and early 1990s. Fashion, though, demands innovation, and in 1993, some designers innovated by applying this "template" to the religious dress of other traditions, including the Amish, Tibetan Buddhists, and Orthodox Jews. For example, Calvin Klein remarked that "I look at the robes that are worn in the clergy, or the pristine white shirts that choirboys wear, or the way the Amish dress, and it all comes together for me."[171] Klein's inspiration mixes together the "elegance" of priests and "the graphic purity of the Amish."[172] Notably, a multipage fashion shoot entitled "The Great Plain," featuring "unadorned simplicity" in the "Amish farmland of Pennsylvania," appeared in the same issue of *Vogue* as Henry Alford's "Simply Divine" article.[173] Geoffrey Beene cited a Tibetan Buddhist inspiration for his designs, but his long black coat worn with a hooded vest "ended up looking like vestments from the Catholic Church, which surprised even him."[174] Knowing his design history, it seems that this should not have been so surprising.

And, having already done an ecclesiastically themed show in 1989, as we have seen, *enfant terrible* Jean Paul Gaultier shifted his inspiration to

Judaism. "Invitations lettered in Hebraic script, a menorah-lined runway and Manischewitz wine set the stage for models wearing the flowing curls of Orthodox Jews, fake fur Orthodox-style hats and long, straight black coats."[175] Fashion's use of the Christian imaginary had expanded beyond cross jewelry and Catholic religious dress to include Judaism, Buddhism, and more.

Having previously established a template of incorporating Catholic religious dress, even if not explicitly acknowledged, fashion designers returned to this pattern and then went further by including the dress of other religious traditions. In doing so, they not only sought to innovate their designs, but they also heightened the possibility for controversy. By the early 1990s, distinct Catholic religious garb for the daily lives of priests, monks, and nuns was the exception, rather than the norm. As a result, in some sense, designers found inspiration in and adapted a historical form of religious dress—a relic from the past. This caused some comment and controversy, but it was muted by the changes within Catholicism itself. However, the same could not be said regarding the dress of Tibetan Buddhists monks, Orthodox Jews, or the Amish.[176] Religious dress in these traditions remained a salient part of everyday religious life, which made its inclusion in fashion design a more fraught endeavor.

In the 1990s, with the exception of Gaultier, who sought to shock and provoke, most designers cultivated a mood of seriousness and simplicity. They wanted publicity and positive coverage, not controversy. Compared to Gernreich and Holmes's earlier designs, the Catholic-inspired designs of 1993 look positively modest and traditional—long sleeves, long skirts, and high collars. The designs themselves do not transgress in the same way that Gaultier did. In addition, the mixing of elements from different religious traditions, such as Catholic with Amish and Catholic with Tibetan Buddhist, diluted the specificity of these garments, which produced a generalized ecclesiastical look. The media grouping of all these collections together and framing them as "religious" and "austere" reinforced this homogenization. It focused attention more on the overall visual appearance, rather than the specifics. Fashion studies scholar Valerie Steele explained, this trend was "about a look," not religiousness.[177]

Steele contrasted fashion's emphasis on a religious "look" with "religiousness," and curator of costumes at the Chicago Historical Society,

Barbara Schreier reinforced this conception in her statement, "if some sociologist or pop-culture professor reads a serious religious message into this, I think they're missing the mark."[178] Steele and Schreier's comments reinforced the interpretation of fashion reporters of the time in seeing this trend as another way to innovate and sell clothes. Their insights helpfully highlight the commercial impulses that drive the fashion industry's use of religious symbols.

At the same time, though, the modern fashion industry's emphasis on a religious look is precisely the point that scholars should not miss. Specifically, by the 1990s we can see that the modern fashion industry had constructed ways of seeing religion focused on visual symbols, material forms, and sensual experiences that could be applied to Catholicism, as well as other religions.[179] By reprocessing religious dress and framing its use in terms of personal biography and taste, the modern fashion industry emphasized the individual's experience and local context over the more global implications of these designs for religious communities. A rationale used, as we will see in chapter 5, to push innovation and religious inspiration further.

Conclusion

In September of 1993, the *New York Times* addressed the "ecclesiastical trend" through a different lens. In this personal piece, journalist and author Emily Prager describes her various thoughts about *The Joy Luck Club*, the latest murder in the headlines, and her most recent shopping adventure. Readers journey through New York's streets and stores accompanied by Prager's reflections on shopping trips past and present. Prager's tale, though, abruptly pauses when she enters a store and sees "what looked to be a black priest's cassock." Prager recounts that her "heart leapt" and "pounded" upon seeing this garment. Unable to justify the expense of the designer outfit, though, Prager continues her shopping journey, but remains "consumed" by it and "how it made [her] feel." In Lord & Taylor, she finds an acceptable substitute and decides to charge "the perfect coat. Black, by Calvin Klein, with a clerical look," which she decides to pair with a new black ballet skirt and a previously purchased hat "that was faintly reminiscent of a French nun's headgear." She then ponders: "I would look like a priestess. Why did I want to?"[180]

In Prager's conclusion, she describes watching the latest news about tourists being murdered in Florida, during which the incarcerated suspects explained, "As long as there are tourists, there'll be murder. Easy money." Prager called the mentality "chilling," "terrifying" evidence of a world lacking in "spirituality." Reflecting on this coverage, Prager comprehends her own attraction to priestly garb: "I realized that I wanted to look like a priest because I wanted to escape that chilling mentality." She continues, "I want to clothe myself in the garb of those who have traditionally dealt in matters of conscience, as if by wearing priest's robes I might be both protected and purified, savior and saved. At the least, I might no longer feel helpless."[181]

Prager's story captures the fashionable religion produced by this ecclesiastical trend in the fashion industry. Prager does not identify herself as religious or even talk about religious identity. Institutional religion does not appear in her article, nor do religious leaders. Rather, Prager emphasizes her personal tastes and experiences of fashion—her own feelings and emotions. She clearly recognizes the priestly look dominating fashion in 1993 and highlights its potential supernatural power. Yet, it is a supernatural power that she accesses through wearing religiously inspired designer garments. Prager's approach highlights what Danièle Hervieu-Léger describes in her theory of religion, that "the constitution and expansion of the modern sacred is a consequence of the direct access individuals have to the stock of cultural symbols available."[182] In shopping for clothes, Prager finds "the modern sacred" in the form of a Calvin Klein coat. Prager's perspective is instructive. Her access to religious symbols and perspective on religion (and fashion) does not simply happen. As we have seen, the fashionable religion constructed by the modern fashion industry and espoused by Prager emerged from the structuring principles of fashion and historical processes that shaped a particular way of seeing Christianity.[183]

The modern fashion industry, governed by novelty, visuality, and personalization, went from using "ecclesiastical bits and pieces" to entire garments inspired by Catholic religious dress—from "mini-medievals" in the 1960s to "dressing ascetic" in the late 1980s. This addition of religious dress to the designer's aesthetic repertoire amplified fashion's use of Christianity. Clothing inspired by Catholic religious dress, in addition to cross jewelry, increased attention on Christianity as something to be seen, felt, and experienced through the individual body. At the same time, though, the fashionable religion produced by this process was not that of Catholic devotionalism or evangelical piety. Instead, the control resided with the individual, her tastes, and her senses. This garb invoked transformative and benevolent supernatural possibilities through acts of consumption and adornment, rather than affiliation with a particular religious community or doctrine. As the spiritual seekers of the 1960s became the "unaffiliated" of the 1990s and people sought alternatives to conservative religiosity, fashionable religion functioned as a beautiful accessory that simultaneously offered spiritual protection and exhibited sartorial style.

Fashion designers continue to return to this inspiration. For example, in 2010, upon seeing Stefano Pilati's collection on the runway, one observer remarked, "There appeared to be a Catholic nunnish theme pervading much of . . . [the] show."[184] And a 2011 article once again proclaimed that "New York Fashion Week Designers Inspired by Nun's Habits, Monk's Robes."[185] In 2018, Dolce & Gabbana's Fall Ready-to-Wear collection returned to this theme as well.[186] In the fashion cycle, the old can become new again. The regular return to and popularity of ecclesiastical dress, as with cross jewelry, suggests the continuing power of religious symbols even as institutional religious affiliation declines. Yet, given the fashion industry's emphasis on novelty, fashion designers must continue to push boundaries and try new things. Chapter 5 examines how designers expanded the design repertoire again when they put the Virgin Mary and other holy figures on garments.

5

Fashioning Holy Figures

Glittering tiaras, designer gowns, and debates about bathing suits dominate beauty pageants and their coverage. The appearance of religion, then, at the 2015 Miss Universe Pageant caused comment and not a little controversy. The "national costume" of Kimberly Castillo, Miss Dominican Republic, focused the audience's attention on Catholicism and, more specifically, the Virgin Mary. Castillo's dress, in shades of blue and yellow accompanied by a veil and halolike headpiece, not only gave her a Marian appearance, but the bodice of the dress also featured an image of the Virgin. More specifically, it depicted the *Virgen de la Altagraci* (translated Highest Grace), protector of the Dominican people. She appears on Castillo's dress in the idiom of her iconography, a reverential pose before her infant son. Some interpreted this sartorial gesture as a respectful homage, while others viewed putting the Mother of God on a dress as an act of profanation.[1] Some clearly saw the beauty pageant and designer gown as an inappropriate setting for the Virgin Mary. Castillo, though, viewed the gown as honoring her faith and country. As the national protector of the nation, the *Virgen* "symbolizes humility and represents the poor, needy and those who find light in the darkness through faith." The inspiration and genesis of the dress by designer Leonel Lirio enhanced this sense of authenticity. Lirio selected the *Virgen de la Altagraci* because Castillo "hails from Higüey where the Virgin is found inside the Basilica," and Lirio's designs and techniques replicated those seen in the Basilica's altarpiece.[2]

The tenor of the controversy over Castillo's dress echoed earlier debates about cross jewelry and Catholic-inspired religious dress. Critics emphasize the disrespectful and profaning context of fashion, while defenders highlight their sincerity and connection to the religious symbol. The controversy then becomes fodder for media headlines, and articles focus solely on these polarized views, which fuels antagonistic conceptualizations of the relationship between religion and fashion.

Figure 5.1. Kimberly Castillo's national costume featuring the *Virgen de la Altagraci* in the 2015 Miss Universe Pageant; Storms Media Group/Alamy Stock Photo.

Placing Castillo's Marian-inspired dress into the history of how God got on a dress, though, highlights a broader, ongoing relationship that entails more than antagonism. Contestant Castillo and designer Lirio personalized the gown and its incorporation of Mary; however, this fashion choice—putting a Christian holy figure on a designer garment— did not occur suddenly or even surprisingly. In the history of Christianity and fashion, we have seen the popularity of Eve as an advertising icon, the rise of the cross as a jewelry fad, and the emergence of ecclesiastically inspired fashions. This trajectory shows that over time the fashion industry has expanded the ways it mediates and incorporates the Christian imaginary from imagery to symbols to designs. Castillo's dress highlights another form of fashion mediation—the inclusion of holy figures on designer garments. Given the industry's demands for innovation, this expansion and amplification of fashion's use of Christianity makes sense, but when did this trend begin? What holy figures appear in haute couture? And how does this illuminate our thinking about broader conversations and trends in American religion?

This chapter answers these questions by examining fashion magazines, fashion columns and blogs, runway shows, and designers' garments from the 1990s. During this decade, the fashion industry added holy figures from the Christian past to its repertoire of design inspirations. Examining these sources and the emergence of fashion garments adorned with Christian figures shows how the fashion industry both reflected *and* shaped religious trends in the 1990s. By analyzing the emergence of this trend in the early 1990s and then its flourishing with Marian imagery in the late 1990s, we can see how fashion designers utilized historical, religious, and artistic references combined with personal style and/or experiences to frame their incorporations of religion. These traits helped position their designs as sincere and authentic expressions of artistic inspiration. This, in turn, enhanced the innovativeness attributed to their work and infused their creations with a sense of awe and wonder—and sometimes caught the attention of the media. Moreover, as the seeking spirituality of midcentury became the "do-it-yourself" religion of the 1990s[3], designers' extraction and personalization of Christian figures modeled a way of seeing and using religion that others could emulate.[4]

Fashion designers added representational religious imagery from the Christian heritage to a list that already included cross jewelry and garments inspired by Catholic religious dress. This expanded repertoire further accustomed people to seeing Christianity in terms of "reprocessed" symbols and imagery—elements extracted from the Christian past and resituated in the sartorial world.[5] It amplified fashionable religion's focus on the spiritual development of the individual accomplished through curating and consuming diverse experiences and products. This addition also emphasized fashionable religion's long-standing promise of "sacred moments" made even more accessible through the viewing and/or purchase of garments featuring these holy figures. This sophisticated spirituality offered personalized transcendent possibilities that avoided the literalism and devotionalism associated with institutional religion.[6]

Holy Figures in High Fashion

When I first began researching fashion designs and magazines for this project, I expected to find garments adorned with religious symbols and figures. Having seen numerous garments of this type in twenty-first-century fashions, I thought to find plentiful examples in the past. I did not—a research finding that then prompted my driving research question (How did God get on a dress?) and shaped the entire structure of this book. Fashion's exclusion and inclusion of holy figures, as with its other mediations of Christianity, has a history.

Part of this history emerges from longstanding debates in Christianity. The controversy that greeted Kimberly Castillo's Marian-inspired gown reflected long-standing doubts about the role of images in the Christian life. For some Christians religious art and icons functioned as a conduit to the sacred, while others feared that such efforts were misleading at best, blasphemous at worst. The demand for monotheism and the prohibition on "graven images" codified in the Ten Commandments caused some Christians to fear that statuary and images of God, Jesus, and other saints of the church could become cause for idolatry. Art historian David Freedberg notes that Byzantine iconoclasts, Protestant reformers, and pagan philosophers shared "a fear of basely materializing the divine, and of contaminating divine prerogative with the efforts of the human hand."[7] He adds that Christians have long debated the status of religious icons not because of their assumed meaninglessness; rather, Freedberg points out, Christians grappled with their potential power— the idea that "what is represented becomes fully present."[8] The success of the Protestant Reformation bolstered these fears and caused many to shy away from religious iconography. This Protestant mentality, as we have seen, infused fashion advertising's *de facto* prohibition on including specific religious figures (with some exceptions) and permeated fashion design.

Protestant reticence about religious imagery combined with fashion designers' embrace of modern art's preference for abstraction heightened the ostensible prohibition on the incorporation of saints and holy figures into garments. Representation implied a less sophisticated design. Fashion historian Richard Martin pointed out "when we have seen representation on clothing, it has generally been silly or juvenile if often charming, such as a rain coat with cats and dogs."[9] Fashion designers left the representation of Christian holy figures in the hands of religious institutions and religious leaders. Thus, their inclusion on garments in the 1990s signaled an important departure from the general norms of the modern fashion industry, a departure fostered by fashion trends of the time.

During this decade, the world of fashion took an international and sometimes religious turn. Some industry observers referred to this trend as "international ethnic," and described designers' source inspirations, including Spain, the Byzantine Empire, Eastern Europe, China, and Tibet. One article, though, took care to state, "this is not the folksy look of the '70s. Today's international ethnic is sophisticated and, at its best, not costumey."[10] Fashion historians also noted that the fashion tenor of the 1990s differed from the excesses of the 1980s. "Clothing design began to reflect a general interest in ecology and spirituality and many designers looked for inspiration to communities whose garments and bodily adornment were not shaped by international fashion trends." In this milieu, "authenticity became the new buzzword" and designers looked to "subcultural style and ethnic clothing" for ideas.[11]

They also continued to mine history, including Christian history, for these "authentic" and "spiritual" inspirations. The Christian heritage provided fashion designers with a repository of design inspirations deemed "authentic" because they reflected the "antimodern" spirituality associated with religious communities and peoples in the past. As we seen have seen throughout, whether in photographs of churches and festivals or references to the Byzantine period and ecclesiastical design, fashion magazines and fashion designers have consistently utilized the visual codes of Christianity, particularly Catholicism. Its historical entanglement with the history of art, its aura of sophistication, and the power of fashion centers in Catholic-dominated countries, especially France and Italy, fostered this pattern of usage. So, too, did the supernatural connotations of Catholicism's material culture and the power of its religious imagery to produce various reactions.

Fashion designers' incorporation of Christian holy figures, then, reflects a long history of incorporating the Christian heritage, but pushes this further amid fashion trends emphasizing spirituality and authenticity. In February of 1991, Richard Martin noticed these fashion currents in his article "Sailing to Byzantium: A Fashion Odyssey, 1990–1991." He argued, "Byzantium is serving in 1990 and 1991 as a reference for dress." This may, he suggested, be part of "the general historicism of recent dress," but he also saw something more—fashion designers using historical references to create narratives.[12] Martin writes:

> What cannot be said about this clothing is that it is meaningless. Right or wrong, we tend to associate representation with meaning, whether it is a religious image or an Andrew Wyeth. We know that a Virgin and Child has meaning; it claims history; it establishes allegory; it begets ideas. When Jasper Johns insisted that we see a flag or a target in the era of Abstract Expressionism, and thereby reinstated referentiality to the image, so Versace takes a supremely recognizable image and applies it to clothing to make explicit his demand that clothing is an eloquent, rhetorical mode.[13]

In this quote, Richard Martin highlights a new fashion trend—the inclusion of Christian holy figures—seen in the collections of Rei Kawakubo, Kansai Yamamoto, and Gianni Versace, among others.[14]

In the early 1990s, these designers began including representational religious imagery, Christian holy figures, in their garments, and these collections established patterns that subsequent designers followed and expanded upon. More specifically, all three designers embraced verisimilitude in their designs. Fashion blogger Anna Battista argues that religion provides fashion designers with cheap, copyright free imagery for their designs.[15] While this may be true, designers' faithfulness to the original referent also highlights the artistic and spiritual gravitas of the garments and the inspiration of the designer. By replicating the original, fashion designers attempt to infuse their work with a sense of the supernatural and thereby elevate its impact. Verisimilitude also fosters an aura of authenticity—imbuing designs with a sense of "respect" and "sincerity" by so closely adapting the original.

The focus on verisimilitude and representational imagery can be seen in Japanese designer Rei Kawakubo's Spring 1991 collection entitled "Ink Dye, Stained Glass." Founder of the fashion house Comme des Garçons, Kawakubo shocked the fashion world in the 1980s with her voluminous shapes, distressed fabrics, and "apocalyptic" style.[16] In contrast to her avant-garde reputation, Kawakubo's "Ink Dye, Stained Glass" collection exhibited a more refined and delicate aesthetic. A company representative stated that "Rei wanted to fill her line with fantasy."[17] She created this effect through chiffon and lace fabrics, models wearing nostalgic pillbox hats and gauzy gowns, while others sported garments featuring stained-glass patterns. Stained-glass designs can be abstract; however, Kawakubo's stained-glass prints looked like exact copies of church windows that included Christian figures. The specific source inspiration for Kawakubo's design goes unmentioned and the small scale of the print makes identification difficult, but close-up examination reveals stained-glass circles featuring various figures, such as a man with a halo in a supplicating position gazing upward, while another circle encompasses crowned figures riding horses, perhaps a depiction of the three kings or wise men.[18]

Japanese designer Kansai Yamamoto, famous for working with David Bowie during his Ziggy Stardust tours, included specific Byzantine-style holy figures in his Fall/Winter 1990–91 collection. At this time, Yamamoto's popularity was waning (he showed his last collection a year later) and his line went unmentioned by all except Richard Martin.[19] Known for his over-the-top designs and use of prints, including figures from Japanese culture, at least two of Yamamoto's jackets exhibited this same exuberant aesthetic using a Christian inspiration. Extensive gilding and embroidery that Yamamoto attributed to techniques learned in the city of Kiryū, Japan adorn the jackets.[20] The back panel of one features a close-up of Mary, *Theotokos*, the god-bearer, with her cheek resting against that of her god-child, Jesus. The image appears to replicate the Virgin of Vladimir, part of Russian iconography that follows the Byzantine style. The back panel of the other jacket includes two of the three "holy hierarchs" of Orthodox Christian iconography, most likely Gregory of Nazianzus on the left and John Chrysostom on the right, wearing the cross-embellished vestments of bishops.[21] Yamamoto's jackets not only boldly feature Christian holy figures, but do so in a detailed way that highlighted a specific historical period and referent—Byzantine icons.

Like designer Coco Chanel before them, Italian designers Romeo Gigli and Gianni Versace also emphasized the Byzantine period, specifically through the mosaics of Ravenna. This city, in northeastern Italy, was the capital of the Western Roman Empire in the fifth century, which greatly enhanced its architectural landscape. The mausoleum of Galla Placidia, the Basilica of Sant'Apollinare Nuovo, and the Church of San Vitale, built in the fifth and sixth centuries CE, constitute the central religious sites of the city and are famous for their mosaics.[22] They were declared a world heritage site in 1996.[23] Galla Placidia includes mosaics of Jesus as the Good Shepherd and the martyrdom of Saint Lawrence. Sant'Apollinare Nuovo has numerous mosaics detailing the life of Christ, the saints, and the Virgin and Child, and the Church of San Vitale features scenes from both the Old and New Testaments, as well as a youthful Christ enthroned and the Emperor Justinian and Empress Theodora.[24]

The mosaic of Empress Theodora at San Vitale is important in examining the shift toward representational imagery in the fashion industry. In the procession, she brings a jeweled eucharistic chalice as an offering to God and the Church. Her regal status emphasized by a jeweled crown and collar. What stands out though, for thinking about religion and fashion, are the figures adorning the hem of her garment—the three kings bearing gifts, just as the Empress herself bears a gift.[25] The three kings motif also appears on a sarcophagus housed at San Vitale and in the mosaics at the nearby Basilica of Sant'Apollinare Nuovo. In drawing inspiration from Ravenna, fashion designers not only found techniques to utilize (embroidery and mosaic) and numerous designs to inspire, but they also discovered an example of holy figures on garments. In his Fall/Winter 1990–91 collection, Romeo Gigli incorporated a mosaiclike design of two of the three kings on one of his tunics.[26]

Italian designer Gianni Versace, though, garnered most of the attention of Richard Martin and fashion journalists. Innovation constituted one of the hallmarks of Versace's famed career. He used unconventional materials and bold prints in his designs. He courted celebrities and rock 'n' roll musicians to forge new fashion alliances and influences. As one observer wrote, "He added risqué factors such as bondage-like fastenings or seductive pleats to superbly crafted suits, created tantalizingly tactile leather garments, and dressed men and women in ebullient prints from head to toe."[27] He also flaunted women's sexuality and was known for what Richard Martin called his "prostitute style."[28] Fashion journalist

Figure 5.2. The three kings on the border of Empress
Theodora's garment from a mosaic at the Church of
San Vitale; photograph courtesy of L. Stephanie
Cobb.

Richard Servin noted that Versace's "S&M" look was "the couture es-
thetic, embraced by supermodels and society ladies alike" in 1992.[29]

Versace, though, also looked to the past, to history, for design inspiration. He was a frequent visitor at the Metropolitan Museum of Art in
New York and the Victoria and Albert Museum (V&A) in London. In
Art and Fashion, Alice Mackrell writes that Versace studied the Byzantine Collection at the Met and was a frequent "student" at the V&A.[30]
Versace himself stated, "When you are born in a place such as Calabria
and there is beauty all around a Roman bath, a Greek remain, you cannot help but be influenced by the classical past."[31] Amy Spindler for the

New York Times noted that "the Italian Baroque, Grecian motifs and Etruscan symbols, were woven into his collections, as were the themes of today."[32] Versace's designs reflect this fusion of past and present, historical referents and contemporary signs.

Versace's Fall/Winter 1991–92 Ready-to-Wear collection, inspired, in part, by the religious mosaics that dominate the sacred sites of Ravenna, embodied these qualities. The runway show featured top supermodels of the day, such as Linda Evangelista, Claudia Schiffer, and Christy Turlington, who started down the runway in sleek black outfits and thigh-high boots accompanied by Joan Jett & the Blackhearts' 1982 hit "I Love Rock 'n' Roll." The "starting point," as journalist Bernadine Morris writes, "is clothes for rock stars."[33] Short slip-like dresses in bright hues, followed by oversize prints, skintight leggings, and pleated mini-skirts highlighted Versace's ability to emphasize the female form. Toward the end of the show, however, the designs become more elaborate with embroidered jackets and beaded tops. Most notable, in terms of religion, were a few looks. Versace fused his rock aesthetic with mosaiclike embellishment to produce a biker jacket with a bejeweled Mary and infant Jesus on the back. And, in another look, he paired a short pleated black skirt with a black leather jacket featuring cross embellishments out of semiprecious gems. Underneath, the model wore an elaborately beaded and mosaiclike halter-top featuring a close-up of the Virgin Mary on the front and another of the Madonna and infant Jesus on the back.[34] Versace demonstrated his artistry and connection to Ravenna through his embellishment technique and by including Christian symbols and holy figures on his garments.[35]

Versace's halter translated the ancient technique of mosaic making into elaborate beadwork and fashion. His use of brightly colored gemstones of various sizes infused the design with a mosaiclike texture and richness. Versace emphasized, like a mosaicist, his ability to bring together smaller components to create a grand whole. Further, his decision to include a cross and Mary in the garment amplified the Christian resonance associated with the mosaic visual code. From the front, the cross element at the neck of the halter echoes the frequent use of the Maltese cross brooch seen so often in fashion history, while the inclusion of Mary adds another innovative design element. The shape of the halter emphasizes Mary's presence. The bustline and halo draw your eye to this

Figure 5.3. Cross-embellished motorcycle jacket and
beaded Marian halter by Gianni Versace, Fall/Winter
1991–92; © Tony Kyriacou/Shutterstock.

holy figure. Similarly, the Virgin and Child create the silhouette for the
back of the halter and dominate the visual display. In both cases, Mary
appears ancient and artistic given Versace's mosaiclike technique, but
at the same time, she seems updated—bejeweled and sparkly. Versace's
"rock star" version of the Madonna and baby Jesus.

Versace's interpretation of religious art in the halter top and in the
jacket not only exhibited verisimilitude enhanced by his Italian roots
but also focused attention on his expertise as an artist who could replicate ancient and valued skills, including mosaic-making and embroidery, in his designs. "He achieved," as one critic stated, "an equilibrium
between the historical and the modern which, though audacious, was

never disrespectful."[36] Further, in his book on Versace, Martin writes that "Versace's translation of Byzantium derived from his inspection of artifacts and his certainty that he could perform something akin." He continues, "it is as if history inspired Versace to say 'I can do that,' even with regard to the most venerated and monumental traditions."[37] For Versace, Ravenna's mosaics provided content and techniques that could be used to enhance the innovation and artistry of his designs—a trend subsequent designers would follow.

Fashion journalists did not emphasize Versace's inclusion of religious symbols or Christian figures; rather, they focused more generally on his celebration of the motorcycle jacket and his embrace of prints. One headline exclaimed, "Black leather, zippered jacket roars back into high fashion," while another article explained, "designers such as Donna Karan, Carmelo Pomodoro and Gianni Versace showed funky leather bomber or motorcycle jackets laced with zippers and buckles."[38] One column simply stated that the "ornate jeweled bodices" included "patterns that mixed dancing girls, religious motifs, classic columns and musical notes," and another described the prints as "Byzantine."[39] Others focused on Versace's workmanship. Fashion editor Bernadine Morris stated that "the designer has used the most extraordinary techniques in constructing these populist styles," while another commented on the "intricately beaded bustiers."[40]

The inclusion of religious figures on designer garments marked a shift in how the modern fashion industry utilized religion, and only Richard Martin seemed to notice. A definitive explanation for why is elusive. It could be that the popularity of cross jewelry and the ecclesiastical fashions of 1993 more clearly represented a religious trend, while the disparate styles of Kawakubo, Yamamoto, and Versace prevented fashion journalists from seeing a connection. Also, the relationship of these particular garments to the larger *oeuvre* of the designer may provide some insight. In comparison to their earlier boundary-pushing work, Kawakubo and Yamamoto's designs and their use of Christian imagery appear almost conservative and sedate. One might think Versace's juxtaposition of sexuality (short skirts) and street style (motorcycle jackets) with religious symbols (Virgin Mary and infant Jesus) would raise some debate, but Versace's embrace of multiple prints and motifs in the collection may have muted the audibility of his religious notes.

This lack of media attention also suggests that by the early 1990s religion in fashion had reached a point where violating the old advertising prohibitions against including Christian religious figures caused little comment. As fashion journalist Nina Hyde put it in 1989, "religious imagery in clothing has been creeping in for a while, though it has never been much of a big deal."[41] Whether or not Hyde and others deemed putting Christian holy figures on a dress, jacket, or a halter-top "a big deal," the fashion industry's incorporation of representational religious imagery *is* "a big deal" in the history of Christianity and fashion. It broadened the available repertoire of religious symbols that designers used to make their collections innovative and meaningful. Further, designers' emphasis on verisimilitude, historical and geographic inspiration, and craftsmanship helped establish the authenticity and legitimacy of these designs, which, in turn, reinforced seeing Christianity in visual, personal, and decontextualized ways. Designers literally provided a model for how to design your own spiritual meaning(s) through the curation and display of Christian symbols and figures.

This taken-for-granted next step in fashion's mediation of Christianity reinforced existing emphases in fashionable religion. Fashionable religion stressed the personal experiences and spiritual journeys available through beauty and artistry, which could become part of your life through the viewing, if not purchasing, of particular garments. Further, designers' mixing of religious motifs with other aesthetic inspirations, such as "dancing girls," likened Christian symbols to other artistic motifs, which downplayed narrow devotional connotations, while introducing the possibility of playful interpretations and juxtapositions. Designer garments adorned with Christian figures did not necessarily mean unsophisticated piety, but, at the same time, they did not eliminate the sacred aura associated with Christian iconography. By drawing their inspiration from and often copying Christian icons from the past, fashion designers invoked the possibility of supernatural presence and power associated with these sacred objects. Icons were not simply representations, but rather powerful artifacts that could "contain or transmit—not just represent—the presence of divinity or supernatural power."[42] Devotees ascribed miraculous and protective powers to them.[43] Invoking and faithfully replicating features of these icons, then, allowed fashion designers to highlight the uniqueness of their garments, even as these garments offered viewer-consumers new ways to access and experience the sacred personage presented. Fashionable religion offered personalized super-natural potential not confined or defined by institutional religion.

These early designs highlight how the modern fashion industry con-tributed images and models to the societal conversation about religion and the visual spirituality beginning to flourish in the 1990s. Holy fig-ures on designer garments, whether Church Fathers, Mary, or Chris-tian saints, supplied "spiritual omnivores" with food for their spiritual journeys.[44] Freed from the constraints of institutional religion, these fashionable religious figures presented people with the opportunity to experience such sacred persons on their own terms.

From Holy Figures to Marian Fashion

The fashion industry's embrace of figural religious representation, though, did not immediately follow these inaugural designs. The Catholic religious dress trend dominated fashion in 1993, as discussed in chapter 4, and in 1994, controversy occurred. In keeping with the "international ethnic" trend and the design process, Karl Lagerfeld, head designer for Chanel, sought historical and artistic inspiration for his collection. He found it in the Arabic calligraphy he had seen in a book on the Taj Mahal. In researching the text, he asked about the mean-ing of the words and reported: "I was told it was a love poem in memory of a maharani."[45] With a specific cultural and historical inspiration, Lagerfeld then faithfully incorporated the calligraphy into the bodices of three dresses. Supermodel Claudia Schiffer wore the most famous of the three on the runway—a sleeveless black cocktail dress that featured a bustier style bodice adorned with the embroidered calligraphy. In dramatic black and white, the dresses are, arguably, quite beautiful and striking. The calligraphy, though, as Lagerfeld soon learned, was not a love poem, but rather words from the Qur'an: "He whom God guides is well-guided, and he who is abandoned by God will find no one to put him on the right road." In this instance, the combination of verisimili-tude, historical inspiration, and designer aesthetic did not create a sense of legitimacy and authenticity. Some subsets of the Muslim community protested and threatened to boycott the brand. The House of Chanel promptly apologized, pleaded with photographers to destroy negatives

Figure 5.4. Claudia Schiffer wearing one of Lagerfeld's "Qur'an" dresses designed for Chanel in 1994; Gérard Julien/AFP/Getty Images.

of the dresses (a plea that went unheeded), and incinerated the three dresses in question.[46]

While Lagerfeld's design does not utilize the Christian imaginary, it sets an important tone and becomes a touchstone event for subsequent journalists writing about fashion and religion. Despite the long and often uncontroversial history of Christianity in fashion and Nina Hyde's claim that religion in fashion was "no big deal," this incident fostered an antagonistic and sacred/secular framework for fashion observers and others thinking about this relationship in the 1990s. The "Satanic Breasts" incident, as one reporter dubbed Lagerfeld's design, alluded to the controversy over Rushdie's *Satanic Verses* in the late 1980s.[47] The

"Qur'an dress" became a battle in the ongoing culture wars that framed fashion as secular and progressive over and against "religion" deemed conservative and intolerant. It became a notable event in constructing an antagonistic plot in the larger the religion and fashion narrative. Later coverage of "controversial" religiously inspired clothing routinely included this incident and the "wrath" the dresses invoked.[48] Iconoclasm was Chanel's response to the offending dresses, and in 1997, Nike did the same thing when a sneaker design accidentally featured flames that resembled the word Allah in Arabic.[49]

These unintended controversies, though, did not deter designers from utilizing representational Christian imagery, as evidenced by the inclusion of Christian religious figures in 1997 and 1998 collections of fashion designers Jean Paul Gaultier and Alexander McQueen; however, the limitation of this imagery to one or two designs in each collection suggests fashion designers figuring out how to navigate these potentially fraught waters. Jean Paul Gaultier's Spring/Summer 1998 collection, inspired by his visit to Cuba and Mexican artist Frida Kahlo, caught the attention of fashion reporters. His models resembled Kahlo with their "bloody tears and lips, heavy dark eyebrows, crowns of thorns and long black locks."[50] Fashion editor Amy Spindler remarked, "it has been many seasons since Mr. Gaultier plumbed the depths of a culture to the extreme as he did this time," and added that "there is no one who does such robber-baron pilfering better."[51] Coverage focused on Gaultier's inspiration and "pilfering," but no fashion columns mentioned the penultimate look, which featured fabric printed with a large image of Jesus and a smaller one of Mary. Their visages appeared upside down as part of the outer layer of a long full skirt. Gaultier's religious image, as with Kawakubo and Yamamoto, embraces verisimilitude as the print appears to replicate a historic and original piece of art.

Similarly, Alexander McQueen's Fall/Winter 1997–98 Ready-to-Wear collection entitled "It's a Jungle Out There" garnered tremendous media attention. Headlines proclaimed: "Law of the Jungle Gives Elegance Quite a Fright," "Briton Fashions the Jungle Look," and "London Bridges Fashion and Rebellion as Alexander McQueen Unleashes a Menagerie."[52] Models sporting animallike makeup, animal prints, and various animal skins created a theatrical spectacle. Some interpreted the collection as McQueen's angry response to harsh criticisms and others

Figure 5.5. Gaultier's skirt featuring the face of Jesus
in his Spring/Summer 1998 collection; Pierre
Vauthey/Getty Images.

saw it as a commentary of "the bleak and sometimes savage beauty of
the modern urban landscape."[53] Themes of savagery, suffering, and religion come through in a jacket featuring a crucifixion scene that goes
unmentioned in the coverage. The jacket's print replicates Northern Renaissance painter Robert Campin's "The Crucified Thief," once part of
larger altarpiece. A close-up of one of the thieves crucified alongside
Jesus appears prominently on the back of the jacket, while the thief's
bleeding legs and the concerned expressions of the Roman soldiers appear in jumbled fashion on the front.

Unlike the more stoic facial expressions that characterize some periods of art history, Campin's painting emphasizes the humanity and

emotion of his painted figures, and in this piece juxtaposes beauty with suffering through the dying thief.[54] The stylized shoulders of the jacket align with McQueen's emphasis on animals and horns, while the close-up of the thief highlights pain and loss.[55] While not an image of the crucified Jesus, McQueen as with other designers incorporated a representational Christian reference that exhibited faithfulness to the religious art reference. On these occasions Gaultier and McQueen's small forays into religious representation went unmentioned, perhaps because it remained a small element of shows emphasizing nonreligious themes.

In contrast, Dolce & Gabbana's incorporation of a religious figure in their Spring/Summer 1998 collection and their embrace of a religious

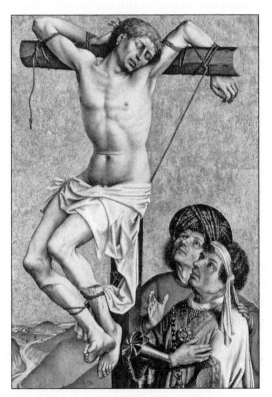

Figure 5.6. Robert Campin's "The Crucified Thief" that was reproduced in jacket form for McQueen's Fall/Winter 1997–98 collection; public domain, courtesy of the Yorck Project.

theme caught the attention of the fashion world. Reporters highlighted its "divine inspiration," described it as a "divine collection," and pondered the implications: "Holy mother of Jesus. Madonna—not to be confused with the pop singer—is the newest fashion trend."[56] Following Gianni Versace's lead, Dolce & Gabbana embraced a Marian inspiration for their "Stromboli" collection, named after the Sicilian volcano and the "earth-shaking" impact of their bold embrace of religious imagery. The collection's title echoes the naming of the bikini bathing suit after the revolutionary events at Bikini atoll, where the United States performed nuclear testing in the 1940s and '50s.

Unlike Gaultier and McQueen, Dolce & Gabbana's entire collection revolved around religious imagery and a religious inspiration, and the positive media reception reflected the design duo's framing of it as an "authentic" expression of their cultural heritage and personal beliefs. They envisioned women, in various states of dress, leaving their homes to join a religious procession honoring "a minor, but locally beloved saint" in Southern Italy.[57] In an interview the design duo explained that "when a procession hits the streets, women flee their houses clad in whatever bathrobes, dresses, cropped pin-striped trousers,"[58] this haphazard fleeing produced a "fractured fairytale of a religious procession."[59] The collection highlighted the designers' Italian and Catholic heritage. One spokeswoman explained that "the designers are Catholics and the design is a celebration of Catholicism and what their background is." The designers themselves reinforced this interpretation. "We realize that the use of religious images in our collection could be controversial because religion is a very personal matter, which is interpreted differently by each of us. Since fashion is the way in which we express ourselves and convey our feelings, the use of religious images was used to praise the Madonna, whom we strongly believe in. We did not want to offend anyone."[60] Their personal statements combined with their invocation of Italian Catholic processions framed the collection as an authentic artistic expression. At least some found this combination of elements persuasive as one fashion columnist remarked, "this current trend is different," and explained that Dolce & Gabbana seemed to be using religious imagery to address a search for spirituality, rather than to shock and provoke.[61]

Dolce & Gabbana's decision to focus on devotional and sentimental images of Mary helped bolster this interpretation. First, they highlighted their personal connection to the inspiration, which enhanced their claims to sincerity and authenticity. Specifically, many of the designs appearing on the collection's garments feature the Madonna del Lavoro, "the Madonna of Work" or "Our Lady of Labor," an image of whom Domenico Dolce's father had in his atelier.[62] Second, their selection, faithful replication, and adornment of a devotional Marian image reinforced the design duo's claims. In iconography, the Madonna del Lavoro appears in a long flowing white dress, a blue belt, a blue veil and cape, and wears a crown. Popular images of her emphasize sentimental themes, such as sweetness and beauty, flowers and emotion. She is beautiful yet approachable, powerful yet benevolent.[63] Dolce & Gabbana invoke these feelings by utilizing the traditional iconography associated with her. This is not Versace's rock star Madonna or a punk parody on the Virgin Mary, but rather a delicately rendered collection that emphasized faithfulness to a specific historical and cultural reference.

The garments in Dolce & Gabbana's collection exhibited a delicacy in their materials and techniques used that emphasizes this point. One observer described how the images of Mary "were hand-painted and jeweled on lean dresses, skirts and tops and covered with the thinnest layer of black veiling."[64] The black veiling over fabrics in muted colors created a softness to the religious imagery that echoed the look of Catholic devotionalism. Some of the garments featured the Madonna del Lavoro, while others showed a maternal and loving Mary holding the Christ child, and some were adorned with cherubic angels crowning Mary the Queen of Heaven. Even for those unfamiliar with Our Lady of Labor and Catholic iconography, more generic cues, such as a crown, a veil, and the holding of the baby Jesus, make Mary's identity clear.

Despite the soft textures and muted tones of the Marian garments, the collection also exhibited some glamour. Dolce & Gabbana adorned the Marian imagery with sparkly sequins and beads. These embellishments draw the viewer's attention to the religious imagery and highlight Mary's special status. Jewelry also enhanced the spiritual glamor quotient as models wore blue miraculous medal earrings, and some garments featured "jeweled Sacred Heart insignias."[65] The effect, though, was not

Figure 5.7. Blouse featuring the Virgin Mary from
Dolce & Gabbana's 1998 Spring/Summer collection;
© Luca Bruno/AP/Shutterstock.

"baroque" or overwhelming, but rather in keeping with the collection's
careful tone. According to one reporter, "It all had a beauty, and even a
peculiar aura of reverence about it," while others described it as "quite
beautiful" and "the best in seasons."[66]

In Dolce & Gabbana's "Stromboli," we see the first high fashion collection focused around a religious inspiration and the representation of
a Christian holy figure, Mary. And, despite the Catholic religious dress
trend of 1993, the enduring popularity of cross jewelry, and numerous
other religiously inspired moments before that, reporters seemed surprised and headlines highlighted controversy: "Heavenly Creatures:
Designers are Plundering Religious Imagery for Divine Inspiration—
and the Vatican is not amused" and "What's Wrong with Having the

Virgin on a T-Shirt?"⁶⁷ Some reinforced this controversial narrative by recounting "the wrath" that emerged in response to Lagerfeld's Qur'an dress,⁶⁸ and quoting Catholic leaders, such as Vatican newspaper columnist's Father Gino Concetti's description of Dolce & Gabbana's collection as in "bad taste."⁶⁹ Fashion news briefs picked up on this framing and emphasized that the design duo had "upset the Vatican," while another remarked that they "have come up with the ultimate in fashion controversy."⁷⁰ Such controversy, though, did not appear to be a problem as reporters asked, "What's fashion without a little controversy?"⁷¹ Indeed, in the years since this collection, numerous fashion designers, fashion houses, and fashion magazines have embraced Marian themes, including Jean Paul Gaultier, Richard Oyarzún, Dolce & Gabbana (again), the House of Holland, *W* magazine, and more. With Dolce & Gabbana's collection, the Virgin Mary, more than other Christian saints, emerged as one of the predominant religious figures appearing in fashion.

The emergence of Mary as a regular part of the fashion designer's repertoire in the late 1990s raises questions about why this holy figure and why at this time. In part, the focus on Mary reflected and reinforced fashion's alliance with the history of high art in the West, which has consistently featured religious themes and figures. Mary, writes Jaroslav Pelikan, "has been portrayed in art and music more than any other woman in history."⁷² Further, it sidestepped the potentially fraught issue of putting God on a dress. Mary's humanity makes her a potentially less controversial choice than Jesus or Arabic calligraphy from the Qur'an. She is relatable, while, at the same time, her religious elevation as the Mother of God and Queen of Heaven amplify her aspirational and supernatural status.

In addition, as we have seen throughout, fashion articles, advertisements, and designers often used the visual code of Christianity to invoke the transcendent, the supernatural. For many people, Mary often connotes enchantment and wonder.⁷³ As a symbol and mediating figure, Mary represents another realm—that of the sacred—but at the same time, her humanity provides people with access to that rarified realm. As a hybrid figure, she is both us and Other—a way to bridge the distance between the seemingly disparate sacred and profane. Similar to angels, she "mediate[s] between sharply opposed realms: religion and history, heaven and earth, spirit and matter," and provides "visionary possibilities."[74] Her presence heightened the drama of photo shoots and runway shows, even as it infused products with divine potential and provided viewers and audience members with a "sacred moment."[75] Unlike holy figures deemed distant or Other, Mary's appearance in fashion emphasized her enchanting presence.[76] Fashion designers incorporation of Mary, in some ways, seemed "real" and "marvelous" because these uses aligned with existing religious and cultural discourses about who Mary is, how she appears, and what she does.[77]

These discourses permeated the 1990s as religious devotion to Mary increased and was fostered by the continuing advent of various apparition sites that drew thousands.[78] Mary was present and active in the world. Europeans and Americans embarked on pilgrimages to old and new sites of apparitions.[79] These sites emphasized Mary's presence and message to the world and were often verified in people's minds by miracles stories, which further enhanced Mary's supernatural status. Further, the presence of countless Marian sites on the web allowed for the sharing and growth of devotion to the Blessed Virgin. It fueled the replication of Marian imagery alongside an increasing variety of Marys. Anthropologist Simon Coleman explains: "On the one hand, the delocalization of Marian imagery has been promoted precisely by its 'virtualization' and endless replication on the internet; on the other, the fragmentary nature of the internet has allowed any number of idiosyncratic and 'localized' expressions of imagery to gain a forum."[80] Thus, in the late twentieth century, Mary simultaneously became more universal and more particular. And, as Simon Coleman points out, "forms of Marianism have expressed opposition to secularizing tendencies . . . [but] they have also proved highly adaptable to modern forms of commercialization, commodification and mobility."[81] Apparitions, pilgrimages, and websites not only emphasized the special status and spiritual powers of Mary but also fostered the replication and commodification of her image.

Such trends also broadened Mary's appeal and accessibility. Historically, as this information suggests, Marian devotion has been considered the province of Catholics, but increasingly in the late twentieth and early twenty-first century, liberal and conservative Protestants started to remember and reclaim Mary and her place in both biblical and Christian history as evidenced by feature articles on her in both *Christian Century* and *Christianity Today*.[82] Further, Andrew Greeley's research on Marian imagery, published in 1990, found that "the image of the Mother of Jesus was as strong for the Protestants in our sample as it was for Jesus."[83] Young Catholics and Protestants alike described her as "warm," "gentle," and "comforting."[84]

Moreover, in the 1990s, Mary also represented, for some, a dimension of the divine feminine and a resource for women. A 1995 article entitled "Goddess Worship," published in *Harper's Bazaar*, emphasized that this movement "help[s] women find spiritual strength in themselves."[85] It problematized dominant male conceptions of the divine and reclaimed goddess traditions in various cultures, including that of Mary. The movement stressed how the goddess, including Mary, "melds the human and the divine." Rather than separation and hierarchies, the goddess embodies "light and shadow, immanence and transcendence, purity and sensuality"—to which one reporter remarked, "no wonder people gravitate to the Goddess."[86]

In addition to Mary's prominence in the 1990s, her emergence on high fashion garments builds on earlier allusions to her in fashion history. As seen in chapter 1, fashion magazine articles included the Virgin Mary and localized versions of her appeared in articles about religious art and Christmas.[87] Visual references to her also occurred in photo shoots where models' prayerful poses mimic religious art depicting Mary's intercessory acts.[88] In two examples from the 1960s, the models wear designer gowns and stand with their arms in prayerlike positions. In one photo shoot, the lighting and drape of the gown emphasize the model's supplication and connote a sense of both mystery and wonder. Her gestures not only highlight features of the gown but also suggest the promise this design holds for transforming the world of fashion. In another photo, your eye is drawn to the model because of her brightly colored dress, large cross pendant, and her body position. Almost frozen in place, she exhibits a sense of enchantment, of disruption—the idea that this design will change things. In these examples, fashion presents itself, like Mary, as a mediator that can help you transform yourself from ordinary to extraordinary.[89]

In addition, at least one fashion designer invoked Mary, not by putting her on garments, but through models portraying her. For example, the debut of French designer Thierry Mugler's Fall/Winter 1984–85 Ready-to-Wear collection embraced a Marian theme. In the 1980s,

Figure 5.8. Charlene Dash wearing a Mollie Parnis dress in a prayerful, Marian-like pose, *Vogue* 154 (July 1969): 71; Gianni Penati/*Vogue* © Condé Nast.

Mugler, often classified alongside fashion leaders Gianni Versace and Jean-Paul Gaultier, was known for his innovative aesthetic and fashion showmanship. Mugler's inspirations "range from the insectoid to the medieval, from the fantastic to the science fictional."[90] In 1983, fashion journalist Bernadine Morris called him one of "today's revolutionaries," and his fashion show in March of 1984 cemented that status.[91] For his show that year Mugler traded the fashion runway for the rock arena, the Zenith (in Paris), and launched his collection in front of the public—six thousand people (four thousand of whom purchased tickets for approximately $22 to $26 a piece).[92] According to one source, "this was the first time that the public was allowed to attend a couture show and marks a trend toward the fashion show as mass entertainment."[93] At times, reporters noted, the spectacle overshadowed the designs.

The show opened with models wearing long gowns accessorized with large golden wings and walking to the "Hallelujah" chorus. They were followed by others wearing large halos and sporting stylized winglike sleeves and posing with their arms outstretched. Their gestures seemed to herald a pending religious revelation, appropriate, perhaps, for a Fall/ Winter collection.[94] Fashion journalists commented on the many angels, and Genevieve Buck described it as "more than two hours of spoof, satire and a little fashion, all laced with a theme that combined religion and Olympic sports."[95] Little more was said in the newspaper accounts about religion or the appearance of Mary.

Yet, partway through the show, the music shifts to *"Il est né le divin enfant,"* a traditional French Christmas carol that celebrates the long-awaited and foretold coming of the Christ child.[96] Then a model wearing a platinum blonde wig and a long-sleeved, high-necked, floor-length gown in a shiny light fabric appears. A rope light–like halo designates her special and holy status, as does the chubby baby she holds in her arms. And in the finale of Mugler's show, a second Marian figure appears. Model Pat Cleveland, three months pregnant, descends from the ceiling wearing a large halo, a veil, and a flowy gown featuring a sequined starburst design.[97] The styling and gestures of this figure suggest a second appearance of a glorified Mary. As she walks down the runway, she bestows grace or blessings upon the audience and serves as a benediction for the show.

Thus, Dolce & Gabbana's decision to focus on Mary not only highlighted their own Catholic and Italian heritage but also drew upon and expanded these existing trends in the history of art, Christianity, and fashion. The Virgin Mary had been a part of the discourse surrounding fashion in some religiously oriented articles featuring nativity art and Catholic processions, while fashion photographers and designer Thierry Mugler invoked her presence through models gesturing or costumed as her. Mary, seen occasionally in the fashion designs of the early 1990s with Versace and Gaultier, became a regular part of the fashion repertoire by the end of the decade with Dolce & Gabbana.

Through the incorporation of holy figures the fashion industry helped accustom people to seeing the Christian heritage reprocessed—bits and pieces of religious symbols and saints divorced from institutional religious contexts and reimagined in other, sometimes unexpected, contexts. These images circulated in fashion magazines, newspapers, and on the emerging World Wide Web. This reinforced already existing tenets in fashionable religion about the centrality of the individual and cultivating one's identity and spirituality through display and consumption. The addition of Christian holy figures, though, strengthened fashionable religion's emphasis on the supernatural and sacred moments made possible through material objects. As seen in chapters 3 and 4, cross jewelry and Catholic religious dress evoked connotations of supernatural protection and sacred auras. Holy figures, particularly references to Marian icons, emphasized the possibility of supernatural presence. David Freedberg explains in relation to Marian imagery that "wanting her to be there, to exist, we willingly concentrate on the image, and what is represented on it becomes present again. She is, quite literally, re-presented."[98] The inclusion of holy figures expanded fashion's incorporation of Christianity and fashionable religion's material offerings. It provided those interested with the possibility of supernatural presence that could be theirs through the world of fashion and consumption. This sophisticated spirituality was not beholden to church or acts of consecration; rather, it offered individuals powerful, personalized religious possibilities.

From Iconoclasts to Iconophiles in the 1990s

The appearance of holy figures, particularly Mary, in fashion constitutes an important moment in the trajectory of Christianity and fashion. At the same time, it also contributes to our understanding of religion in the '90s. In 1996, Wade Clark Roof suggested, "Perhaps it is best to think of religious change in the United States neither as religious revival nor as secular decline but as somewhat like a religious kaleidoscope—as always changing in its forms."[99] The fashion industry's embrace of Christian holy figures encourages us to think about this kaleidoscope and religion's changing forms in the 1990s.

Roof and other scholars noted how "generational cultures" exhibited different patterns of religious belief and affiliation, and that the declines in institutional religion that began in the 1960s had continued. The "seeking" trend described by Wuthnow flourished in the 1990s. According to Roof in 1995, this burgeoning form of faith emphasized the affective and sensual. It "privilege[d] experience over belief, exploration over certitude, affirm[ed] the body as a feeling, sensing self," while also "emphasizing the insights and emotions garnered in experiential encounters."[100] In April of 1994, a national poll captured these divergent trends. Almost two-thirds of Americans thought that religion's influence on American life was waning, yet almost the same number reported that religion was increasingly important in their own personal lives.[101] Roof concluded that the "religious energies" of the 1990s revolved around "two major foci of concerns—personal meaning and social belonging."[102] The fashion industry's mediation of religion both reflected and shaped these concerns.

Events in the 1990s made creating personal religious meaning particularly significant, if not urgent. As the battles and skirmishes of the culture wars continued, Americans grappled with the meaning of religion and violence as the United States engaged in the Gulf War, and religious violence unfolded at numerous sites around the country. Further, fears about "Y2K" and the religious potential of the pending millennium heightened the stakes. Participants in the fashion industry tuned into these cultural currents. For example, in March of 1998, a spokeswoman for Nieman Marcus observed: "With the millennium approaching, people are seeking solace in religion, spirituality, yoga and meditation. And since fashion designers are at the forefront of the trend, there's an abundance of spiritual designs."[103] Spiritual designs, though, as we have seen, did not begin in 1998; they appeared in both the ecclesiastical trend examined in chapter 4 and in the incorporation of Christian holy figures—throughout the decade.

While millennial fears may have heightened the spiritual turn of the '90s, popular culture also helped foster this trend. As fears swirled and battles raged, popular culture offered a wealth of resources for spiritual seekers hoping to allay fears, cultivate assurance, and experience sacred moments. Books, videos, and television shows focused on "near-death experiences, angels, mythology, visualization, dream states, ancient wisdom, self-help, or journey and recovery theology."[104] Supernatural beings, particularly angels, garnered much popular attention. For example, *Touched by an Angel*, which debuted in 1994, became a top-ten show in 1996 and maintained this popularity through the year 2000. Angels also made their presence felt in the print culture of the decade. In his article

"Awash with Angels," Roger Gilbert writes, "Heavenly beings swarmed the decade's books and magazines like locusts." Movies, such as *City of Angels* and *Angels in the Outfield*, also promoted this theme.[105] Popular culture provided people in the 1990s with a wealth of resources for the increasingly dominant "do-it-yourself-kind-of-religion."[106]

These various popular culture forms privileged the visual, which altered dominant ways of seeing religion.[107] According to scholar Catherine Albanese, the new "shamanic" spirituality of the 1990s privileged "sight and vision." She explains that this new form "substitutes image for word, using the resources of the pictorial imagination to journey to places and times that modify everyday reality."[108] The reliance on "sight and vision" alters how we think and make sense of reality. It privileges the subjective over the objective, and disrupts "the coherent, orderly arrangement of ideas." Wade Clark Roof describes it this way: "Fleeting images have the capacity of creating a sense of reality as itself in flux and without permanence, and of moving us freely from one psychological world to another—making us something like pilgrims wandering through a galaxy of shifting ontologies."[109] The result is an ever-accessible and changing visual buffet for the spiritual seeking omnivore—a smorgasbord supplied, in part, by fashion designers and the fashion industry.

Amid this visual turn, it is not surprising that "imageries of God," angels, and other Christian holy figures circulated more widely and changed.[110] Fashion constitutes one arena where images of the divine can be and are altered and, as a result, shapes the societal conversation about religion through its visual and material forms. As Gilbert notes in his analysis of angels, artists in the '90s found inspiration in representational religious imagery once deemed unfashionable and "illicit."[111] The fashion industry adaptation of "antifashion," Catholic religious dress, exemplifies this idea.

So, too, does the fashion industry's incorporation of Christian holy figures, which from the 1970s onward often resided in the unfashionable hands of evangelical Protestants. Despite their iconoclastic rhetoric, Protestants have a long and rich history filled with religious visual and material culture, as scholars Colleen McDannell and David Morgan have documented.[112] In the mid to late 1970s, evangelical Christians added a large chapter to this history. Their subculture flourished as they sought to make their religious priorities known and share their faith through material objects, including fashion. Colleen McDannell in *Material Christianity* observes, "These Christians fully exploited popular culture to express their new-found religious spirit."[113] One of the dominant fashion results was and continues to be a proliferation of Christian T-shirts featuring religious imagery, biblical verses, inspirational slogans, and playful puns. Initially produced by Christian companies, these T-shirts could be purchased by Christian consumers in the 1980s and 1990s at an increasing number of Christian bookstores.[114] Notably, these T-shirts did not shy away from incorporating illustrations of religious figures.

The parochial and communicative purpose of these efforts, though, distinguished evangelical efforts from those of the fashion industry. Unlike the interpretive possibilities emphasized and valued by fashion designers and consumers, evangelical T-shirts endorsed a strict and specific theology that reinforced the alignment of one's identity and their attire. This perspective emphasized longstanding notions that clothing could and should act as a clear communicator of identity. Within evangelicalism, these T-shirts became a way to publicly indicate Christian identity and values, while simultaneously prompting others to ponder religious questions through the Christian imagery and slogans on it.[115]

In thinking about the larger evolution of religion in fashion, it is important to note that, before fashion designers put Mary on a halter-top and dress, conservative Protestants put Jesus on a T-shirt. This highlights how the fashion system was not alone in its emphasis on the visual elements of religion or in uncoupling religious symbols from their institutional moorings. By placing religious imagery on T-shirts, evangelicals alongside other cultural forces and forms helped pave the way for others to do likewise. As one scholar notes, "the privatization of religion cannot be successfully accomplished unless religious ideologies are packaged and marketed through public channels in order to attract seekers."[116] Evangelical Christians made their individually focused religion public through their various commercial products, which in turn encouraged others to copy and parody them.[117]

Evangelical efforts to be stylish through T-shirts referencing popular culture brands and slogans put them in the decidedly unfashionable camp. As scholars have noted, people construct and evaluate edginess and sophistication through traits, such as emotional control, rebellion against authority, and irony.[118] Fashion designers' increasing incorporation of Christian holy figures offered such a stylish and sophisticated alternative. By using historical and artistic references, focusing on the "Catholic" Mary rather than the "Protestant" Jesus, and utilizing prized sewing techniques, such as mosaic and embroidery, the designs of Dolce & Gabbana and subsequent designers distanced themselves from the casual, devotional, and graphic fashion efforts of conservative Protestantism. In contrast to the communicative clarity and authority associated with evangelical T-shirts, the fashionable religion provided by couture designs featuring Christian holy figures emphasized the separation of religious symbols and ideas from a particular theology and played with the relationship between identity and clothing, while at the same time preserving the possibility of sacred moments and supernatural potential.

Conclusion

In thinking through the significance of the Virgin Mary's appearance on designer clothing, Catholic journalist Annabel Miller provided a more in-depth consideration. Miller noted Dolce & Gabbana's intention, but she highlighted and pondered Catholic imagery's appeal to potential fashion consumers. Miller writes from a British perspective, but her explanation implicitly highlights changes in the 1990s American religious landscape documented by sociologists Robert Wuthnow and Wade Clark Roof. She explained that because young people did not grow up in a "traditional Christian culture," they do not associate religious imagery with repressive institutional religious dictates. She also added that such imagery, associated with "love, heart, and deep emotion," addressed an unconscious desire for spirituality. She writes, "They might admit to a vague fascination with 'spirituality' without knowing what they mean by the word. They might also admit to feeling a sense of protection from these images, and to be using them as a kind of talisman. They may not understand that these images are about sacrifice and discipline, as well as about love." She concluded, "People are fascinated by the transcendent and will not let go of that longing."[119]

Miller's insights highlight how the strands of fashionable religion intersect with the "seeking" and "do-it-yourself" spirituality described by scholars of religion. Removed from the confines of the institutional, Mary remains familiar and recognizable. At the same time, though, her location on high fashion garments and her embellishment makes her more modern and accessible. She is supernatural and special but also personalized and available. Such a vision of Mary highlights the individual and her sensual reaction and personal experience of Mary, as well as the garments in question. The fashionable religion constructed and reinforced by this mediation offers wearers of these garments access to a benevolent supernatural that promises protection, good luck, feelings of love, and a stylish outfit. Such supernatural gifts do not depend on right belief or religious affiliation but rather on personal experience, taste, and consumption.

In the 1990s, this fashionable religion offered spiritual seekers and other consumers a way to engage religion and religious symbols in a sophisticated way. By representing Mary and offering consumers the opportunity to wear her, Dolce & Gabbana offered a fashionable take on devotional clothing, the upscale "catholic" (in the universal sense of the word) version of the evangelical T-shirt. What helps make the clothing stylish, though, is the high fashion context. Placing Mary in this "secular" context raises questions of authenticity that evangelical apparel seeks to avoid. Evangelicals seek to align the creator's intentions, the product's message, and the wearer's body (and attitude) so that Christian T-shirts function as clear indications of one's identity as a certain type of Christian. While Dolce & Gabbana stated their ostensibly devout intentions in ways that resembled those articulated by evangelical T-shirt creators, the high fashion context amplifies Mary's possible meanings and raises questions about the wearer's identity.[120] In this collection, Mary's appearance could be read as a symbol of faith, devotion, and the supernatural; a tongue-in-cheek act of fashion provocation; and/or an ironic statement about the entanglement of religion and fashion. Further, Dolce & Gabbana's collection problematizes the assumption that clothing functions as a transparent communicator of one's individual identity. Rightly or wrongly, people often assume that someone wearing a "Jesus Saves" T-shirt is Christian, and a conservative one at that, but seeing a celebrity, socialite, or fashion blogger wearing a Marian piece from the "Stromboli" collection offers no such illusion of clarity. The garment could be worn out of devotion, nostalgia, or a desire for protection, but it could also be worn because it is designer, pretty, or provocative, or some complicated combination of all these various reasons. Part of this collection's fashionability, then, revolves around the ways it challenges dominant understandings of how clothing works and disrupts traditional conceptualizations of religion and religious identity.

In 2015, the media focused on the controversy associated with Kimberly Castillo's dress featuring the *Virgen de la Altagraci*. Emphasizing controversy, though, obscures the broader historical relationship between Christianity and fashion, notably its historical shift toward more representational Christian imagery. It prevents us from seeing how the modern fashion industry's incorporation of Christian holy figures has a history. This history illuminates how the fashion system not only supplied garments to be purchased but also provided visual and material resources for the "do-it-yourself-religion" of the 1990s. These visual and material resources emphasized the spiritual presence and supernatural power of the divine through the individual's sensory experience—seeing a particular designer's collection, purchasing a garment, or wearing the clothes. And, as the twentieth century gave way to the twenty-first, this trend continued when fashion designers put God on a dress.

Figure 1. Kimberly Castillo's national costume featuring the *Virgen de la Altagraci* in the 2015 Miss Universe Pageant; Storms Media Group/Alamy Stock Photo.

Figure 2. The three kings on the border of Empress Theodora's garment from a mosaic at the Church of San Vitale; photograph courtesy of L. Stephanie Cobb.

Figure 3. Cross-embellished motorcycle jacket and beaded Marian halter by Gianni Versace, Fall/Winter 1991–92; © Tony Kyriacou/Shutterstock.

Figure 4. Claudia Schiffer wearing one of Lagerfeld's "Qur'an" dresses designed for Chanel in 1994; Gérard Julien/AFP/Getty Images.

Figure 5. Gaultier's skirt featuring the face of Jesus in his Spring/Summer 1998 collection; Pierre Vauthey/Getty Images.

Figure 6. Robert Campin's "The Crucified Thief" that was reproduced in jacket form for McQueen's Fall/Winter 1997–98 collection; public domain, courtesy of the Yorck Project.

Figure 7. Blouse featuring the Virgin Mary from Dolce & Gabbana's 1998 Spring/Summer collection; © Luca Bruno/AP/Shutterstock.

Figure 8. Charlene Dash wearing a Mollie Parnis dress in a prayerful, Marian-like pose, *Vogue* 154 (July 1969): 71; Gianni Penati/*Vogue* © Condé Nast.

Figure 9. Jesus dress from Karla Špetić's Fall 2013 "Faith" collection; Mark Metcalfe/Getty Images.

Figure 10. "Christian lord and savior" dress from Dolce & Gabbana's "Tailored Mosaic" collection that accompanied Anibundel's blog; Venturelli/WireImage/Getty Images.

Figure 11. "Queen Mosaic Print" dress from Dolce & Gabbana's 2013 "Tailored Mosaic" collection that reproduces a mosaic of the biblical Rebekah; Venturelli/WireImage/Getty Images.

Conclusion

Putting God on a Dress

In 2013, so many designers incorporated Christian imagery that British *Vogue* proclaimed that a "Holy Spirit" infused the season's fashions.[1] Croatian-born Australian designer Karla Špetić contributed to this atmosphere with her "Faith" collection.[2] A number of the blouses, skirts, and dresses in the line utilized stained-glass prints in "ice cream carnival colours" that boldly featured Jesus. One observer described it this way: "A richly coloured stained glass Jesus—holding a lamb no less—found his way onto blouses, full skirts and dresses. Like the naive curves of Špetić's floral lace, this illustration was not quite crude, but a little cartoony. The humour in Jesus' expression helped to soften the intensity of the print's palette."[3] Another stated, "the digital prints feature flattering portraits of Biblical superstar Jesus himself—skin ex-foliated, beard groomed and eyebrows sculpted—pouting, praying, and getting a cuddle from a cute little lamb."[4] Špetić's collection is one of the first to feature the Son of God to this extent.

That same year Dolce & Gabbana once again embraced their Italian heritage and captured headlines with their beautifully crafted collection entitled "Tailored Mosaic." Inspired by the Byzantine mosaics at the Cathedral of Monreale in Sicily, the duo's designs included numerous Christian holy figures. Fashion journalist Lou Stoppard wrote, "From the gilded crowns that sat atop the models' heads to the bejewelled crosses that decorated gowns, this was all about the mite and majesty of Italian faith."[5] Blogger Anibundel described the drama of the show, including its "hits and misses," and then wondered: "It seems odd to be going to a party wearing a golden dress with the Christian lord and savior front and center on your skirt, like it was the new 21st century vision of the poodle skirt."[6] Fashion designers put the Christian God, or at least the Christian Savior, on a dress.

Figure C.1. Jesus dress from Karla Špetić's Fall 2013 "Faith" collection; Mark Metcalfe/Getty Images.

Jesus had appeared occasionally in prior fashion lines. We saw earlier that Jean Paul Gaultier's 1998 collection included a skirt printed with Jesus wearing a crown of thorns alongside a devout Mary, and in 2007 his Marian-inspired collection, "Les Virgenes," featured a stained-glass printed gown adorned with Mary carrying the infant Jesus. Prior to that, some advertisements and fashion brands, such as Jesus Jeans in the 1970s, invoked the name of Jesus alongside biblical puns, such as "Thou shalt not have any other jeans before me" and "He who loves me follows me."[7] They did not include imagery of Jesus, though, unlike some of the jeans available today. In this trajectory, Špetić's collection stands out for its extensive inclusion of Jesus imagery.

As the twentieth century gave way to the twenty-first, the fashion industry expanded its incorporation of the Christian imaginary yet again. Having already utilized prominent Christian symbols, Catholic religious attire, and Christian holy figures, designers pushed their inspirations and innovations further to include the divine. This move constituted the next step in fashion's long and intertwined relationship with religion. This book has analyzed the fashion industry's longstanding and increasing mediation of Christianity over time. In articles, Christianity appeared alongside fashion news, while advertisements combined

Figure C.2. "Christian lord and savior" dress from Dolce & Gabbana's 2013 "Tailored Mosaic" collection that accompanied Anibundel's blog; Venturelli/ WireImage/Getty Images.

Christian language and imagery with fashion products. The popularity of cross jewelry in the 1960s and again in the 1980s highlighted fashion's incorporation of a Christian symbol into accessories, while Catholic religious dress inspired fashion designs with increasing frequency. The addition of couture creations adorned with Christian holy figures, especially Mary, in the 1990s paved the way for designers to place the divine on a dress. At this point, few, if any, dimensions of Christianity seem off limits to the artistic inclinations of fashion designers.

As with these earlier mediations, putting God on a dress connotes the possibility and power of sacred presence. For Catholics and Protestants, iconic as well as popular imagery of Jesus can serve multiple functions, such as mediating divine presence, providing protection, and affirming theology.[8] Designers' incorporation of Jesus imagery into fashion invokes these meanings and, in some ways, extends them. "The reproductions," as one scholar argues, "are the aura" that sacralize the religious art or object in question.[9] Thus, placing Jesus within the fashion context highlights and enhances the spiritual power and meaning attributed to images of the divine. Seeing Jesus in this way helps construct and reinforce fashionable religion's emphasis on a benevolent and accessible supernatural that meets people's needs, provides sacred moments, and bestows good things.

Fashionable Religion's Ways of Seeing

Fashion designers' putting God on a dress again emphasizes the fashion industry's particular ways of seeing Christianity.[10] Throughout, we have seen how articles, advertisements, designs, and adornments foreground the transformative power of Christianity's symbols, images, and figures. This perspective assumes a particular vision of the Christian past. Specifically, it assumes that the supernatural permeated Christian history and now resides in its material relics, the remaining bits and pieces of this heritage. The challenge, then, becomes how to access these sacred objects. By materializing and visualizing elements of the Christian heritage—religious art, cross jewelry, "mini-medievals," and Jesus on a dress—fashion designers, and the fashion industry more broadly, offer potential ways to gain such access. This reinforces, as we have seen throughout this book, the notion that "reality and authenticity are thought to be elsewhere: in other historical periods and other cultures, in purer, simpler lifestyles."[11] Consequently, fashionable religion communicates that the power, wonder, and benevolence of the Christian supernatural reside in its visual and material heritage, which can be experienced in the present. Fashionable religion highlights the richness of this visual and material heritage as a way for people to experience "sacred moments" and "spiritual vistas" that promise to transform their lives, at least temporarily.

Designers, as we have seen, highlight the "authenticity" of their collections by emphasizing their personal connections to particular historical or geographic inspirations. Naming the Byzantine era, the priest's cassock, or Our Lady of Labor as the source of their creative vision and explaining their connection to it emphasizes the "purity" of their inspiration. It focuses attention on the personal and artistic intentions of designers and their ability to access the Christian past and make it present. This framing directs attention to the past and underscores the importance of the individual, while also accentuating the particularities of a given collection.

We can see this way of constructing authenticity in how Karla Špetić and Dolce & Gabbana describe their 2013 collections. When interviewed about her "Faith" line, Karla Špetić explained, "Growing up in Croatia, I was raised Roman Catholic, so religion played an important role in my upbringing. What fascinates me about religious iconography is the sense of power it represents. It's a sense of belief and hope. It's interesting how our minds can capture these emotions through visual symbolism." In this quote, Špetić cited her personal connection to Christianity and stressed the power of its material legacy. She went on to state that she has "faith in the truth" and would like those who are "unaffected" and with "their own true style" to wear her clothes.[12] In this brief interview, Špetić also highlights other elements of fashionable religion, namely the visual power of Christianity to convey ideas and produce emotions. Further, by citing her Catholic background and the importance of "truth," Špetić frames her collection in terms of authenticity—being true to herself and hoping consumers would do likewise.

Dolce & Gabbana's framing of "Tailored Mosaic" also combined the inspirational and the personal to underscore the authenticity of their creations. The press release for the collection named their particular inspiration, the Cathedral of Monreale. It then chronicled the building's history and described the mosaics inside. Similar to Versace in the 1990s, Dolce & Gabbana utilized a mosaic-making process and motif in their construction, while the designs featured various Christian holy figures that resembled those adorning the walls of the Cathedral.[13] The designers further validated the particularity of this inspiration by emphasizing their connections to Sicily. Not only had previous collections used Sicily as an inspiration, but Domenico Dolce was born and raised in Sicily. As with Špetić, the designers stated in an interview: "[R]eligious iconography 'reminds us of our beloved Sicily, and of the roots and traditions that have become such an important part of our DNA.'"[14] Dolce & Gabbana wove together Sicily and Catholicism with their personal identities. Their connection to Sicily and its religious heritage, then, prompted people to understand the collection as an authentic expression of who they are and where they come from.[15] Very little controversy accompanied either of these collections, which suggests that critics and consumers found this framing persuasive and deemed their collections to be authentic reflections of their artistic and personal experiences.

Further, designers' embrace of verisimilitude in their sewing techniques, design choices, and content selection heightened the authenticity and "aura" associated with these Christian objects, symbols, and figures. Kansai Yamamoto's Byzantine-inspired jackets replicated existing icons, Kawakubo and McQueen's digitized prints reproduced stained-glass windows and Campin's crucifixion painting respectively, and Dolce & Gabbana's mosaic-inspired garments looked like the mosaics in the Cathedral. After the latter's collection debuted, numerous bloggers posted photographs showing a particular mosaic alongside its appearance in fashion form to emphasize the likeness. Even those designers not digitizing a print or replicating a particular image emphasized elements of their Christian referents. For example, while Špetić personalized her color palette and did not name a specific historical inspiration, her designs utilized the lines, shapes, and iconography of stained-glass windows. Similarly, designers inspired by Catholic religious dress retained enough features of the monk's robe or nun's habit to make the referent known. This framing reinforced designers' claims to artistry and authenticity, while displaying their ability to tap into the power of the Christian past and make it present again.[16]

Fashion designers' presentation of this heritage, though, privileges some Christian objects and figures more than others and represents them in particular ways. In their analysis of how Scottish heritage was constructed, David McCrone, Angela Morris, and Richard Kiely, authors of *Scotland—the Brand*, explain how Sir Walter Scott's literature envisioned a "highly romantic picture of the Scottish past," which "encouraged nineteenth-century Scottish historians to recover and study historical documents and records, and recreate for themselves similar pictures of the past."[17] Persuaded by Scott's prose, historians located and utilized sources that helped them create this idealized Scottish past.[18]

In a similar way, the fashion industry's selection of Christian symbols, designs, and figures contribute to a particular vision of the tradition. More specifically, fashionable religion constructs a romanticized and idealized vision of Christianity and its past. Throughout this book— from churches filled with art to products promising miracles to the power associated with the cross, Catholic religious dress, and images of Mary, the saints, and Jesus—we have seen how the fashion industry has produced a vision of Christianity filled with beautiful things, abundant gifts, and sacred moments. For example, designers' specific focus on Mary, an intermediary figure known for her intercessory powers, privileges this idea of Christian supernatural benevolence and assurance, rather than judgment or fear. The bits and pieces selected chronicle a Christian past devoid of turmoil and strife. Readers experience only the wonder of "miraculous" churches and the enchantment of Lourdes without seeing the inevitable decay of old architecture or battling crowds of tourists at an apparition site. Fashionable religion utilizes this idealized past to construct a beautiful and present Christianity characterized by a diffuse and generous supernatural that promises partakers only good things. Consuming visual and material objects provides access to the supernatural power of this past and its promises of transformation.

Designers' presentations of these elements reinforce these idyllic visions. For example, Karla Špetić uses a "bubble gum colour palette" rather than the bold, saturated hues traditionally associated with stained glass. These brighter colors—associated with candy, ice cream, and childhood—connote a sense of fun, joy, and lightness. Further, she combines this palette with images of Jesus the Good Shepherd, rather than the crucified Jesus or Pantocrator (Judge) Jesus. This friendly Jesus emphasizes his accessibility—the love and care of this Shepherd, not his sacrifice or judgment.[19] Similarly, Dolce & Gabbana's use of sentimental Marian imagery, soft pastels, and delicate overlays in the Stromboli collection simultaneously emphasizes her human accessibility and her spiritual elevation. Throughout, we have seen how these design features help construct a beautiful and benevolent, inspiring and enchanting fashionable religion.

This fashionable religion, though, tells us less about the Christianity of the past and more about the spiritual landscape of the present. In their analysis of Scottish heritage construction, McCrone, Morris, and Kiely explain that a "boom" of interest in the past occurs "because of what we want to use [it] for in the context of our own lives, and [its] potential for mapping out the future."[20] Throughout its various Christian mediations, whether fashion magazine articles, advertisements, accessories, or adornments, the fashion industry has emphasized the accessibility of this Christian past and its potential power in the present. Fashion designers, in some ways, model how to do this in their appeals to history, inspiration, and authenticity. In this way, we can see that the fashion industry participates in the spiritual marketplace and the societal conversations about religion by supplying spiritual omnivores with models to emulate, as well as a visual and material buffet to satiate their hunger.

In the late twentieth and early twenty-first centuries, museum leaders and advocates for historical sites have increasingly emphasized the idea of accessing the past through re-enactments, interactive exhibits, and virtual reality.[21] In a similar way, the fashion industry highlights how to participate in and access the aura of these Christian objects. Fashion's reprocessing of these artifacts frees these powerful relics of the Christian heritage from the theological and interpretive constraints of institutional Christianity. It then makes them available to people in beautiful garments and accessories that they can wear on their bodies. In this way, the fashion industry encourages people to view commodified Christian symbols, designs, and figures as potentially transformative. They model how to find inspiration and personalize it. The consumption and curation of these commodified sacred objects provides a way for people to participate in fashionable religion—to cultivate their own "authentic" spiritual moments through sacred objects.

Accessing this Christian past through the visual and material realm of fashion emphasizes one's personal sensory experience of it—seeing, touching, hearing, and smelling these bits and pieces of the Christian heritage. The focus on sensory participation, in turn, highlights one's "immediate" and "unmediated" response to the sacred object. This is not to say that these Christian objects are unmediated, but rather that fashionable religion focuses attention on sacred objects and one's sensory response to them. Individuals often interpret this response as "unmediated" and "personal." This way of seeing shapes fashionable religion in that it emphasizes one's "immediate" sensory pleasure or displeasure upon engaging with these relics, which enhances the authenticity accorded the experience.[22] Thus, fashionable religion grounds the concept of authentic "sacred moments" in the individual's sensory response.

At the same time, though, to be seen as sophisticated and fashionable the sensory experience of these "sacred moments" demands a sense of distance. Fashionable religion creates this distance through reprocessing.[23] It decontextualizes sacred objects from their theological and institutional homes and recontextualizes them within the broader visual and material world, including fashion. This reprocessing of the relic offers people a sense of direct, immediate access to the sacred, while simultaneously shifting their perspective from that of participants to spectators, from naive religious devotees to cosmopolitan spiritual connoisseurs.[24]

Fashionable religion celebrates individual, sensory responses to and experiences of reprocessed Christian objects. In this framework, individuals practice Christianity not through church attendance or theological commitments but by consuming sophisticated sacred moments and spiritual vistas. The articulation of faith occurs through their cultivation of these moments or the display of a tasteful sacred object. Fashionable religion, then, defines Christianity in the aesthetic terms of "lifestyle, taste, and patterns of consumption and appreciat[ion] of the visual, the sensual, and the unique."[25] This valorization of the individual and her experiences necessarily obscures the authority of institutional Christianity, the power of global capitalism, and the importance of cultural ownership.[26]

Fashionable religion romanticizes the Christian past, highlights the accessibility and power of its visual and material heritage, and emphasizes the centrality of sensory experience. It focuses on individuals and their quest for spiritual meaning and fulfillment through acts of consumption. In her theory of religion, sociologist Danièle Hervieu-Léger explains:

> From the moment that contrasting modern societies no longer asked established religion to provide a framework for social organization, religion has become fragmented across an array of specialized spheres and institutions. Individuals, in groups or on their own, hence are free to construct a universe of meaning on the basis of a chosen dimension of their experience—family, sexuality, aesthetics and so on. The constitution and expansion of the modern sacred is a consequence of the direct access individuals have to the stock of cultural symbols available.[27]

Through this examination, we can see, as Hervieu-Léger notes, the ability of individuals to access Christian symbols, designs, and figures, as well as the ways the fashion industry encourages an aesthetic perspective on and interpretation of them. The point here is not to celebrate or lament fashionable religion or to debate the sincerity of designers or the experience of fashion consumers, but rather to emphasize how fashionable religion's ways of seeing enhance our understanding of the religious landscape of the early 2000s. Examining the long and intertwined history of religion and fashion as we have done in this book enriches our understanding of significant changes in American religious life in the latter half of the twentieth century. It illuminates how the fashion industry supplied and reinforced the spiritual seeking trends of the 1950s and 1960s, which have flourished in the twenty-first century.

The Flourishing of Fashionable Religion

In 2012, magazines and newspapers proclaimed "the rise of the nones." The Pew Research Center reported that 20 percent of the American public and a third of adults under thirty were religiously unaffiliated—"the highest percentages ever" in their history of polling.[28] The *Christian Century* examined the impact of this trend on the political landscape, citing the "liberal" tendencies of the unaffiliated and the idea that politicians may stop "pandering to the religious" as this becomes a less salient factor in Americans' lives.[29] Other headlines emphasized that the "nones" represented "the nation's second-largest category only to Catholics, and outnumbered the top Protestant denomination, the Southern Baptists,"[30] and in its March 12, 2012 issue, *TIME Magazine* included the trend in its coverage of "10 Ideas That Are Changing Your Life."[31]

This religious shift had its roots in the soil of the 1950s and 1960s. In his commentary on the rise of the "nones," religious studies scholar Gary Laderman writes, "the 1960s are coming home to roost."[32] The seekers of the mid-twentieth century gave rise to the spirituality of the late twentieth and then the "nones" of the twenty-first. The unaffiliated, though, continue to report high rates of belief in God, and over a third define themselves as "spiritual," while one-fifth report praying every day.[33] These trends resemble those in Western Europe, where people exhibit what sociologist Grace Davie calls "believing without belonging." She argues that "a marked falling-off in religious attendance . . . has not yet resulted in a parallel abdication of religious belief. In short, many Europeans have ceased to belong to their religious institutions in any meaningful sense, but so far they have not abandoned many of their deep-seated religious aspirations."[34] For Americans and Western Europeans, elements of Christianity, and practices associated with the category of religion—the supernatural, prayer, faith—continue to resonate outside the confines of theology and church.

Fashionable religion flourishes as it reflects and reinforces these trends. This book has chronicled how the fashion industry supplied people with ways of seeing Christianity that fostered the shift from "religious dwelling" to "spiritual seeking."[35] The fashion industry was not the only source of this shift or supplier of these ideas, but it was an important one, particularly with the rise of visual imagery and technologies in the latter half of the twentieth century. The fashion industry not only modeled how to reprocess elements of Christianity but also provided some of the visual and material tools for people to do likewise.

Fashionable religion encourages a personalized faith that romanticizes the Christian past. It emphasizes individuals and their ability to remain connected to Christianity through visual practices and material objects. It underscores the idea that the sensory experience of these images and objects produces authentic spiritual moments that will help develop and transform the self. Fashionable religion envisions the supernatural as a diffuse, benevolent force that protects, comforts, and enchants. In a context of increasingly unaffiliated and "believing without belonging" people, fashionable religion highlights powerful and personalized ways of engaging Christianity.

Rather than framing these religious shifts in terms of secularization, the idea that societies are becoming "less religious" because of increasing rationality, Hervieu-Léger offers an alternative perspective. She argues that Western societies are increasingly incapable of sustaining the collective memory "which lies at the heart of their religious existence."[36] The result, she explains, is a type of amnesia regarding the authority, history, and context of institutional religion. Such forgetting helps foster "devotion where practice is a la carte in accordance with personal needs; and in its more extreme forms, where authorized memory no longer plays a role at all, there is a pick-and-mix attitude to belief."[37] Hervieu-Léger's insights provide a framework for understanding some of the religious shifts occurring in the twenty-first century and the flourishing of fashionable religion.

Fashionable religion reflects and reinforces this "pick-and-mix" form of devotion. It highlights how decontextualized Christian symbols, images, and designs provide sophisticated access to the supernatural. The precise historical and theological meaning of these Christian symbols, objects and figures is less important than what the personalized meanings and experiences they offer designers and their consumers. Fashionable religion's idealized construction of the past, its mediation of these objects, and its emphasis on the individual's sensory experience of them, foreground the spiritual look and feel of Christian images and objects.

This simultaneously encourages a recognition and experience of these Christian mediations and the amnesia of which Hervieu-Léger writes. For example, blogger Anibundel extolled the virtues of Dolce & Gabbana's "Tailored Mosaic" collection but also worried about the appropriateness of a party dress adorned with "the Christian Lord and Savior." The gilded mosaic dress in question features a bearded man wearing a crown on the skirt. He looks regal and majestic, resembles existing imagery of Jesus, and evokes the Christian past. Further, given the religious inspiration of the collection, Anibundel's interpretation (and that of others) makes sense. Except the figure on the dress is *not* Jesus. The dress depicts King Roger II of Sicily, prominently featured in the Monreale mosaics. Similarly, Katy Perry wore a dress from this collection to the 2013 Met Gala for the "PUNK: Chaos to Couture" exhibit. Perry delighted onlookers as a "Goth Medieval Queen," according to MTV style.[38] Prior to the event, Perry tweeted that she was "channeling the OG [original] queen of PUNK, JOAN of ARC," along with a picture of her embellished nails.[39] Twitter followers complimented her nail art, commented on her beauty, and then retweeted her post more than five thousand times. Many thereafter referred to it as the "Joan of Arc" dress, even though the dress depicted a Byzantine angel and not Joan of Arc. Dolce & Gabbana's online store also displayed some misrecognition. They labeled one digitized print dress of a woman looking out of a doorway as "Queen Mosaic Print Hourglass Dress." The woman, however, is the biblical Rebekah, not a queen, and duplicates a Monreale mosaic in which she watches her favorite son Jacob secure the blessing of his father, Isaac.[40] These examples highlight the amnesiac tendencies outlined by Hervieu-Léger. The collective memory of the Christian tradition that helps people correctly distinguish Jesus from King Roger, an angel from Joan of Arc or Mary (as some identified the figure), or Rebekah from a queen, has diminished.

Anibundel, Dolce & Gabbana, and Katy Perry are not the only ones suffering from these amnesiac tendencies. In an online survey of more than one hundred people on the topic of religion and fashion, respondents were shown an image of the Katy Perry dress and asked to identify the figure depicted. Of the seventy-one people who answered this question, more than half (43) identified it as some type of religious person, such as Mary, Jesus, or a saint, and of those, most (33) suspected that it was Mary. Similarly, almost all of the respondents surveyed identified the figure in McQueen's crucifixion jacket as Jesus, rather than the thief crucified next to him.[41] While this raises questions about secularization, religious illiteracy, and the emerging "nones," fashionable religion draws our attention to how people recognized these figures as religious even as they misidentified them. They identified these figures as "sacred" or "religious" relics from the Christian past through the visual look and display of religion. This demonstrates fashionable religion's success in fostering a particular way of seeing Christianity.

The modern fashion industry with its emphasis on the visual, as well as the evolving ways it has and continues to mediate religion, has fostered this forgetfulness and individualization. Throughout the last half

Figure C.3. "Queen Mosaic Print" dress from Dolce &
Gabbana's 2013 "Tailored Mosaic" collection that
reproduces a mosaic of the biblical Rebekah;
Venturelli/WireImage/Getty Images.

of the twentieth century and now in the twenty-first, the fashion system has supplied people with numerous reprocessed religious stories,
images, and designs. This reprocessing de-emphasized the historical
and institutional religious context even as it privileged individual pref-
erences and interpretations. In a world increasingly dominated by the
visual and the continual circulation of images, fashion's contribution to
this conversation should not be overlooked.

Further, in the "pick-and-mix" religious milieu of the twenty-first century, the valorization of individuals and their self-development through
the "sacred moments" and "spiritual vistas" afforded by reprocessed

religious relics fosters expansive and omnivorous tendencies. Sacred moments are temporary, necessitating an ongoing search for and collection of such experiences through an ever-expanding array of visual and material objects. Further, fashionable religion's idealization of the religious past for use in the present combined with its emphasis on the personal and sensual over the collective and cognitive, diminishes the importance of institutional authorities and cultural context. Add to this fashionable religion's inclusive, liberal ethos that ostensibly celebrates the heritage of other religions, and it is not surprising that the fashion industry has sought additional resources in the visual and material culture of other religions.

While this book has focused on the relationship between Christianity and fashion, other religious traditions exhibit equally complex connections to it. I leave it to others to advance this scholarly project, but it is worth noting that the appearance of Jesus in Špetić's collection occurred *after* the sometimes-controversial incorporation of figural religious imagery from Buddhism and Hinduism. In 2003, prior to his "downfall" for making anti-Semitic remarks, designer John Galliano's Spring Ready-to-Wear Collection celebrated the Hindu festival of Holi. Models were painted blue and wore designs decorated with the vibrant colored powders of the rite. In this collection, one model's voluminous top sported an image of the Hindu Goddess Kali. A year later, in 2004, Victoria's Secret sold swimsuits made by OndadeMar featuring images of Shakyamuni Buddha, and in 2011, the Hindu goddess Lakshmi appeared on a bathing suit designed by Lisa Burke. Before Jesus appeared so boldly in Špetić's collection in 2013, Hindu goddesses and depictions of Buddhas had already found their way into high fashion.

These collections met with varied responses. Fashion columnists celebrated Galliano's "ongoing ethnic obsession" with his Holi theme. Suzy Menkes reported, "His sari drapes and tinsel hoods turned the runway into a Rajasthani parade of exultant glamour and festivity."[42] Fashion critics' valorization of Galliano's artistry and aesthetic helped this collection avoid the controversy it likely would have garnered even a year or two later, which is what happened when consumers saw bathing suits featuring Buddhas and Lakshmi. When groups of Buddhists from the United States and other nations protested "Buddha's image on the breast and crotch areas" of two-piece bathing suits, OndadeMar and

Victoria's Secret stopped sales of the swimsuits in question.[43] Similarly, when some Hindus protested Australian designer Lisa Burke's swimsuit featuring Lakshmi, Burke promptly apologized and pulled the suit. Her ties to India (she had lived there for a time) and her explanation that the suit was meant to "celebrate different cultures," not give offense, did little to stem the tide of criticisms. In her apology, she assured her critics that it "will never be for sale" and concluded, "It was a lesson to me to be super-sensitive and careful of other cultures."[44] It was a lesson that Karl Lagerfeld learned in the mid-1990s with his "Qur'an dress" controversy.

This expansive and inclusive attitude that would lead one to put Lakshmi on a bathing suit or to purchase a hamsa keychain, though, reflects the ethos of fashionable religion. In this aestheticized perspective, personal inspiration and connection to the particular religious object, image, or locale overrides the theological context for those images and their broader global meanings.[45] If the benevolent supernatural can be accessed through Christian-inspired accessories and designs, why would such potential not also be obtainable through the sacred objects, symbols, and figures of other religious traditions? This is not to say that analyses focused on appropriation, Orientalism, and global capitalism's commodification of other cultures are misguided, but rather to highlight that the current "do-it-yourself" religious trends combined with fashionable religion's aestheticized perspective foster this type of religious eclecticism and consumption. It encourages people to construct their spiritual and sartorial selves through mixing and matching religious symbols, designs, and figures according to their personal tastes. The fashionable religion envisioned through this perspective may not be "religious enough" for some[46], but in a "pick-and-mix" religious landscape we must consider different forms of religiosity that defy the boundaries of religious institutions and traditions. Examining these eclectic collections and hybrid religious identities present scholars with challenging and exciting research opportunities for the future.

This book began with a consideration of *Vogue's* November 1988 cover featuring Israeli model Michaela Bercu wearing a cross-embellished Lacroix jacket. Analyzing Lacroix's design, at this point, we can see that this Catholic-reared designer utilized a Byzantine, mosaic-style inspiration that coincided with the popularity of oversized, bejeweled cross jewelry in the 1980s. The use of the cross recalled and reinforced the belief that this and other religious symbols could work as amulets and talismans, as well as markers of identity and taste. As with other fashion designers, his inspiration appealed to the Christian past and a sacred symbol and, at the same time, participated in the fashion and religious trends of the time. While Anna Wintour denied she was making a religious statement with this cover, we have seen in this example and throughout this book that the fashion industry does more than make statements. The fashion industry has supplied and reinforced a particular way of seeing Christianity that has flourished in the twenty-first century. Fashion history *is* religious history.

ACKNOWLEDGMENTS

In June 2018, shortly after finishing the manuscript for this book, I entered the Metropolitan Museum of Art to experience the "Heavenly Bodies: Fashion and the Catholic Imagination" exhibit. I entered the Met a little afraid that the exhibit would reveal some vital piece of information that I had missed, but at the same time, I was excited to see these fashion designs that I had only seen in two dimensions come to life. Upon viewing the exhibit, my fears proved groundless and my excitement only increased. While some have criticized the exhibit for its various failings, my appreciation for and understanding of these fashion designs was heightened by seeing the textures, colors, and details of the garments. As I made my way through the exhibit with hundreds of others, the material dimension of fashion *and* religion, as well as the public's fascination with it, could not be denied. My hope is that this book captures these material and aesthetic qualities, and like the exhibit, introduces readers to the longstanding and significant relationship between religion and fashion.

A number of people aided my journey into fashion studies. A series of annual international conferences hosted by Interdisciplinary.net introduced me to the exciting and dynamic work being done in fashion studies, as well as a host of amazing scholars. Patricia Hunt-Hurst, Deidra Arrington, Elizabeth Way, Luca Lo Sicco, and Rosie Findlay generously shared their expertise and emailed resources. They modeled scholarly collegiality and helped make this interdisciplinary work possible. So, too, did the kindness of numerous people and companies who answered my email queries and phone calls and then granted permission to use their photographs and illustrations.

My colleagues in the Department for the Study of Religions dispensed advice, provided technical support, answered questions, and helped create an environment in which my scholarship could flourish. The generosity of the Wake Forest Publication Fund enabled the book to include color images. Further, Kelly Besecke provided crucial editorial feedback during the early stages of writing and revision, and my editor, Jennifer Hammer, patiently endured my slow progress and constant questions with a ready smile and a quick reply.

I am also indebted to a number of friends and fellow scholars. Susan Ridgely provided endless encouragement over the phone and during quick summer visits. Pat Lord forced me to explain my work to a scientist, cheered me on over countless meals, and helped me remember my passion for this work when it seemed to fade. Stephanie Cobb organized my work calendar during a rough patch, commented on an early version of the entire manuscript, and then invited me to go to Italy so I could see Ravenna. Their support made this project more than it would have been otherwise and I am grateful. My writing accountability partner and dear friend David Yamane has read more drafts of this book than anyone should have ever had to do. During our weekly meetings when I couldn't find the words or struggled to revise a chapter, he helped me remember my voice, think through the issues, and develop a way to move forward. Through it all he understood, supported, and sharpened my vision for the project. I am thankful for his steadfast help and even more so for his friendship.

My family remains a constant source of encouragement. While they all keep me motivated and moving forward through phone calls and visits, Sarah Anderton, Emily Steffler, and Brandon Neal especially played key roles in making sure this project came to fruition. Such support was needed as during the process of researching and writing, my dad battled Alzheimer's disease. This often made it hard to research and write, but when I talked to him on the phone or visited with him, he would still ask me about the project. Even as his world became smaller and he eventually lost his battle, his example of concern for others and curiosity about the world continues to shape my life and work. This book is dedicated to him.

NOTES

INTRODUCTION. FASHION HISTORY IS RELIGIOUS HISTORY

1 The title of this introduction is inspired by Braude, "Women's History *Is* American Religious History," 87.

2 Anna Wintour, "Honoring the 120th Anniversary: Anna Wintour Shares Her *Vogue* Story," *Vogue.com*, August 14, 2012, www.vogue.com; Dhani Mau, "Anna Wintour's First *Vogue* Covergirl Only Wore Jeans Because She Was Too Big for That Lacroix Suit," *Fashionista.com*, August 14, 2012, www.fashionista.com; Geraldine Fabrikant, "Vogue Tries a More Relaxed Look," *New York Times*, October 31, 1988, D1, D9; Elizabeth A. Brown, "Wintour Harvest," *Chicago Tribune*, January 25, 1989, CN18.

3 I examined all available volumes of *Vogue* from 1944 through 2014; I supplemented this with a systematic review of three years from every decade of *Harper's Bazaar* from 1950 to 2010, and every available year of *W* from 1993 through 2012. *Harper's Bazaar* began in 1867. Under the inaugural editorial guidance of Mary Louise Booth, the magazine's readership grew to 80,000 within ten years. In the 2010s, its circulation averages 700,000 per issue. See "*Harper's Bazaar* Circulation," *Harpersbazaar.com*, www.harpersbazaarmediakit.com, accessed September 29, 2014. Founded in 1972 as a sister publication to *Women's Wear Daily*, *W* (owned by Condé Nast since 1999), with its oversize format, features coverage of the latest styles as well as provocative photo shoots and hence prides itself on being a more "artistic" fashion magazine.

4 "Condé Nast Facts," *Your Dictionary*, http://biography.yourdictionary.com, accessed December 8, 2014.

5 Condé Nast, "Media Kit," www.condenast.com, accessed September 29, 2014.

6 Entwistle, *The Fashioned Body*, 117.

7 Finkelstein, *Fashion: An Introduction*, 46.

8 The average is based on issues of *Vogue* from 2014.

9 The format of *Vogue* remains relatively stable over time. In 1955, the table of contents included the following sections—Fashion, In Vogue for Men, Features-Articles-People, Beauty, and Departments—while in 1965, regular features included Fashion, Fashion-Articles-People, Beauty, Departments. In 1975, Fashion, Beauty and Health, Features, Fashion in Living, and Travel constituted the main headings, and in 1985, they were Fashion, Beauty and Health, Living, Travel, and People Are Talking About.

10 Rabine, "A Woman's Two Bodies," 59; also see Finkelstein, *Fashion: An Introduction.*

11 Seebohm, *The Man Who Was Vogue,* 9.

12 Morgan, *The Sacred Gaze,* 6.

13 Tortora and Eubank, *Survey of Historic Costume,* 543. See also Barber and Lobel, "'Fashion' in Women's Clothes and the American Social System," 124–31.

14 Meyer, *Mediation and the Genesis of Presence,* 26.

15 Ibid., 11.

16 *Oxford English Dictionary, s.v.* "fashionable, adj. and n.," accessed January 17, 2018, OED Online. Oxford University Press.

17 Thank you to fellow scholar Martha Finch, who helpfully pointed out the problems with "window" language in a conversation at AAR. This choice also reflects how the fashion sources, particularly through the 1960s, equated the concept of religion with Christianity. Christianity operates as the *de facto* religion of the fashion industry. When articles on religion appear in fashion magazines, they assume Christianity. The Christian imaginary also provides the backdrop for numerous advertisements and eventually inspires numerous fashion designs. Yet, Christianity's dominance does not mean the absence of "other" religious traditions. While it is beyond the scope of this book to examine the relationship between fashion and Native American religions, Hinduism, Buddhism, Judaism, I hope that the phrase "fashionable religion" will provoke future scholarship in these areas.

18 Hervieu-Léger, *Religion as a Chain of Memory,* 158.

19 Duncan and Duncan, "The Aestheticization of the Politics of Landscape Preservation," 387, 391–92, 398.

20 Porterfield, *The Transformation of American Religion,* 4.

21 There is much debate in fashion studies about the terms fashion, costume, dress, and clothing. While illuminating, these debates are not the focus of this research. Throughout the book I use the term "fashion" to denote specific items of adornment, such as dresses and jewelry, as well as the larger industry that elevates certain styles and clothing items above others. For more on these debates, see Kawamura, *Doing Research in Fashion and Dress,* 8–9.

22 Phillips, *Jewelry,* 73–74.

23 Ibid.

24 John Wesley, *Advice to the People Called Methodists, with Regard to Dress* (London: 1795). Eighteenth Century Collections Online. Gale CW 121281298, Wake Forest University.

25 Finch, "'Fashions of Worldly Dames,'" 494.

26 Durkheim, *The Elementary Forms of Religious Life,* 140–49, 52, 55. Durkheim divided the world into two domains—the sacred and the profane. In this system, Durkheim explained that the powerful and dangerous realm of the sacred existed apart from the profane dimensions of ordinary life. In Durkheim's theory, these two realms were separate and hostile rivals. Over the past century, scholars have

nuanced and challenged Durkheim's views; however, his dichotomy captures the way people, past and present, often make sense of the relationship between religion and fashion.

27 Arthur, *Religion, Dress, and the Body*, 1.

28 Ibid., 5.

29 Joselit, *A Perfect Fit*.

30 Klassen, "The Robes of Womanhood," 39–82. See also Payne, "'Pants Don't Make Preachers,'" 83–113.

31 Tarlo, *Visibly Muslim*, 17; Bucar, *Pious Fashion*.

32 McDannell, *Material Christianity*, 8.

33 Gloria Guinness, "Eve and the First Dress," *Harper's Bazaar* 97 (March 1964): 156–57.

34 Lofton, *Oprah: The Gospel of an Icon*, 9–10; Meyer, "Praise the Lord," 106.

35 Meyer, "Praise the Lord," 94.

36 Barnard, *Fashion as Communication*, 26.

37 Davis, *Fashion, Culture, and Identity*, 4.

38 McDannell, *Material Christianity*, 1–2.

39 Meyer, *Mediation and the Genesis of Presence*, 28.

40 Morgan, *The Sacred Gaze*, 33, 6.

41 Ibid., 6.

42 Ellwood, *The Fifties Spiritual Marketplace*, 12–13.

43 Roof, *Spiritual Marketplace*, 65.

44 Ibid., 69. Also see MacCannell, *The Tourist*, 3.

45 Wuthnow, *After Heaven*, 4, 30–34.

46 Roof, *Spiritual Marketplace*, 68.

47 Ibid., 73.

48 Greeley, *The Catholic Myth*, 4, 44–45.

49 Fessenden, *Culture and Redemption*, 4.

50 Ibid., 5. See also Moore, "Religion, Secularization, and the Shaping of the Culture Industry in Antebellum America," 216–42, and Hervieu-Léger, *Religion as a Chain of Memory*, 109.

51 Demerath, "Cultural Victory and Organizational Defeat in the Paradoxical Decline of Liberal Protestantism," 458–69.

52 Greeley, *The Catholic Myth*, 4, 44–45.

53 Porterfield, *The Transformation of American Religion*, 64.

54 Dwyer-McNulty, *Common Threads*, 6.

55 Besecke, "Seeing Invisible Religion," 181.

56 Joselit, *A Perfect Fit*, 24, 37, 43.

57 Roof, *Spiritual Marketplace*, 3.

58 Ibid., 6–7; Wuthnow, *After Heaven*, viii.

59 Meyer, *Mediation and the Genesis of Presence*, 24.

60 Morgan, *The Sacred Gaze*, 6.

61 Ibid.

62 Ibid.

63 Maggie Maloney, "25 Coco Chanel Quotes Every Woman Should Live By," *TownandCountryMag.com*, August 16, 2017, www.townandcountrymag.com.

CHAPTER 1. DESIGNING NEW WAYS OF SEEING CHRISTIANITY

1 Elizabeth Bowen, "The Light in the Dark," *Vogue* 116 (December 1950): 157.

2 Ibid.

3 Ibid., 90.

4 Ibid., 157.

5 To find these articles, I went through every year of American *Vogue* from 1945 to 2013. I defined "religion" broadly, looking at article titles and topics, as well as language and images used. In addition, I systematically examined three years per decade of *Harper's Bazaar* from 1950 through 2010.

6 Besecke, "Seeing Invisible Religion," 181.

7 Morgan, *The Sacred Gaze*, 6.

8 Wuthnow, *After Heaven*, 4.

9 Morgan, *The Sacred Gaze*, 6.

10 Demerath, "Cultural Victory and Organizational Defeat," 458–69.

11 "People Are Talking About," *Vogue* 124 (August 15, 1954): 98–99.

12 Ellwood, *1950*, 117.

13 Roof, *Spiritual Marketplace*, 67.

14 Demerath, "Cultural Victory and Organizational Defeat," 460; Greeley, *The Catholic Myth*, 4, 56, 59.

15 Saler, "Modernity and Enchantment," 714.

16 Porterfield, *The Transformation of American Religion*, 4.

17 Saler, "Modernity and Enchantment," 714.

18 Ibid., 713–14; Stearns, *American Cool*, 7–8.

19 Quoted in Cook, *The Arts of Deception*, 158.

20 MacCannell, *The Tourist*, 3.

21 Ibid., 13.

22 Roof, *Spiritual Marketplace*, 69; Wuthnow, *After Heaven*, 4.

23 Hutchison, *The Modernist Impulse in American Protestantism*, 4.

24 Demerath, "Cultural Victory and Organizational Defeat," 460.

25 Morgan, *The Sacred Gaze*, 6; Besecke, "Seeing Invisible Religion," 181.

26 Ellwood, *The Fifties Spiritual Marketplace*, 1.

27 Allitt, *Religion in America since 1945*, 16.

28 Special to the *New York Times*, "'No. 1 Problem' Seen as Mental Health," *New York Times* February 7, 1950, 21.

29 PBS, "Timeline: Treatments for Mental Illness," *American Experience: A Brilliant Madness*, www.pbs.org, accessed August 22, 2016.

30 "Lists Mental Ills as Major Health Issue," *Chicago Daily Tribune*, May 3, 1955, C11.

31 Roy Gibbons, "Sees Society as Living near Mental Abyss," *Chicago Daily Tribune*, November 21, 1959, 9.

32 Smith, *What Would Jesus Read*, 137.

33 Ibid., 135.

34 Ibid.

35 Gibbons, "Sees Society as Living near Mental Abyss," 9.

36 James A. Pike, "A God-Shaped Blank in Man's Heart," *Vogue* 116 (July 1950): 74.

37 Robert R. Wicks, "Finding Faith," *Vogue* 120 (November 15, 1952): 106. Also see Francine Du Plessix Gray, "Exorcising Ourselves," *Vogue* 163 (May 1974): 149.

38 "The Heroic Encounter," *Vogue* 131 (April 1, 1958): 94.

39 René Dubos, "Mankind Does Become Better," *Vogue* 140 (September 1, 1962): 218.

40 Morgan, *The Sacred Gaze*, 6.

41 Smith, *What Would Jesus Read?*, 143.

42 Ellwood, *1950*, 136.

43 Fulton J. Sheen, "Hope," *Vogue* 148 (December 1, 1966): 216–17.

44 Pike, "A God-Shaped Blank in Man's Heart," 74–76.

45 Hutchison, *The Modernist Impulse*, 2–3, 7–8; Demerath, "Cultural Victory and Organizational Defeat," 460.

46 Wicks, "Finding Faith," 106–7.

47 Hutchison, *The Modernist Impulse*, 3–4.

48 Phyllis McGinley, "A Little Grace," *Vogue* 137 (January 1961): 60.

49 Ibid., 61.

50 Phyllis McGinley, "The Wit of the Saints," *Vogue* 139 (August 1, 1962): 124.

51 Ibid., 176.

52 "The Wisdom of the Desert," *Harper's Bazaar* 93 (December 1960): 82.

53 Ibid., 84.

54 Forbes, *Christmas*, 133.

55 Ibid., 169.

56 Restad, *Christmas in America*, 158–59; Moore, *Christmas*, 213.

57 Restad, *Christmas in America*, 155.

58 Morgan, *The Sacred Gaze*, 6.

59 "Christmas Night," *Vogue* 114 (December 1949): 33; "The Light in the Dark," 88; "Christmas: The Children's Miracle," *Vogue* 122 (December 1953): 79–85.

60 "Christmas Night," 33–34.

61 Ibid., 33.

62 "A Tribute of Love," *Vogue* 160 (December 1972): 114–17; "Michelangelo's Divine Circle," *Vogue* 164 (December 1974): 138–39.

63 Restad, *Christmas in America*, 169.

64 "Christmas: The Children's Miracle," 79–85.

65 "The Children," *Harper's Bazaar* 92 (December 1959): 75.

66 "Christmas: The Children's Miracle," 79–85. Also see Rumer Godden, "The Feast of Christmas," *Vogue* 126 (December 1955): 98–103.

67 "Nativity," *Vogue* 146 (December 1965): 170.

68 Thomas Merton, "The Holy Child's Song," *Vogue* 156 (December 1970): 112.

69 "The Land of Jesus," *Vogue* 142 (December 1963): 93–101.

70 Ibid., 97, 99.

71 "Christmas Night," 34.

72 "A Child's Religion," *Vogue* 122 (December 1953): 87; see also "A Season for Grace," *Harper's Bazaar* 93 (November 1960): 121–22.

73 Morgan, *The Sacred Gaze*, 6.

74 Stallybrass and White, *The Politics and Poetics of Transgression*, 42, 119, 139.

75 Edward Sackville-West, "Church Art," *Vogue* 111 (March 1, 1948): 202.

76 Ibid., 238.

77 Ibid.

78 "What Is Modern Art?," *MoMA Learning*, www.moma.org, accessed April 24, 2017.

79 Sackville-West, "Church Art," 240.

80 Morgan, *The Sacred Gaze*, 6.

81 "Matisse Designs a New Church," *Vogue* 113 (February 15, 1949): 79, 131.

82 Ibid., 76.

83 "Church Full of Joy," *Vogue* 118 (December 1951), 174.

84 Ibid., 129.

85 Greeley, *The Catholic Myth*, 4; Hutchison, *The Modernist Impulse*, 3–4.

86 "Church Full of Joy," 174.

87 Morgan, *The Sacred Gaze*, 6.

88 "Miracles of Faith, *Vogue* 150 (December 1967): 180–91; "Miraculous Churches of Khizi," *Vogue* 154 (December 1969): 156–61; "Celebrations of Genius at the Rothko Chapel," *Vogue* 157 (March 1, 1971): 109–11.

89 "Miracles of Faith," 180.

90 Ibid., 180, 191.

91 Morgan, *The Sacred Gaze*, 6, 8.

92 Ibid., 33.

93 "Miracles of Faith," 182–88.

94 Ibid., 191.

95 "Byzantine Art," *Vogue* 122 (December 1953): 95; "The Painted Churches of Moldavia," *Vogue* 157 (May 1971): 194.

96 Roloff Beny, "The Pleasure of Ruins," *Harper's Bazaar* 97 (December 1964): 98–103.

97 Ibid., 100–101.

98 "The House of Shiva," *Harper's Bazaar* 88 (May 1955): 112–13; Morgan, *The Sacred Gaze*, 6.

99 Wuthnow, *After Heaven*, 4.

100 Hansen, *Roman Catholicism in Fantastic Film*, 4.

101 Ibid., 4–5.

102 Kathryn Hulme, "River of Light," *Vogue* 131 (January 1, 1958): 144.

103 Cook, *The Arts of Deception*, 23.

104 Herbert Kubly, "Procession of Mysteries," *Vogue* 127 (April 1, 1956): 92.

105 Ibid., 93, 148.
106 Ibid., 148.
107 Ibid., 93.
108 Ibid., 149.
109 Ibid., 150.
110 Hansen, *Roman Catholicism*, 4–5; Wuthnow, *After Heaven*, 4.
111 Hulme, "River of Light," 96.
112 Ibid., 97.
113 Ibid., 97, 142.
114 Ibid., 144.
115 Ibid.
116 Ibid., 145.
117 Ibid., 146.
118 Saler, "Modernity and Enchantment," 697; Cook, *The Arts of Deception*, 118, 158.
119 "Holy Week in Seville," *Vogue* 119 (April 15, 1952): 80–81.
120 "The Angels of Campobasso," *Harper's Bazaar* 88 (December 1955): 78.
121 "The Virgin in Cuzco," *Harper's Bazaar* 87 (December 1954): 72–73; "The Healing Saints," *Harper's Bazaar* 88 (December 1955): 77.
122 Bowen, "The Light in the Dark," 90.
123 "Ecstasy of the Eye," *Vogue* 152 (December 1968): 188–90.
124 Wuthnow, *After Heaven*, 4; Morgan, *The Sacred Gaze*, 6.
125 Rumer Godden, "The Feast of Christmas," *Vogue* 126 (December 1955): 99–103.

CHAPTER 2. MAKING OVER CHRISTIANITY

1 Kayser glove advertisement, *Vogue* 127 (March 1, 1956): 45.
2 Morgan, *The Sacred Gaze*, 6.
3 For more on the relationship between religion and advertising, see Sheffield, *The Religious Dimensions of Advertising*, and Jhally, "Advertising as Religion: The Dialectic of Technology and Magic," 217–29.
4 Moore, *Selling God*; Moore, "Religion, Secularization, and the Shaping of the Culture Industry in Antebellum America," 216–42.
5 Porterfield, *The Transformation of American Religion*, 4; Wuthnow, *After Heaven*, 4; Lears, *Fables of Abundance*, 57.
6 Benjamin, *Illuminations*, 221; Dillon, "It's Here, It's That Time," 41.
7 Hervieu-Léger, *Religion as a Chain of Memory*, 158.
8 Payne, Winakor, and Farrell-Beck, *The History of Costume*, 594.
9 Tortora and Eubank, *Survey of Historic Costume*, 495; Mendes and de la Haye, *Fashion since 1900*, 126.
10 Farrell-Beck and Parsons, *20th-Century Dress in the United States*, 147.
11 Lears, *Fables of Abundance*, 154.
12 Marchand, *Advertising the American Dream*, 206–8, 217–18.
13 Ibid., 237–38.
14 Ibid., 267–69.

15 Ibid., 264–65.
16 Ibid., xviii.
17 Besecke, "Seeing Invisible Religion," 179–96.
18 Morgan, *The Sacred Gaze*, 6.
19 Avon advertisement, *Vogue* 108 (November 1, 1946): 27.
20 William Winkler advertisement, *Vogue* 117 (April 1, 1951): inside front cover.
21 Winthrop Mills advertisement, *Vogue* 107 (April 15, 1946): 25.
22 Winthrop Mills advertisement, *Vogue* 108 (August 15, 1946): 88; Evans Case Company advertisement, *Vogue* 109 (April 1, 1947): 131; Fabergette perfume ensemble advertisement, *Vogue* 112 (August 15, 1948): 10–11.
23 Etta Gaynes advertisement, *Vogue* 109 (March 15, 1947): 122.
24 DuPont advertisement, *Vogue* 124 (September 15, 1954): 34; R.A.R. Fashions advertisement, *Vogue* 127 (March 1, 1956): 69; DuPont advertisement, *Vogue* 129 (March 15, 1957): 36; DuPont advertisement, *Vogue* 129 (April 1, 1957): 98; Kimberly advertisement, *Vogue* 145 (March 1, 1965): 17; Kate Greenaway advertisement, *Vogue* 125 (March 1, 1955): 38.
25 DuPont nylon advertisement, *Vogue* 129 (March 15, 1957): 36; DuPont nylon advertisement, *Vogue* 129 (April 1, 1957): 98.
26 Jaquet cosmetics advertisement, *Vogue* 105 (March 15, 1945): 6; Celanese Corporation advertisement, *Vogue* 122 (September 15, 1953): 15; Saks Fifth Avenue advertisement, *Vogue* 127 (March 1, 1956): 11.
27 Jaquet cosmetics advertisement, *Vogue* 105 (March 15, 1945): 6.
28 American Cotton advertisement, *Vogue* 106 (August 1, 1945): 36; McDannell, *Material Christianity*, 46.
29 Granat advertisement, *Vogue* 105 (April 1, 1945): 16; Henri Bendel advertisement, *Vogue* 109 (March 15, 1947): 4; Tula advertisement, *Vogue* 110 (November 1, 1947): 41.
30 Shannon Hosiery Mills advertisement, *Vogue* 109 (May 1, 1947): 92; Lovable Brassiere Company advertisement, *Vogue* 109 (June 15, 1947): 17; Jordan Marsh advertisement, *Vogue* 115 (May 1, 1950): 13; Oneida Community Sterling advertisement, *Vogue* 120 (December 1952), 41.
31 Gorham sterling advertisement, *Vogue* 111 (April 15, 1948): 14; Burlington Mills Corporation of New York advertisement, *Vogue* 110 (November 15, 1947): 43; The International Nickel Company advertisement, *Vogue* 116 (July 1950): 4.
32 Oneida Community sterling advertisement, *Vogue* 120 (November 15, 1952): 29.
33 Wuthnow, *After Heaven*, 34–36.
34 Lowenstein Signature Fine Art Fabrics advertisement, *Vogue* 129 (January 1, 1957): 20.
35 Gala Spectaculars advertisement, *Vogue* 141 (Mary 1963): 73.
36 Hutzler's advertisement, *Vogue* 152 (September 1, 1968): 141; Alitalia advertisement, *Vogue* 153 (April 1, 1969): 15.
37 Roof, *Spiritual Marketplace*, 69; Wuthnow, *After Heaven*, 30–34, 4.
38 Morgan, *The Sacred Gaze*, 6.

39 Lears, *Fables of Abundance*, 20.

40 Marghanita Laski, "Advertising—Sacred and Profane," 122.

41 Coty advertisement, *Vogue* 103 (June 1944): 157; Lenthéric advertisement, *Vogue* 105 (May 1945): 117.

42 Countess Maritza Cosmetics Company advertisement, *Vogue* 106 (November 1, 1945): 197; Avon cosmetics advertisement, *Vogue* 107 (April 1, 1946): 41; Macshore Classics advertisement, *Vogue* 128 (September 1, 1956): 128. Also see Helene Curtis advertisement, *Vogue* 125 (April 1, 1955): 177; Titche-Goettinger Company advertisement, *Vogue* 126 (October 15, 1955): 17; J. P. Stevens & Company Inc. advertisement, *Vogue* 128 (September 1, 1956): 122–23.

43 Golden Fleece advertisement, *Vogue* 108 (November 15, 1946): 232; Avon cosmetics advertisement, *Vogue* 107 (April 1, 1946): 41; Van Raalte advertisement, *Vogue* 109 (May 15, 1947): 24–25.

44 Lenthéric advertisement, *Vogue* 103 (March 1, 1944): 62; Lenthéric advertisement, *Vogue* 105 (May 1945): 117. Also see: Lenthéric advertisement, *Harper's Bazaar* 87 (March 1954): 204–205.

45 DuBarry advertisement, *Vogue* 129 (March 1, 1957): 67.

46 Radway, "Reading Is Not Eating," 7–29.

47 Cook, *The Arts of Deception*, 17–19.

48 Vanderlaan, *Fundamentalism versus Modernism*, 21.

49 DuBarry advertisement, *Vogue* 129 (March 1, 1957): 67.

50 "Miracles of Faith," *Vogue* 150 (December 1967): 180–91.

51 Mendes and de la Haye, *Fashion since 1900*, 189–91.

52 Carter's advertisement, *Vogue* 118 (December 1951): 99; Peck and Peck advertisement, *Vogue* 123 (March 15, 1954): 19.

53 Helena Rubinstein advertisement, *Vogue* 131 (January 15, 1958): 19; Helena Rubinstein advertisement, *Vogue* 132 (September 15, 1958): 53; Helena Rubinstein advertisement, *Vogue* 134 (September 15, 1959): 16.

54 Cook, *The Arts of Deception*, 19, 28–29.

55 Germaine Monteil advertisement, *Vogue* 134 (October 1, 1959): 112; Germaine Monteil advertisement, *Vogue* 135 (May 1960): 138; Germaine Monteil advertisement, *Vogue* 141 (February 1, 1963): 90; Germaine Monteil advertisement, *Vogue* 149 (February 1, 1967): 118.

56 Wohl Shoe Company advertisement, *Vogue* 109 (March 15, 1947): 101.

57 Wimbelbacher and Rice Incorporated advertisement, *Vogue* 118 (November 1, 1951): 71.

58 Dorothy Gray advertisement, *Vogue* 108 (November 1, 1946): 258; Pond's advertisement, *Vogue* 108 (November 1, 1946): 245; Pond's advertisement, *Vogue* 109 (January 15, 1947): 131.

59 Avon cosmetics advertisement, *Vogue* 107 (April 1, 1946): 41. See also Stylecraft advertisement, *Vogue* 108 (August 1, 1946): 39.

60 Jones, *Angels*, 48, 54, 71, 87.

61 Pountain and Robbins, *Cool Rules*, 19.

62 Nolde Westminster Hosiery advertisement, *Vogue* 118 (October 15, 1951): 62.

63 Angelique advertisement, *Vogue* 126 (September 1, 1955): 82.

64 Skinner's Satin advertisement, *Vogue* 106 (September 1, 1945): 44.

65 Bates Fabrics advertisement, *Vogue* 112 (October 1, 1948): back cover.

66 Hansen advertisement, *Vogue* 134 (September 1, 1959): 99. Also see Barbizon advertisement, *Vogue* 135 (May 1960): 40; Macshore Classics advertisement, *Vogue* 128 (September 1, 1956): 128.

67 Lears, *Fables*, 139, 212.

68 Marchand, *Advertising the American Dream*, 237–38.

69 Chen Yu advertisement, *Vogue* 103 (April 1, 1944): 17.

70 Hanes advertisement, *Vogue* 125 (March 15, 1955): 54; Laguna advertisement, *Vogue* 140 (November 15, 1962): 63.

71 Jenks, *Transgression*, 3.

72 Ibid., 7.

73 Sanders, *Approaching Eden*, 9.

74 Gloria Guinness, "Eve and the First Dress," *Harper's Bazaar* 97 (March 1964): 156–57.

75 Kimball advertisement, *Vogue* 104 (August 1, 1944): 118.

76 Lenthéric advertisement, *Vogue* 120 (September 1, 1952): 198; Lenthéric advertisement, *Vogue* 131 (April 1, 1958): 143; Lenthéric advertisement, *Harper's Bazaar* 87 (April 1954): 199; Lenthéric advertisement, *Harper's Bazaar* 87 (September 1954): 265.

77 Revlon advertisement, *Vogue* 106 (December 15, 1945): 10–11.

78 Nina Ricci advertisement, *Vogue* 124 (November 1, 1954): 21.

79 Formfit advertisement, *Vogue* 131 (June 1958): 51.

80 Dorothy Gray advertisement, *Vogue* 132 (September 1, 1958): 74; Burlington Hosiery Co. advertisement, *Vogue* 133 (February 15, 1959): 25; Parfums Ciro advertisement, *Vogue* 139 (March 1, 1962): 179; Sarah Coventry advertisement, *Vogue* 138 (August 15, 1961): 124; My Own advertisement, *Vogue* 152 (September 1, 1968): 208; Max Factor advertisement, *Vogue* 153 (April 1, 1969): 125; Coty advertisement, *Vogue* 138 (September 15, 1961): 95.

81 Crepe de Chine advertisement, *Vogue* 132 (October 13, 1958): 119; Fleming Joffe advertisement, *Vogue* 142 (December 1963): 29; Cobra advertisement, *Vogue* 147 (March 1, 1966): 62; Princeton Knitting Mills advertisement, *Vogue* 132 (November 1, 1958): 20; Kayser lingerie advertisement, *Vogue* 134 (September 15, 1959): 69.

82 Lears, *Fables of Abundance*, 57.

83 Ibid., 161.

84 Humming Bird advertisement, *Vogue* 130 (September 15, 1957): 79.

85 Registered Fabrics Corp. advertisement, *Vogue* 149 (March 1, 1967): 91.

86 Maybelline advertisement, *Vogue* 138 (September 15, 1961): 62–63.

87 Hanes advertisement, *Vogue* 127 (March 15, 1956): 29.

88 D'Orsay advertisement, *Vogue* 128 (October 1, 1956): 213.

89 Catalina advertisement, *Vogue* 139 (January 1, 1962): 15; Catalina advertisement, *Vogue* 139 (January 1, 1962): 23; Catalina advertisement, *Vogue* 139 (May 1962): 49;

Catalina advertisement, *Vogue* 139 (May 1962): 53; Catalina advertisement, *Vogue* 141 (January 1, 1963): 39; Catalina advertisement, *Vogue* 141 (May 1963): 89.

90 Aziza advertisement, *Vogue* 146 (October 1, 1965): 77; Aziza advertisement, *Vogue* 146 (December 1965): 75; Aziza advertisement, *Vogue* 147 (March 1, 1966): back cover.

91 Lady Manhattan advertisement, *Vogue* 147 (February 1, 1966): 85; Lady Manhattan advertisement, *Vogue* 148 (September 1, 1966): 213; Lady Manhattan advertisement, *Vogue* 149 (February 1, 1967): 86.

92 Wuthnow, *After Heaven*, 30–34, 4–5; Roof, *Spiritual Marketplace*, 68–69.

93 A number of advertisements also use the statuary of Asian religions to connote ideas of sophistication and contagious magic. Asian religions simultaneously connote the "high culture" of artistic accomplishment and the "low" culture of religious primitivism and idolatry. These visual cues often occur in advertisements for jewelry and will be discussed more fully in chapter 3.

94 Hutchinson, *The Modernist Impulse*, 4.

95 Wuthnow, *After Heaven*, 140.

96 Styers, *Making Magic*, 4–20.

97 Stallybrass and White, *The Politics and Poetics of Transgression*, 89.

98 Maybelline advertisement, *Harper's Bazaar* 92 (October 1959): 36.

99 Tussy Shado-Rama advertisement, *Harper's Bazaar* 93 (June 1960): 44–45. Also see Surprise Brassiere Company advertisement, *Harper's Bazaar* 98 (September 1965): 329; Fabergé and Bueche-Girod advertisement, *Harper's Bazaar* 102 (May 1969): 68–69.

100 Fischer advertisement, *Vogue* 135 (April 1, 1960): 35; Nolde Westminster Hosiery advertisement, *Vogue* 118 (October 15, 1951): 62; Belle-Sharmeer advertisement, *Vogue* 128 (October 15, 1956): 6; Wohl Shoe Company advertisement, *Vogue* 136 (August 15, 1960): 23.

101 Rosewood Fabric advertisement, *Vogue* 108 (November 1, 1946): 124; also see Fischer advertisement, *Vogue* 135 (April 1, 1960): 35.

102 Relax-A-cizor advertisement, *Vogue* 142 (July 1963): 16, 19; Relax-A-cizor advertisement, *Vogue* 142 (November 1, 1963): 90–91.

103 Jaquet advertisement, *Vogue* 142 (September 1, 1963): 77. Also see Helene Curtis advertisement, *Vogue* 143 (June 1964): 28–29; Emmons advertisement, *Vogue* 146 (November 1, 1965): 218; Lilly Pulitzer advertisement, *Vogue* 152 (December 1968): 42.

104 Max Factor advertisement, *Vogue* 134 (October 1, 1959): 58–59.

105 Tussy Shado-Rama advertisement, *Harper's Bazaar* 93 (June 1960): 44–45.

106 Max Factor advertisement, *Harper's Bazaar* 93 (October 1960): 61.

107 Pola Cosmetics advertisement, *Vogue* 154 (December 1969): 104.

108 Davenport Hosiery Mills advertisement, *Vogue* 134 (September 15, 1959): 60; Pola Cosmetics advertisement, *Vogue* 154 (December 1969): 104.

109 Hudson Hosiery advertisement, *Vogue* 104 (August 1, 1944): 69; Evyan advertisement, *Vogue* 108 (September 15, 1946): 265; Lancôme advertisement, *Vogue* 122 (September 15, 1953): 173.

110 Black Magic advertisement, *Vogue* 108 (September 15, 1946): 265.

111 NoMend advertisement, *Vogue* 134 (November 15, 1959): 79; Fischer advertisement, *Vogue* 135 (April 1, 1960): 35; Carter's advertisement, *Vogue* 118 (December 1951): 99; Magic Latex Corporation advertisement, *Vogue* 134 (November 1, 1959); 190,

112 Morgan, *The Sacred Gaze*, 6.

CHAPTER 3. ACCESSORIZING THE CROSS

1 Ruth Hilton, "Vatican Gets Cross at Stars' Fashion for Wearing Crucifixes," *Daily Express* (May 23, 2002): 5; "Vatican Cross at Stars' Crucifixes," *BBC News*, May 23, 2002, http://news.bbc.co.uk; Bill Hoffmann, "Pope's Cross Words: Vatican Rips Stars' Gaudy Crucifixes," *New York Post*, May 24, 2002, http://nypost.com; "Crucifix Fashion Jewelry Makes Vatican Cross," www.antiques-art-collectibles.com, accessed January 15, 2015.

2 Bill Hoffmann, "Pope's Cross Words: Vatican Rips Stars' Gaudy Crucifixes," *New York Post,* May 24, 2002, http://nypost.com; Ruth Hilton, "Vatican Gets Cross at Stars' Fashion for Wearing Crucifixes," *Daily Express* (May 23, 2002): 5.

3 Madonna, "Madonna - Like A Virgin (Live MTV VMAs 1984)," https://youtu.be/gkSxhG4cbPo; Chris Willman, "How Madonna's 1984 VMAs Wedding Dress Wed Her to Pop Culture Forever," *Yahoo Music*, August 31, 2012, www.yahoo.com.

4 James Wolcott, "Madonna," *Vanity Fair* (August 1985), www.vanityfair.com.

5 Michael Gross, "Rock Videos Shape Fashion for the Young," *New York Times*, December 27, 1985, B8.

6 Morgan, *The Sacred Gaze*, 6; Porterfield, *The Transformation of American Religion*, 4.

7 Given its focus on jewelry, I have incorporated an analysis of jewelry advertisements in this chapter, rather than the previous one.

8 Benjamin, *Illuminations*, 220–22.

9 Baucom, *Specters of the Atlantic*, 24; Dillon, "It's Here, It's That Time," 38–51.

10 Plate, *A History of Religion in 5½ Objects*, 149; Sherry B. Ortner, "On Key Symbols," 158–67.

11 O'Hara Callan, *The Thames and Hudson Dictionary of Fashion and Fashion Designers*, 75.

12 Pond's Cold Cream advertisement, *Vogue* 109 (February 1, 1947): 217.

13 "Paris Collections Full Report," *Vogue* 117 (March 15, 1951): 97.

14 "The Upkeep of Costume," *Vogue* 118 (October 1, 1951): 150.

15 "27 Fashion Presents," *Vogue* 126 (November 15, 1955): 110–11.

16 Marchal Jewelers advertisement, "Charms for Easter!," *Vogue* 123 (March 1, 1954): 93; Charm and Treasure advertisement, *Vogue* 134 (November 1, 1959): 95.

17 Charles-Roux, *Chanel and Her World*; de la Haye and Tobin, *Chanel*.

18 Charles-Roux, *Chanel and Her World*, 367.

19 De la Haye and Tobin, *Chanel*, 51.

20 Koda and Bolton, *Chanel*, 26.
21 De la Haye and Tobin, *Chanel*, 7; Charles-Roux, *Chanel and Her World*, 5.
22 De la Haye and Tobin, *Chanel*, 9.
23 Charles-Roux, *Chanel and Her World*, 286.
24 Davie, *Religion in Modern Europe*, 6.
25 De La Haye and Tobin, *Chanel*, 72–73; Jean Nathan, "America's Crown Jeweler," *New York Times*, November 22, 1998, ST1, 8.
26 "Knights of St. John," *Visit Malta*, www.visitmalta.com, accessed January 22, 2015; Mica Calfe, "The History of the 'Maltese Cross,'" www.fireserviceinfo.com, accessed July 4, 2017.
27 Benjamin, *Illuminations*, 221.
28 Cook, *The Arts of Deception*, 17–28.
29 Meyer, *Religious Sensations*, 713.
30 Rhea Seeger, "New Fashions in Accessories Offer Thrills," *Chicago Daily Tribune*, April 30, 1932, 13; "By Wireless from Paris," *New York Times*, February 25, 1934, X9; K. C. "By Wireless from Paris," *New York Times*, February 6, 1938, 86.
31 Koda and Bolton, *Chanel*, 26–27; Sandra Ballentine "Cuff Love: Coco Adored Them, and So Does Lynn Wyatt," *New York Times*, February 20, 2005.
32 Rita Reif, "Auctions," *New York Times*, August 7, 1987, C29; Anne-Marie Schiro, "Costume Jewelry: Closer to the Real Thing," *New York Times*, October 20, 1987, C14.
33 *Jewelry: Ancient to Modern*, 149.
34 Phillips, *Jewelry*, 37.
35 Mausoleum of Galla Placidia, www.turismo.ra.it, accessed January 30, 2015.
36 Mauriès, *Jewelry by Chanel*, 32.
37 "History of Byzantine and Chainmaille Jewelry," The Sacred Art of Adornment, http://sacredartofadornment.com, accessed January 22, 2015.
38 Mauriès, *Jewelry by Chanel*, 99, 101–103, 106, 108, 121, 124–25.
39 Phyllis Lee Levin, "Spring Clothes Deserve Medals," *New York Times*, March 20, 1957, 41.
40 John Duka, "Notes on Fashion," *New York Times*, July 7, 1981, C5; John Duka, "Notes on Fashion," *New York Times*, July 27, 1982, B4; John Duka, "Notes on Fashion," *New York Times*, December 18, 1984, C15.
41 Bernadine Morris, "Yves Saint Laurent Reasserts His Mastery of Line and Color," *New York Times*, July 28, 1988, C1.
42 Plate, *A History of Religion in 5½ Objects*, 149; Ortner, "On Key Symbols," 158–67.
43 Wuthnow, *After Heaven*, 140; Duncan and Duncan, "The Aestheticization of the Landscape Preservation," 396; Spooner, "Weavers and Dealers," 199–202.
44 Ortner, "On Key Symbols," 161.
45 Marylin Bender, "Ancient Symbol Becomes Fashion Fad," *New York Times*, November 28, 1969, 45.
46 "Vogue's Own Boutique: Now It's Fashion," *Vogue* 154 (July 1969): 154.

47 Examples of models wearing Chanel attire and cross jewelry include "Chanel: The Great Little Tweed Suits . . . Smaller, Narrower," *Vogue* 147 (March 15, 1966): 88–91, and "Chanel," *Vogue* 154 (November 1, 1969): 158.

48 "The Good Grey Jersey," *Vogue* 142 (October 15, 1963): 29, 124–25.

49 "The Poet's Blouse," *Vogue* 142 (December 1963): 164–67.

50 "Trifari Sees Mosaics in a Whole New Light," Trifari advertisement, *Vogue* 148 (September 1, 1966): 179; "Shop Hound: Maltese Cross," *Vogue* 148 (November 15, 1966): 201; "Shop Hound: Maltese Cross," *Vogue* 149 (February 15, 1967): 152.

51 "The NY Collection," *Vogue* 152 (September 1, 1968): 392; "Crompton is Corduroy," *Vogue* 152 (September 15, 1968): 34; "Short Dress, Longer Coat: Evening's Double Image," *Vogue* 152 (October 1, 1968): 191.

52 "Shop Hound: Maltese Cross," *Vogue* 148 (November 15, 1966): 201.

53 "Turkey: Eastward to Eden," *Vogue* 148 (December 1966): 198, 212–13.

54 "Vogue's Own Boutique," *Vogue* 152 (September 1, 1968): 162.

55 David Webb, Inc. advertisement, *Vogue* 144 (December 1964): 37; Van Cleef & Arpels advertisement, *Vogue* 150 (December 1967): 21.

56 Kay Jewelers advertisement, *Vogue* 148 (November 15, 1966): 85.

57 Shopping International advertisement, "Crusader's Cross from Jerusalem," *Vogue* 142 (November 1, 1963): 192; Lilly advertisement, "Nature's Cross," *Vogue* 142 (December 1963): 190.

58 "Shop Hound," Saint Christopher Medal, *Vogue* 139 (March 1, 1962): 80.

59 Johnston Jewels, Ltd., "The Eternal Tree of Life Brooch," *Vogue* 148 (December 1966): 275.

60 Trifari's Ark advertisement, *Vogue* 148 (October 1, 1966): 149.

61 Coty advertisement, *Vogue* 149 (April 1, 1967): 18; "Vogue Patterns: Navy Crossed by White," *Vogue* 152 (July 1968): 100.

62 "The New York Collections: Spangled Tennis Dress," *Vogue* 150 (September 1, 1967): 306.

63 "Beauty Bulletin," *Vogue* 150 (September 15, 1967): 132–33.

64 "Best of Spring, U.S.A.," *Vogue* 149 (February 1, 1967): 142; Photograph of Mrs. Angier Biddle Duke, *Vogue* 149 (May 1967): 182–83; "Pendleton Country Clothes," *Vogue* 150 (September 1, 1967): 174; "Heavenly: The New Metallics," *Vogue* 150 (June 1967): 104–105; "Celanese Acetate," *Vogue* 150 (September 15, 1967): 6; "The Courtliness of Cotton," *Vogue* 150 (September 15, 1967): 18; Trevira advertisement, *Vogue* 152 (September 1, 1968): 304.

65 "The New York Collection," *Vogue* 152 (September 1, 1968): 390.

66 "Florida Beachwear," *Vogue* 153 (January 15, 1969): 178; "Spring: The Clothes You'll Love to Wear," *Vogue* 153 (February 15, 1969): 66; "Sun-Seers: Clothes for a Great Summer . . . ," *Vogue* 153 (June 1969): 82–103; "Fashion Forecast," *Vogue* 154 (July 1969): 71, 90; "Chanel," *Vogue* 154 (November 1, 1969): 158.

67 Marylin Bender, "Ancient Symbol Becomes Fashion Fad," *New York Times*, November 28, 1969: 45.

68 Ibid.

69 Ibid.

70 Supreme Court cases revolving around religion in the 1950s and 1960s, including *Burstyn v. Wilson* 343 U.S. 495 (1952), *Torcaso v. Watkins* 367 U.S. 488 (1961), *Engel v. Vitale* 370 U.S. 421 (1962), *Sherbert v. Verner* 374 U.S. 398 (1962), and *Abington v. Schempp* 374 U.S. 203 (1963), highlighted and shaped this questioning of Christianity and its dominance in the American landscape.

71 Eskridge, *God's Forever Family*, 7–8.

72 Bender, "Ancient Symbol," 45.

73 Ibid.

74 MacCannell, *The Tourist*, 3.

75 Spooner, "Weavers and Dealers," 200.

76 Cohen, "Authenticity and Commoditization in Tourism," 372; MacCannell, "Staged Authenticity," 593.

77 Bender, "Ancient Symbol," 45.

78 Allitt, *Religion in America since 1945*, xi–xii.

79 Geary, "Sacred Commodities," 169–91.

80 Phillips, *Jewelry*, 12, 40; also see *Jewelry: Ancient to Modern*, 10, 152–53, 165.

81 Phillips, *Jewelry*, 58–59; Lightbown, *Mediaeval European Jewelry*, 96.

82 Ibid.

83 *Jewelry: Ancient to Modern*, 165.

84 Phillips, *Jewelry*, 33.

85 Benjamin, "The Work of Art," 218–34.

86 Lears, *Fables,* 17; Twitchell, *Lead Us into Temptation,* 59.

87 Personal interview with James L. Ford, December 13, 2016.

88 Bulgari advertisement, *Vogue* 154 (December 1969): 81. Also see Bailey, Banks, and Biddle advertisements, *Vogue* 152 (December 1968): 171; "Extravagant Gestures," *Harper's Bazaar* 92 (April 1959): 134–35.

89 Personal interview with James L. Ford, December 13, 2016.

90 Bailey Banks & Biddle advertisement, *Vogue* 152 (December 1968): 171; Haniwa figure draped in jewelry, *Vogue* 138 (September 15, 1961): 142–43; Lady Coventry advertisement, *Vogue* 148 (October 15, 1966): 68.

91 Rice-Weiner & Company advertisement, *Vogue* 109 (March 15, 1947): 244; Lord & Taylor advertisement, *Vogue* 138 (November 15, 1961): 80.

92 Ortner, "On Key Symbols," 161.

93 Morgan, "Art and Religion in the Modern Age," 25.

94 "American Spring Collections," *Vogue* 155 (February 1, 1970): 204–5; "Springs: The Tiger Splits," *Vogue* 155 (April 15, 1970): 84–85; "New York Collections," *Vogue* 156 (September 1, 1970): 362, 370.

95 "Your Best Bets '71," *Vogue* 157 (January 1, 1971): 77.

96 "The Nonstop Coats," *Vogue* 157 (February 1, 1971): 129; "First Look at Summer," *Vogue* (April 1, 1972): 102; "Beach Report," *Vogue* 159 (May 1972): 161; "The New

Ease in Fashion," *Vogue* 160 (July 1972): 42–43; "Wool's Got Life," *Vogue* 160 (September 15, 1972): 42–43; "Diane Love for Trifari," *Vogue* 160 (November 1, 1972): 79; "Venice . . . September '72," *Vogue* 160 (November 15, 1972): 124.

97 "Men in Vogue," *Vogue* 155 (March 1, 1970): 121; photograph of Desi Arnaz Jr., *Vogue* 158 (November 1, 1971); 95; "Fashion for Pleasure," *Vogue* 161 (June 1973): 118–29.

98 "Fall Now," *Vogue* 165 (July 1975): 56; "Gelsey Kirkland," *Vogue* 165 (December 1975): 13.

99 Tiffany & Co. advertisement, *Vogue* 166 (December 1976): 4.

100 "Two Stars," *Harper's Bazaar* 104 (March 1971): 112; "Peekaboo Shorts," *Harper's Bazaar* 104 (July 1971): 42; La Costa Resort advertisement, *Harper's Bazaar* 104 (September 1971): 29; Elsa Peretti cross advertisement, *Harper's Bazaar* 108 (October 1975): 106–7; Bailey Banks & Biddle advertisement, *Harper's Bazaar* 108 (November 1975): 53.

101 Cover, *Newsweek*, October 25, 1976.

102 McDannell, *Material Christianity*; Hendershot, *Shaking the World for Jesus*.

103 Wuthnow, *After Heaven*, 4.

104 Bruce Buursma, "'Holy Hardware' Is the Trendiest Cross to Bear," *Chicago Tribune*, December 30, 1980, B2.

105 Grazian, "Demystifying Authenticity in the Sociology of Culture," 196.

106 Pountain and Robbins, *Cool Rules*, 19, 23.

107 Anne-Marie Schiro, "Notes on Fashion," *New York Times*, July 6, 1982, C6; John Duka, "Notes on Fashion," Special to the *New York Times*, April 10, 1984, C13; Rita Reif, "Jewelry Inspired by Antiquity," *New York Times*, July 15, 1984, 78; Genevieve Buck, "Bold Baubles," *Chicago Tribune*, October 2, 1985, S15.

108 Deborah Hoffmann, "In Jewelry, Choices Sacred and Profane, Ancient and New Age," *New York Times*, May 7, 1989, 66; Bernadette Morra, "Must Haves for Fall," *Toronto Star*, September 14, 1989, J1; Frank DeCaro, "Sacred, It's Not," *Newsday, Combined Editions*, May 10, 1989, O4.

109 William E. Geist, "Time for Religion: Hard Times Bring Out Lots of Shoppers," Special to the *New York Times*, April 6, 1982, B3; Hoffmann, "In Jewelry," 66.

110 Anne-Marie Schiro, "Notes on Fashion," *New York Times*, July 6, 1982, C6; Rita Reif, "Jewelry Inspired by Antiquity," *New York Times*, July 15, 1984, 78; Brenda Butler, "Medals and Badges Take Top Honors for Fall," *Chicago Tribune*, October 7, 1984, 143.

111 Butler, "Medals and Badges," 143; Buck, "Bold Baubles," S15, emphasis added.

112 "Vogue's View: Paris Couture," *Vogue* 178 (October 1988): 117.

113 "Evening Temptations," *Vogue* 172 (November 1982): 38; "New York Collections," *Vogue* 175 (September 1985): 63; Allison Kyle Leopold, *Vogue* 177 (October 1987): 464, 484.

114 "Vogue's View: Paris Couture," *Vogue* 178 (October 1988): 117; cover, *Vogue* 179 (November 1988); Bernadette Morra, *Toronto Star*, September 14, 1989, J1; John Duka, "Notes on Fashion," *New York Times*, November 3, 1981, B14.

115 Geary, "Sacred Commodities," 180.

116 Cohen, "Authenticity and Commoditization in Tourism," 372.

117 Buursma, "'Holy Hardware' Is the Trendiest Cross to Bear," B2; Hoffmann, "In Jewelry, Choices Sacred and Profane, Ancient and New Age," 66; Bernadette Morra, *Toronto Star*, September 14, 1989, J1.

118 Madonna, "Like a Prayer," Wikipedia, http://en.wikipedia.org; Shekhar Bhatia, "Thriller Scares Off Rivals for Video Crown," *Daily Express* (May 3, 2001): News 5.

119 "Pepsi Cans Madonna's TV Advert," *Daily Express* (April 5, 1989): 3. This was not the first time Madonna faced controversy in Italy and the United States. In 1986, in response to some of the Vatican's conservative tendencies, Madonna dedicated her hit song "Papa Don't Preach" to Pope John Paul II, who, in turn, urged Italian Catholics to boycott her "Who's That Girl" tour. Jim Farber, "When it Comes to Controversy on Tour, Madonna's Been Down this Road," *Daily News* (New York), October 21, 2008, www.nydailynews.com.

120 Jamie Portman, Southam News, "Madonna Has Stopped Commenting on the Controversy," *CanWest News* (March 19, 1989): 1.

121 Andrew M. Greeley, "Madonna's Challenge to Her Church," *America: The Jesuit Review*, May 13, 1989, www.americamagzine.org.

122 Christopher Bryson, "The American Anti-Hero," *Guardian* (London), September 15, 1990.

123 "Pepsi Cans Madonna's TV Advert," *Daily Express* (April 5, 1989): 3; "Pepsi Cancels Madonna Ad," *New York Times*, April 5, 1989.

124 Reuters, *St. Louis Post-Dispatch*, March 5, 1989, A2; Aly Sujo, "MTV Runs with Madonna Video," *Philadelphia Daily News*, March 7, 1989, 37.

125 Davison Hunter, *Culture Wars*, 42.

126 Ibid.

127 Ibid., 232.

128 Ibid., 236.

129 Davison Hunter, *Culture Wars*, 233–34. Also see J. Leo, M. Michaels, and J. Willwerth, "A Holy Furor," *Time* 132 (August 15, 1988): 7, 34; "Violence for Fun," *Christianity Today* 30 (February 21, 1986): 16–17.

130 Davison Hunter, *Culture Wars*, 231.

131 The rise of fundamentalism and the "culture wars" went beyond the American Protestant context. Global Catholicism saw some significant changes that fostered increasing conservatism. Pope John Paul II took over leadership of the Catholic Church in 1978 (until his death in 2005) and left what theologian Hans Küng calls a "contradictory" legacy. Küng contrasts the Pope's advocacy for human rights and his battles against communism with his unwillingness to sign the European Council's Declaration of Human Rights. Similarly, Küng points out the tension between the Pope's dedication to the Virgin Mary and his refusal to ordain women. Further, despite advocating for social justice in various parts of the world, he upheld traditional Catholic positions on birth control, abortion, celibate clergy, and homosexuality. In addition, Pope John Paul II strongly supported

the lay organization Opus Dei, characterized by many as very conservative and traditional. Thus, while not fundamentalist in the same way as the Moral Majority, conservative strains characterized Pope John Paul II and Catholicism more broadly during this time (documented by scholars in "The Fundamentalism Project"). See Hans Küng, "Crisis in the Catholic Church: The Pope's Contradictions," *Spiegel Online*, August 13, 2005, www.spiegel.de. Also see Joel Roberts, "John Paul's Conservative Legacy," *CBS News*, www.cbsnews.com, accessed February 20, 2015; William D. Dinges and James Hitchcock, "Roman Catholic Traditionalism and Activist Conservatism in the US," in *Fundamentalisms Observed*, edited by Martin E. Marty and R. Scott Appelby (Chicago: University of Chicago Press, 1991), 119.

132 Davison Hunter, *Culture Wars*, 147.

133 Carl Arrington, "Madonna," *People* 23:10 (March 11, 1985); Stephen Holden, "Madonna Re-Creates Herself—Again," *New York Times*, March 19, 1989, H1, 12.

134 R. Davies, "Beating Off the Backward Bigots," *Sunday Mail (QLD)*, July 8, 1990.

135 Bruce Buursma, "'Holy Hardware' Is the Trendiest Cross to Bear," *Chicago Tribune*, December 30, 1980, B2; J. A. Sargent, "Astrology's Rising Star," *Christianity Today*, February 4, 1983, 37–39.

136 Hoffmann, "In Jewelry," 66.

137 Sutcliffe and Gihus, *New Age Spirituality*, 3–6.

138 Lynn Snowden, "Crystal Power," *Vogue* 178 (August 1988): 340–42, 390, 392.

139 Ibid., 396.

140 Hoffmann, "In Jewelry, Choices Sacred and Profane, Ancient and New Age," 66.

141 Ibid., 66; also see Snowden, "Crystal Power," 340–42, 390, 392.

142 Patricia McLaughlin, "Instant Chic," *Chicago Tribune*, November 26, 1989, 131.

143 Wuthnow, *After Heaven*, 4.

144 Sturken, *Tangled Memories*, 9; Morgan, *The Sacred Gaze*, 9; also see "Understanding Visual Literacy: The Visual Thinking Strategies Approach," by Dabney Hailey, Alexa Miller and Philip Yenawine, pp. 49–73 in Danilo M. Baylen and Adriana D'Alba, eds., *Essentials of Teaching and Integrating Visual and Media Literacy: Visualizing Learning* (Switzerland: Springer International Publishing, 2015), 56.

145 Connerton, *How Societies Remember*, 39.

146 Hervieu-Léger, *Religion as a Chain of Memory*, 158.

147 Jenks, *Transgression*, 2.

CHAPTER 4. INNOVATING RELIGIOUS DRESS

1 Henry Alford, "Simply Divine," *Vogue* 183 (August 1993): 130–31, 136.

2 Morgan, *The Sacred Gaze*, 6.

3 Wuthnow, *After Heaven*, 4.

4 Alford, "Simply Divine," 136.

5 Here my approach is influenced by anthropologists of religion, notably Meyer, "Praise the Lord," 92–110, and Van de Port, "Visualizing the Sacred," 444–61.

6 Morgan, *The Sacred Gaze*, 6.

7   Davis, *Fashion, Culture, and Identity*, 103–4; Braham, "Fashion," 131.

8   My focus is on the design and supply side of the modern fashion industry; however, wonderful scholarship on the relationship between fashion and embodiment exists. For an excellent starting point, see Entwistle, *The Fashioned Body*.

9   Finkelstein, *Fashion*, 19.

10 Nika Mavrody, "At a Glance: See How These Six Corporations Control the Luxury Fashion Industry," www.thefashionspot.com, April 30, 2014.

11 For more on the use of Christian symbols and imagery prior to 1945, see the work of American designer Claire McCardell, who designed a very popular and famous "monastic" dress. Further, French designer Jeanne Lanvin incorporated elements of Catholicism into her designs. For more on these designers, see Kohle Yohannan, *Claire McCardell: Redefining Modernism* (New York: Harry N. Abrams, 1998); Dean L. Merceron, *Lanvin* (New York: Rizzoli International Publications, 2007).

12 "What Is Modern Art?," MoMA Learning, www.moma.org, accessed April 24, 2017.

13 Haas, "The Fabric of Religion," 199, 194, 204–5.

14 Mendes and de la Haye, *Fashion since 1900*, 144–45; Farrell-Beck and Parsons, *20th-Century Dress in the United States*, 145.

15 "Florence Fashions Add a Fancy Fillip," special to the *New York Times*, January 21, 1952, 18; "Richness Prevails in Rome," *Washington Post*, July 22, 1953, 23; Dina Tangari, "Rome, Too, Dictates Styles," *Christian Science Monitor*, January 31, 1957, 10.

16 Merlo and Polese, "Turning Fashion into Business," 429.

17 Ibid., 422.

18 "Florence Fashions Add a Fancy Fillip," special to the *New York Times*, January 21, 1952, 18; "Richness Prevails in Rome," *Washington Post*, July 22, 1953, 23; "2 Rome Designers Raise Hemlines," special to the *New York Times*, January 26, 1954, 19.

19 For more on the construction of authenticity, see Grazian, "Demystifying Authenticity in the Sociology of Culture," 191–200; Jenß, "Dressed in History," 387–404.

20 "An Italian Designer at Work Here," *New York Times*, May 21, 1952, 24.

21 Nan Robertson, "'Family Acts' from Italy Parade Their Fashions in New York Ring," *New York Times*, November 21, 1955, 32.

22 Virginia Pope, "75-Year-Old Matriarch and 3 Daughters Thrust Casa Fontana in Fashion Spotlight," *New York Times*, July 17, 1954, 16.

23 Merlo and Polese, "Turning Fashion into Business," 423.

24 Davie, *Religion in Modern Europe*, 6; Burke Smith, *The Look of Catholics*, 9–13. See also Dwyer-McNulty, *Common Threads*, 129.

25 Bishop Fulton J. Sheen, "Hope," *Vogue* 148 (December 1, 1966): 216–17; Thomas Merton, "The Wisdom of the Desert," *Harper's Bazaar* 93 (December 1960): 82–83; "Pope John XXIII," *Vogue* 140 (October 1, 1962): 170–71; "Gifts of Silence," *Harper's Bazaar* 93 (May 1960): 150–53; Gerald Brenan, "Spanish Seminarists," *Harper's Bazaar* 88 (April 1955): 172–73; "Holy Week in Seville," *Vogue* 119 (April 15, 1952): 80–81; "The Angels of Campobasso," *Harper's Bazaar* 88 (December 1955): 78; Lenthéric Perfume advertisement, *Vogue* 105 (May 1945): 117; Elizabeth Arden advertisement, *Vogue* 133 (February 1, 1959): 81.

26 Smith, *The Look of Catholics*, 1.

27 "People Are Talking About," *Vogue* 122 (September 15, 1953): 138; "Advance Notice," *Vogue* 132 (August 14, 1958): 81.

28 Porterfield, *The Transformation of American Religion*, 58. In some ways, Protestant anti-Catholic rhetoric focused on the materiality of Catholicism is reframed as a positive answer to the spiritual questions being asked by religious progressives and seekers. For more on the discourse of Catholic materiality, see Jenny Franchot, "Unseemly Commemoration: Religion, Fragments, and the Icon," *American Literary History* 9:3 (Autumn 1997): 502–21.

29 Porterfield, *The Transformation of American Religion*, 64.

30 Hansen, *Roman Catholicism in Fantastic Film*, 5.

31 Keenan, "From Friars to Fornicators," 390. Also see Mayo, *A History of Ecclesiastical Dress*.

32 Wuthnow, *After Heaven*, 140; Duncan and Duncan, "The Aestheticization of the Landscape Preservation," 396; Spooner, "Weavers and Dealers," 199–202; Conklin, "Body Paint, Feathers, and VCRs," 715.

33 For more on the history of Catholic religious dress, see Dwyer-McNulty, *Common Threads*. This implicitly constructed a mainline Protestant gaze that located religion in the lives and dress of Others, while making their own religious and spiritual choices simultaneously "normal" and invisible.

34 Dwyer-McNulty, *Common Threads*, 1.

35 Jenß, "Dressed in History," 396.

36 Raymond advertisement, "Monks Robes," *Vogue* 109 (May 1, 1947): 80. The incorporation of Catholic religious dress appears rarely in the 1940s; however, it is mentioned a few times in the 1930s. See "Cleric Mode Will Feature Bridal Gown," *Washington Post*, September 17, 1933, S6; Virginia Pope, "Monks' Hoods Play a Lay Style Role," *New York Times*, September 24, 1933, X8; "Paris Fashions Reflect Nuns' and Monks' Habits," *New York Times*, March 23, 1934, 25. Also, see the work of Claire McCardell. Constance C. R. White, "Celebrating Claire McCardell," *New York Times*, November 17, 1998, B15; "Claire McCardell and the American Look," http://articles.baltimoresun.com, accessed March 20, 2015; also see Claire McCardell, "Monastic Dress," Metropolitan Museum of Art, www.metmuseum.org, accessed March 20, 2015.

37 Cele Wohl, "Fashions Go Ecclesiastical in Roman Show," *Chicago Daily Tribune*, July 21, 1956, 17.

38 "The Windswept Drapery from Rome," *Sydney Morning Herald*, September 20, 1956, 7.

39 "Ava Gardner and the Shocking Dress," *London Daily Express*, September 14, 1956, 3.

40 "The Windswept Drapery from Rome," *Sydney Morning Herald*, September 20, 1956, 7; "The 'Pretino' of the Sorelle Fontana, Italian Glamour: 1950s, www.italianglamour.it, accessed July 17, 2017; personal correspondence with Salvatore Lo Sicco, September 27, 2014; "Micol, 100 Years for Fashion," www.lifestyle43.com, accessed February 14, 2014.

41 "Italy Follows the Curve in Fashions for Autumn by Fontana and Garnett," *New York Times*, July 24, 1956, 28.

42 Judith Cass, "Present Fontana Fashion Show Today," *Chicago Daily Tribune*, October 12, 1956, B1.

43 Edith Beeson Smith, "Roman Designer Seeks Boutique Fashions Here," *New York Times*, February 16, 1961, 35.

44 "Zoe Fontana's Daughter: 'Princess' of Fashion House Becomes Nun," *Los Angeles Times*, January 8, 1962, 17; "Rome Designer Takes Veil," *Washington Post, Times Herald*, January 9, 1962, A22.

45 McLeod, *The Religious Crisis of the 1960s*, 60.

46 Morgan, *The Sacred Gaze*, 6.

47 McLeod, *The Religious Crisis of the 1960s*, 67.

48 Herberg, *Protestant, Catholic, Jew*.

49 McLeod, *The Religious Crisis of the 1960s*, 83–101.

50 McLeod, *The Religious Crisis of the 1960s*, 60–82; Wuthnow, *After Heaven*, 4.

51 McLeod, *The Religious Crisis of the 1960s*, 140.

52 Enid Nemy, "The 1967 Fashion Story," *New York Times*, January 1, 1968, 22.

53 Farrell-Beck and Parsons, *20th-Century Dress in the United States*, 167–68; Tortora and Eubanks, *Survey of Historic Costume*, 529.

54 Tortora and Eubank, *Survey of Historic Costume*, 543; Gloria Steinem, "Gernreich's Progress; Or, Eve Unbound," *New York Times*, January 31, 1965, SM18. For more on imitation and the fashion system, see Simmel, "Fashion," 541–58.

55 Tortora and Eubank, *Survey of Historic Costume*, 541–43.

56 Evelyn Livingston, "Christian Churches," *Chicago Tribune*, November 25, 1968, D2.

57 Steinem, "Gernreich's Progress," SM18-SM23; Moffitt and Claxton, *The Rudi Gernreich Book*, 8–9.

58 Steinem, "Gernreich's Progress," SM18; Evelyn Livingstone, "Ahead of His Time," *Chicago Tribune*, September 19, 1966, C2.

59 Steinem, "Gernreich's Progress," SM20; Livingstone, "Ahead of His Time," C2.

60 Bernadine Morris, "Gernreich on the Dress," *New York Times*, February 14, 1967, 46.

61 Bernadine Morris, "Was Rudi Gernreich Kidding?," *New York Times*, October 19, 1966, 40.

62 Morris, "Gernreich on the Dress," 46.

63 Bill Cunningham, "The Ecclesiastical Look," *Chicago Tribune*, May 6, 1968, C8. Another designer who utilized the visual code of the nun prior to Vatican II and World War II was Valentina, a Russian émigré who designed in the United States. She considered nuns "the most stylish people on earth" and dressed her famous clients, including Greta Garbo and Katharine Hepburn, in "long-sleeved, severe dresses with peaked caps." See "New York Fashion Week Designers Inspired by Nun's Habits, Monk's Robes," www.forbes.com, accessed March 20, 2015.

64 Moffitt and Claxton, *The Rudi Gernreich Book*, 138–39, 121.

65 Ibid., 138–39.

66 "From Nude to Nun Look: Gernreich's Fashions Run Gamut," *Standard-Speaker* (Hazleton, Pennsylvania), May 18, 1967, 19; Ruth Olis, "Gernreich Unveils Shockers Again," *Courier-Post* (Camden, NJ), 6. It is interesting to note that the media did not highlight Gernreich's Jewish identity and its relationship to these designs. They instead focused on his artistry and aesthetics.

67 Enid Nemy, "Halston, the Hat Man, Designs First Dresses," *New York Times*, June 29, 1966, 43; "Besides Those Scares, There's a Whole New World of Accessories," *Chicago Tribune*, August 1, 1966, B2.

68 Cunningham, "The Ecclesiastical Look," C8; Patricia Shelton, "Spring Silhouettes," *Christian Science Monitor*, January 10, 1967, 6; "Witching Black," *Vogue* 150 (August 1, 1967): 50–51.

69 Joanna Leite, "Exhibition: Cristóbal Balenciaga," August 12, 2012, http://modecon nect.com.

70 Cunningham, "The Ecclesiastical Look," C8. Also see Evelyn Livingstone, "Christian Churches Have Long Had," *Chicago Tribune*, November 25, 1968, D2.

71 "Balenciaga's Marvels of Form—the Bride's Dress, the Cape Dress; All Bias Ovals," *Vogue* 150 (July 1967): 80–81.

72 Jouve, *Balenciaga*, 7.

73 Cristóbal Balenciaga, "Evening Ensemble," Victoria & Albert Museum, http://col lections.vam.ac.uk, accessed March 18, 2015.

74 Tamara W. Hill, "Cristóbal Balenciaga," www.ornamentmagazine.com, accessed March 18, 2015.

75 Evelyn Livingstone, "Chicagoan's Designs for Dinah," *Chicago Daily Tribune*, January 20, 1963, E1; Evelyn Livingstone, "You, Too, Can Have a Personal Designer," *Chicago Daily Tribune*, January 27, 1963, F3; "Chicago Styles by a Londoner in Store Here," *New York Times*, February 18, 1965, 37; Evelyn Livingstone, "Walter Holmes Wants Full Coverage," *Chicago Tribune*, December 26, 1965, H3; Eleanor Page, "Chicago Designer Wins Fashion Award," *Chicago Tribune*, April 28, 1966, E2.

76 Evelyn Livingstone, "Designers Vie for Coveted Award," *Chicago Tribune*, April 25, 1967, B3.

77 Michele Majer, "Boutique," in *The Berg Companion to Fashion*, edited by Valerie Steele. Oxford: Bloomsbury Academic, 2010, accessed July 18, 2017. www.blooms buryfashioncentral.com.

78 Eleanor Nangle, "Way-Out Styles Get 'In' Welcome to Rush Street," *Chicago Tribune*, September 1, 1966, D3.

79 Irene Powers, "An Electric Mixture of Their Own," *Chicago Tribune*, April 4, 1968, B6.

80 Judy Klemesrud, "Way-Out Designer with Solemn Task," *New York Times*, October 7, 1968, 54; "Get Thee to a Boutique," *Newsweek* 72 (July 8, 1968): 48. See also "Medieval Minis," *Chicago Tribune*, June 28, 1968, 2.

81 Klemesrud, "Way-Out Designer with Solemn Task," 54.

82 Ibid., 54.

83 Ibid.

84 Dorothea Nicholas, "Priesthood Training Hits High of 2,275 Students," *Chicago Daily Tribune*, June 14, 1962, S A6.

85 Dwyer-McNulty, *Common Threads*, 176, 185; see also John McLaughlin, "Of Many Things: The Garb of European Priests," *America* 117:15 (October 7, 1967): inside cover.

86 Eleanor Nangle, "For the Record," *Chicago Tribune*, May 6, 1968, Section 2–9, Feminique. Also see "Designing Nun Knows Her Way around Seventh Avenue," special to the *New York Times*, January 9, 1968, 46.

87 Cunningham, "The Ecclesiastical Look," C8.

88 Judy Klemesrud, "Designer Adapts Nuns' Garb for Public," *New York Times*, June 27, 1968, 38; "Get Thee to a Boutique," *Newsweek* 72 (July 8, 1968): 48.

89 Judy Klemesrud, "Mini-Medievals—Some Say They're Sacrilegious," *Akron Beacon Journal* (Akron, OH), June 28, 1968, A14; "Mini-Medievals Stir Storm," *Battle Creek Enquirer* (Battle Creek, MI), July 1, 1968, 6; Judy Klemesrud, "Nun-Like Mini Fashions: Sacrilegious or Prudent?," *Arizona Republic*, June 28, 1968, 35.

90 Keenan, "From Friars to Fornicators," 396–97.

91 Jonathan Walford, "Fashion Hall of Obscurity—Walter Holmes," posted July 24, 2012, https://kickshawproductions.com, accessed July 17, 2017.

92 Klemesrud, "Way-Out Designer with Solemn Task," 54.

93 Cover of Feminique, *Chicago Tribune*, November 25, 1968, D1.

94 Evelyn Livingston, "Christian Churches," *Chicago Tribune*, November 25, 1968, D2.

95 "Get Thee to a Boutique," *Newsweek* 72 (July 8, 1968): 48.

96 Cunningham, "The Ecclesiastical Look," C8.

97 Klemesrud, "Designer Adapts Nuns' Garb for Public."

98 Van de Port, "Visualizing the Sacred," 445.

99 Morgan, *The Sacred Gaze*, 6.

100 Thomas Luckmann, "Shrinking Transcendence, Expanding Religion," 138.

101 Stanley Korshak advertisement, *Vogue* 159 (February 1, 1972): 10.

102 "Ready-to-Wear: The Best of the New Looks from Paris and Italy," *Vogue* 164 (July 1974): 76; "Ready-to-Wear," *Vogue* 165 (August 1975): 144.

103 Geary, "Sacred Commodities," 180.

104 Davison Hunter, *Culture Wars*, 42. Chapter 3 examines this context in more detail.

105 Tortora and Eubank, *Survey of Historic Costume: A History of Western Dress*, 596.

106 Farrell-Beck and Parsons, *20th-Century Dress in the United States*, 214.

107 Ibid., 210–11.

108 Ibid., 223.

109 Mendes and de la Haye, *Fashion since 1900*, 223.

110 Nina Hyde, "Fashion Notes," *Washington Post*, April 12, 1981, L3.

111 Nina Hyde, "On Their Avant-Garde," *Washington Post*, March 10, 1987, D1; "Dressing Ascetic," *Vogue* 177 (September 1987): 641, 660.

112 Hyde, "On Their Avant-Garde," D1.

113 Ibid.; "Dressing Ascetic," *Vogue* 177 (September 1987): 641, 660.

114 Angelo Tarlazzi was the head designer for Callaghan. You can see video footage of the show at "Callaghan Spring Summer 1986 Milan Pret a Porter Woman by Canale Mode," Fashion Channel Milan, https://youtu.be/nzOdKXmN4Zo, accessed March 23, 2015.

115 Carol Brennan, "Geoffrey Beene," *The Encyclopedia of World Biography*, www .notablebiographies.com, accessed March 20, 2015.

116 Nina Hyde, "Geoffrey Beene, Simply Elegant," *Washington Post*, posted April 19, 1987, www.washingtonpost.com, accessed July 20, 2017.

117 "The World of Geoffrey Beene," *Vogue* 177 (September 1, 1987): 688–97.

118 Woody Hochswender, "Fashion Iconoclasts Rediscover Subtleties," *New York Times*, April 2, 1989, 46.

119 Michael Gross, "Gaultier: Fashion Designed to Provoke," *New York Times*, October 31, 1986, A32; Marina Sturdza, "Anarchy by Gaultier," *Globe and Mail* (Canada), July 8, 1986, Fashion C4; Nina Hyde, "Couture's Bad Boy," *Washington Post*, October 20, 1986, Style C1.

120 Gross, "Gaultier: Fashion Designed to Provoke," A32.

121 Hyde, "Couture's Bad Boy," C1.

122 Nina Hyde, "The Cutting Edge," *Washington Post*, October 24, 1989, C1.

123 Bernadine Morris, "In Paris, Ready-to-Wear Forgoes Understatement," *New York Times*, October 23, 1989, B9; also see David Livingstone, "Showmanship on Display at Gaultier Presentation," *Globe and Mail* (Canada), October 26, 1989.

124 Matthew D. Herrera, "Holy Smoke—the Use of Incense in the Catholic Church," *Adoremus Bulletin* Online Edition, February 2012, Vol. XVII, No. 10, www .adoremus.org.

125 The word "nunnish" is used by blogger "Klng"; see "Yves Saint Laurent: Fall 2010 . . . and the High-Fashion Nun?," March 22, 2010, http://klngsartorial .blogspot.com.

126 Cook, *The Arts of Deception*, 19.

127 Jan Greeve, "Jean Paul Gaultier 1990 Spring Summer Collection," http://youtu .be/50B7u2m2WHE, accessed March 24, 2015.

128 "Fashion: French, Italian Designers Shed Light onto the Future," *Los Angeles Times*, October 23, 1989, E3, emphasis added.

129 Pat Morgan, "Paris: The Hourglass' Time Has Come," *Detroit Free Press*, October 26, 1989, 2C.

130 Morris, "In Paris," B9; also see David Livingstone, "Showmanship on Display at Gaultier Presentation," *Globe and Mail* (Canada), October 26, 1989.

131 Hyde, "The Cutting Edge," C9.

132 "Fashion: French, Italian Designers . . . ," *Los Angeles Times*, E3.

133 Jill Gerston, "Barely There," *Philadelphia Inquirer*, October 29, 1989, I3.

134 Pat Morgan, "Paris," 2C.

135 Nina Hyde, "Fashion Notes: Gaultier Gets Religion," *Washington Post*, October 29, 1989, F3; see also Janice G. McCoart, "Image and Social Responsibility: Catholic Values and Fashion Advertising," in *Mapping the Catholic Cultural Landscape*,

edited by Sister Paula Jean Miller, FSE, and Richard Fossey (Lanham, MD: Rowman & Littlefield, 2004), 239–48.

136 Hyde, "Fashion Notes," F3.

137 For more on Gaultier's Catholicism and past, see Sarah Raper Laurenaudie, "Gaul of the Wild," *W* 28 (December 1999): 300–305.

138 Morgan, *The Sacred Gaze*, 6.

139 Keenan, "From Friars to Fornicators: The Eroticization of Sacred Dress," 397. See also William J. F. Keenan, "Of Mammon Clothed Divinely: The Profanization of Sacred Dress," *Body & Society* 5:1 (1999): 73–92.

140 Van de Port, "Visualizing the Sacred," 444–45.

141 Pountain and Robbins, *Cool Rules*, 19.

142 Jenks, *Transgression*, 9.

143 Monk et al., *Awful Disclosures of Maria Monk*; Nakahara, "Barred Nuns: Italian Nunsploitation Films." See also the controversy surrounding Benetton's provocative advertising campaign in 1991, which included an image of a priest and nun kissing. Genevieve Buck, "F.Y.I.: There's a Controversy at Benetton—and It's Not over Clothes," *Chicago Tribune*, August 14, 1991, F6; Paul Antick, "Bloody Jumpers: Benetton and the Mechanics of Cultural Exclusion," *Fashion Theory* 6:1 (2002): 83–109.

144 Keenan, "From Friars to Fornicators," 401.

145 Jenks, *Transgression*, 2.

146 Mendes and de la Haye, *Fashion since 1900*, 252.

147 Fashion Channel, "Krizia Fall 1991/1992 Milan – Fashion Channel," https://youtu .be/MMPeQYoxhHg.

148 Marylou Luther, "The New Fashion Austerity: U.S. Designers Tone It Down," *Christian Science Monitor*, April 15, 1993, 11; Trish Donnally, "Fashion Designers Are Finding Religion," *Clarion-Ledger* (Jackson, MS), April 24, 1993, 2D; Genevieve Buck, "Simply Divine," *Chicago Tribune*, July 18, 1993, SM22; Amy M. Spindler, "Piety on Parade: Fashion Seeks Inspiration," *New York Times*, September 5, 1993, 1.

149 Donnally, "Fashion Designers Are Finding Religion," 2D. "Christian Dior Autumn Winter 1993 1994 Paris 3 of 4 Pret a Porter Woman by Fashion Channel," https:// youtu.be/PocabE9lQjU, accessed March 23, 2015.

150 Luther, "The New Fashion Austerity," 11.

151 Buck, "Simply Divine," SM22.

152 Luther, "The New Fashion Austerity," 11.

153 Vida Roberts, "The Spiritual Look Becomes a Fashion Statement," *Star Tribune* (Minneapolis, MN), August 4, 1993, 3E.

154 Buck, "Simply Divine," SM22.

155 Ibid.

156 Donnally, "Fashion Designers Are Finding Religion," 2D.

157 Ibid.

158 "Fashion," *Muncie Evening Press*, April 23, 1993, 10.

159 Buck, "Simply Divine," SM22; Luther, "The New Fashion Austerity," 11.

160 Jackie White, "Fashion Gets Religion?" *Town Talk* (Alexandria, LA), October 26, 1993, C2.

161 Patricia McLaughlin, "Style: Cross Currents," *Philadelphia Inquirer*, November 14, 1993, Style 31.

162 Janet McCue "Designers Say Less Is More," *St. Louis Post-Dispatch*, November 11, 1993, 14WF.

163 Spindler, "Piety on Parade," 30.

164 Alford, "Simply Divine," 136.

165 Spindler, "Piety on Parade," 1, 30.

166 Luther, "The New Fashion Austerity," 11.

167 Spindler, "Piety on Parade," 30.

168 Ibid.; Jackie White, "Fashion Turns to Cross and Cloister," *Salina Journal* (Salina, KS), October 23, 1993, 21.

169 Davison Hunter, *Culture Wars*, 147.

170 Morgan, *Visual Piety*, 14.

171 Spindler, "Piety on Parade," 1.

172 Alford, "Simply Divine," *Vogue* 183 (August 1993): 131.

173 "The Great Plain," *Vogue* 183 (August 1993): 278–91; also see "Nervous Parents Meet the Devil," *New York Times*, January 2, 1994, H31.

174 "Fashion," *Muncie Evening Press*, April 23, 1993, 10.

175 Donnally, "Fashion Designers Are Finding Religion," 2D; see also Alford, "Simply Divine," 136. This book's focus on Christianity's relationship to fashion does not mean that Judaism was absent. Jewish imagery and design inspirations appear occasionally as in Gaultier's collection. In addition, Jewish men and women were influential in the fashion industry through department and jewelry stores, such as Saks Fifth Avenue, Henri Bendel, and Kay Jewelers, as well as the cosmetics industry (e.g., Helena Rubinstein, Max Factor), and through numerous Jewish designers—Kenneth Cole, Diane von Fürstenberg, Ralph Lauren, Isaac Mizrahi, and others. Jenna Weissman Joselit's *A Perfect Fit* provides some insight into this relationship, as does Kerri Steinberg's *Jewish Mad Men: Advertising and the Design of the American Jewish Experience* (New Brunswick, NJ: Rutgers University Press, 2015). Yet more scholarship on the relationship between Judaism and the modern fashion industry specifically needs to be done.

176 Spindler, "Piety on Parade," 30.

177 Ibid.; also see Patricia McLaughlin, "Style: Cross Currents," Style 31.

178 Buck, "Simply Divine," SM22.

179 Morgan, *The Sacred Gaze*, 6.

180 Emily Prager, "The Going Got Tough," *New York Times*, September 26, 1993, 10v.

181 Ibid.

182 Hervieu-Léger, *Religion as a Chain of Memory*, 33.

183 Morgan, *The Sacred Gaze*, 6.

184 "Yves Saint Laurent: Fall 2010 . . . and the High-Fashion Nun?," March 22, 2010, http://klngsartorial.blogspot.com; Suzy Menkes, "Good Habits," November 29,

2010, http://tmagazine.blogs.nytimes.com; Sarah Mower, "Saint Laurent Fall 2010 Ready-to-Wear," *Style.com*, March 8, 2010, www.style.com; "Yves Saint Laurent Fall Winter 2010/2010 Full Fashion Show Exclusive," https://youtu.be/xoaYoA7_ i2M, accessed March 25, 2015; "Yves Saint Laurent Fall 2010: Social and Religious Customs," Fashion Windows, March 10, 2010; "Yves Saint Laurent's Stefano Pilati Does Stark, Puritan Chic, Complete with Starched Collars," *Guelph Mercury*, March 8, 2010, www.guelphmercury.com; Eric Wilson, "Fashion Review: Can Sackcloth Have Fur Trim?," *New York Times*, March 10, 2010, B12; Cathy Horyn, "Stefano Pilati to Leave YSL," *New York Times*, February 27, 2012, http://runway .blogs.nytimes.com; Alexander McQueen, Fall 2013 RTW, *Style.com*, www.style .com, accessed April 3, 2015.

185 "New York Fashion Week Designers Inspired by Nun's Habits, Monk's Robes," www.forbes.com, accessed March 20, 2015.

186 Sarah Mower, "Fall 2018 Ready-to-Wear: Dolce & Gabbana," *Vogue.com*, February 25, 2018, www.vogue.com.

CHAPTER 5. FASHIONING HOLY FIGURES

1 "Miss Dominican Republic National Costume Stirs Controversy," *DominicanToday. com*, January 24, 2015, www.dominicantoday.com; Yara Simon, "Miss Universe 2014 Date: Contestant Kimberly Castillo, Miss Dominican Republic, Sparks Controversy with Virgin Mary Dress," *Latin Post*, January 15, 2015, www.latinpost.com.

2 Simon, "Miss Universe 2014 Date."

3 Roof, *Spiritual Marketplace*, 7–10.

4 Morgan, *The Sacred Gaze*, 6.

5 Hervieu-Léger, *Religion as a Chain of Memory*, 158.

6 Luckmann, "Shrinking Transcendence, Expanding Religion?," 127–38.

7 Freedberg, *The Power of Images*, 62.

8 Ibid., 28.

9 Martin, "Sailing to Byzantium: A Fashion Odyssey," 9.

10 Women's Wear Daily, "Designers Reach for 'International Ethnic,'" *Palm Beach Daily News*, March 20, 1990, 1.

11 Mendes and de la Haye, *Fashion since 1900*, 252.

12 Martin, "Sailing to Byzantium," 4.

13 Ibid.

14 Elizabeth Snead, "Japanese Collections Chart New Course," *Times Herald* (Port Huron, MI), October 29, 1990, The Express, 12; Nicola Jeal, "Fashion Buyers Wary at Paris Shows," *Salina Journal* (Salina, KS), October 21, 1990, 32. See Todd Oldham collections, Fall 1991–92, www.toddoldhamstudio.com, accessed August 3, 2017.

15 Anna Battista, "How a Fake Search for the Spiritual Became an Unfashionable Trend," *Irenebrination*, August 29, 2013, www.irenebrination.typepad.com.

16 Claire Wilcox, "Comme des Garçons" in *The Berg Companion to Fashion*, edited by Valerie Steele (Oxford: Bloomsbury Academic, 2010), accessed August 03, 2017. www.bloomsburyfashioncentral.com.

17 Trish Donnally, "Fantasy, Nostalgia Fill Paris Spring," *Honolulu Star-Bulletin* (Honolulu, HI), October 21, 1990, 73; Snead, "Japanese Collections Chart New Course," 32.

18 "Comme des Garçons: Spring 1991 Ready-to-Wear," www.vogue.com, accessed August 3, 2014.

19 Martin, "Sailing to Byzantium," 8–9.

20 Kansai Yamamoto Official, Instagram post March 29, 2016, accessed June 17, 2018.

21 Personal correspondence with Laura Veneskey, assistant professor of art history, Wake Forest University, August 8, 2017.

22 "Ravenna, Italy," Encyclopaedia Britannica, www.britannica.com, accessed March 30, 2015.

23 "Early Christian Monuments of Ravenna," *Whc.Unesco.org*, http://whc.unesco.org, accessed April 1, 2015.

24 "Mausoleum of Galla Placidia, Ravenna," *Sacred-Destinations.com*, www.sacred -destinations.com, accessed April 1, 2015; "Sant'Apollinare Nuovo, Ravenna," *Sacred-Destinations.com*, www.sacred-destinations.com, accessed April 1, 2015; "San Vitale Basilica, Ravenna," *Saared-Destinations.com*, www.sacred-destinations.com, accessed April 1, 2015. For a more detailed and historical treatment of Ravenna and its mosaics, see Lowden, *Early Christian & Byzantine Art*, 101–44.

25 Nazanin Hedayat Munroe, "Dress Styles in the Mosaics of San Vitale," *Metropolitan Museum of Art*, June 25, 2012, www.metmuseum.org.

26 Martin, "Sailing to Byzantium," 6.

27 "Gianni Versace," *Victoria & Albert Museum, VAM.ac.uk*, www.vam.ac.uk, accessed March 31, 2015.

28 Martin, *Gianni Versace*, 12.

29 Richard Servin, "Chic or Cruel?: Gianni Versace's Style Takes a Cue from the World of S&M," *New York Times*, November 1, 1992, V1, V10.

30 Mackrell, *Fashion and Art*, 155.

31 Amy M. Spindler, "Gianni Versace, 50, the Designer Who Infused Fashion with Life and Art," *New York Times*, July 16, 1997, A14.

32 Ibid.

33 Bernadine Morris, "Versace Provides the Razzle and Lacroix the Dazzle in Paris," *New York Times*, July 23, 1991, B6.

34 Fashion Central, "Gianni Versace Fall 1991/1992 Milan - Fashion Channel," https://youtu.be/S8xRputSXlk.

35 Other figural religious representations in the collection include a beaded bolero jacket that includes a large cross and Madonna with child on the back panel and a beaded bustier-style halter that suggests a Christian personage.

36 Versace, *VAM.ac.uk*, www.vam.ac.uk, accessed March 31, 2015.

37 Martin, *Gianni Versace*, 65.

38 Tracy Achor Hayes, "Black Leather, Zippered Jacket Roars Back into High Fashion," *Arizona Daily Star*, September 6, 1991, D4; "Fall Fashion," *Philadelphia Inquirer*, April 21, 1991, 6K.

39 "Milan," *Chicago Tribune*, March 13, 1991, Style 6, Section 7; Daniela Petroff, "War, Recession in Style," *Times Herald* (Port Huron, MI), March 17, 1991, 6G.

40 Morris, "Versace Provides the Razzle," B6; Rod Stafford Hagwood, "Less Flash in Eurofash," *South Florida Sun Sentinel* (Fort Lauderdale, FL), March 21, 1991, 6E. There are a few brief mentions of Versace's inclusion of religious themes in 1991. See Lindsay Baker, "Long Live Leggings," *Guardian* (London), June 3, 1991, Style 33; "Talking a Blue Streak," *Los Angeles Times*, August 23, 1991, E8.

41 Nina Hyde, "In London, Pop Profanity," *Washington Post*, March 14, 1989, E1.

42 Lowden, *Early Christian & Byzantine Art*, 7.

43 Ibid., 149–50.

44 Roof, *Spiritual Marketplace*, 69.

45 Nadine Brozan, "Style," NewYorkTimes.com, January 21, 1994, www.nytimes.com.

46 Ibid.; Julian Nundy, "Chanel Apologises to Muslims for 'Satanic Breasts' Dress," Independent.co.uk, January 24, 1994, www.independent.co.uk.

47 Nundy, "Chanel Apologises to Muslims."

48 Susannah Frankel, "Fashion: Heavenly Creatures," *Guardian* (London), January 24, 1998, 32; Robert O'Byrne, "Fashion Designers Display Catholic Tastes with Some Inspiration from Religious Art," *Irish Times*, October 7, 1997, Home News, 5.

49 Louise Jury, "Nike to Trash Trainers That Offended Islam," *Independent* (UK), June 24, 1997, www.independent.co.uk.

50 "Fashion's Newest Star," *Philadelphia Inquirer*, October 20, 1997, D5. The collection can be seen at "Spring 1998 Ready-to-Wear: Jean Paul Gaultier," *Vogue.com*, www.vogue.com, accessed June 18, 2018.

51 Amy M. Spindler, "Dressing Them Like Artists," *New York Times*, October 21, 1997, B6.

52 Jane de Teliga, "Law of the Jungle Gives Elegance Quite a Fright," *Sydney Morning Herald*, March 1, 1997, 5; Amy M. Spindler, "Briton Fashions the Jungle Look," *Cincinnati Enquirer*, March 5, 1997, E4; "London Bridges Fashion and Rebellion as Alexander McQueen Unleashes a Menagerie," *Chicago Tribune*, March 6, 1997, Tempo Section 5.

53 Sally Brampton, "McQueen's Head Rules His Heart," *Guardian* (London), March 13, 1997, Home News 5.

54 "The Crucified Thief by Robert Campin," *RationalSensualArt.Blogspot*, April 7, 2012, http://rationalsensualart.blogspot.com.

55 "Fall 1997 Ready-to-Wear: Alexander McQueen," *Vogue.com*, www.vogue.com, accessed August 10, 2017.

56 Barbara DeWitt, "Madonna (Not Her) Sets Fashion Trend," *Santa Cruz Sentinel*, March 14, 1998, D3; "Milan Shows Chic and Cheeky Spring/Summer Collections Range from Cute to Divine," *Toronto Star*, October 14, 1997, H2; "A Divine Collection from Dolce & Gabbana," LosAngelesTimes.com, October 7, 1997, http://articles.latimes.com.

57 A Divine Collection from Dolce & Gabbana," LosAngelesTimes.com, October 7, 1997, http://articles.latimes.com.

58 "Milan Shows Chic and Cheeky Spring/Summer Collections Range from Cute to Divine," *Toronto Star*, October 14, 1997, H2.

59 Jane de Teliga, "Anything Goes: The Collections," *Sydney Morning Herald*, October 14, 1997, Good Living 12.

60 Frankel, "Fashion: Heavenly Creatures," 32.

61 Annabel Miller, "What's Wrong with Having the Virgin on a T-Shirt?" *Guardian* (London), January 31, 1998, 19.

62 Valentina Zannoni, "1998: Dolce and Gabbana Printed the Virgin Mary on T-Shirts," *Swide.com*, September 9, 2013, www.swide.com.

63 Robert O'Byrne, "Fashion Designers Display Catholic Tastes with Some Inspiration from Religious Art," *Irish Times*, October 7, 1997, Home News, 5; Rebecca Bedell, "What Is Sentimental Art?," *American Art* 25:3 (Fall 2011): 9–12.

64 Tsaprailis and Roston, with Drolet, "New Fashions a Religious Experience," A3.

65 Ibid.

66 "Milan Shows Chic and Cheeky Spring/Summer Collections," *Toronto Star*, October 14, 1997, H2; O'Byrne, "Fashion Designers Display Catholic Tastes with Some Inspiration from Religious Art."

67 Frankel, "Fashion: Heavenly Creatures," 32; Miller, "What's Wrong with Having the Virgin on a T-Shirt?," 19.

68 O'Byrne, "Fashion Designers Display Catholic Tastes with Some Inspiration from Religious Art."

69 Frankel, "Fashion: Heavenly Creatures," 32.

70 "Fashion News," *Philadelphia Daily News*, March 18, 1998, 41; "Copycats," *Observer* (London), April 19, 1998, 32. Also see Alessandra Stanley, "Religion in Vogue and the Vatican Is Scandalized," *New York Times*, July 16, 1998, A4.

71 "Milan Shows Chic and Cheeky Spring/Summer Collections," *Toronto Star*, October 14, 1997, H2.

72 Pelikan, *Mary through the Centuries*, 1.

73 Hansen, ed., *Roman Catholicism in Fantastic Film*, 4. Also see Greeley, *The Catholic Myth*, 61–62, 253.

74 Gilbert, "Awash with Angels," 239.

75 Wuthnow, *After Heaven*, 4.

76 Gilbert, "Awash with Angels," 244.

77 Pieto, "The Devil Made Me Do It," 52–53, 3–4.

78 Tweed, *Our Lady of the Exile*, 58; Pelikan, *Mary through the Centuries*, 3.

79 Hermkens, Jansen, and Notermans, *Moved by Mary*, 1.

80 Coleman, "Mary: Images and Objects," 408.

81 Ibid., 406.

82 David Van Biema, "Hail, Mary," *Time* 165:2 (March 21, 2005): 60–69; Jason Byassee, "What about Mary?," *Christian Century* 121:25 (December 14, 2004): 28–32; Timothy George, "The Blessed Evangelical Mary," *Christianity Today* 47:12

(December 2003): 34–39; Scott McKnight, "The Mary We Never Knew," *Christianity Today* 50:12 (December 2006): 26–30.

83 Greeley, *The Catholic Myth*, 244.

84 Ibid., 244, 248.

85 Francine Prose, "Goddess Worship," *Harper's Bazaar* 128 (August 1995): 76, 82.

86 "What's Your Image of God?," *St. Cloud Times* (St. Cloud, MN), January 2, 1998, 7A.

87 "Christmas Night," *Vogue* (December 1949): 82–85; Bowen, "The Light in the Dark," 88–91; "Nativity," *Vogue* 146 (December 1965): 170–173; "Michelangelo's Divine Circle," *Vogue* 164 (December 1974): 138–39; Pál Kelemen, "The Virgin in Cuzco," *Harper's Bazaar* 87 (December 1954): 72–73; "Majorca," *Harper's Bazaar* 87 (September 1954): 189. Also see "The Healing Saints" and "The Angels of Campobasso," *Harper's Bazaar* 88 (December 1955): 76–79.

88 For more on Marian art and iconography, see Vloberg, "The Iconographic Types of the Virgin in Western Art," 542.

89 *Vogue* 139 (March 1, 1962): 131; *Vogue* 154 (July 1969): 71. Similar Marian-like imagery also appeared in some advertisements. See *Vogue* 170 (December 1980): 9 and *Vogue* 173 (December 1983): 13.

90 Gregory Votolato, updated by Daryl F. Mallett, "Thierry Mugler," *Fashion Encyclopedia*, www.fashionencyclopedia.com, accessed May 11, 2015; also see Anne-Marie Schiro, "A New York Encounter with Futuristic Fashions," *New York Times*, May 8, 1980, C10.

91 Bernadine Morris, "The Directions of the Innovators," *New York Times*, February 27, 1983, FS132–33, 166.

92 Genevieve Buck, "Show Biz: Mugler Throws a Knockout of a Spectacle," *Chicago Tribune*, March 29, 1984, G8; John Duka, "In Fashion, the Show's the Thing," *New York Times*, March 28, 1984, C1.

93 Michelle Finamore, "Fashion Shows," *A–Z of Fashion*, Berg Fashion Library.

94 "Thierry Mugler, 1984," Garmento, http://garmentozine.com, May 11, 2015; "Mugler A/W RTW 1984," https://youtu.be/QJyzRzj2py4, May 11, 2015.

95 Buck, "Mugler Throws a Knockout of a Spectacle," G8.

96 "Thierry Mugler, 1984"; "*Il est né divin Enfant*," Wikipedia, http://en.m.wikipedia.org, May 11, 2015.

97 Duka, "In Fashion, the Show's the Thing," C1.

98 Freedberg, *The Power of Images*, 28.

99 Roof, "Religious Kaleidoscope," 184.

100 Roof, "God Is in the Details," 152.

101 Ibid., 153.

102 Ibid., 154.

103 Barbara De Witt, "Madonna (Not Her) Sets Fashion Trend," *Santa Cruz Sentinel*, March 14, 1998, D3.

104 Roof, "God Is in the Details," 152.

105 Gilbert, "Awash with Angels," 238, 239.
106 Roof, "Religious Kaleidoscope," 190.
107 Morgan, *The Sacred Gaze*, 6.
108 Albanese, "From New Thought to New Vision: The Shamanic Paradigm in Contemporary Spirituality," 338.
109 Roof, "God Is in the Details," 154.
110 Ibid., 151.
111 Gilbert, "Awash with Angels," 239.
112 McDannell, *Material Christianity*; Morgan, *Visual Piety*.
113 McDannell, *Material Christianity*, 247.
114 Ibid., 249–51.
115 For more on Christian T-shirts, see Neal, "OMG," 223–44, and Blum and Harvey, *The Color of Christ*, 252.
116 Lee, "The Globalization of Religious Markets: International Innovations, Malaysian Consumption," 39.
117 Neal, "OMG," 223–44. Also see Nina Hyde, "In London, Pop Profanity," *Washington Post*, March 14, 1989, E1.
118 For more on cool, see Pountain and Robbins, *Cool Rules*, and Stearns, *American Cool*.
119 Miller, "What's Wrong," 19.
120 Neal, "OMG," 223–44. Some might also view Dolce & Gabbana's statement of intent and relationship with the Catholic Church with more skepticism. The designers are not afraid to juxtapose religious symbols, such as the cross, with some of their more overtly sexualized designs. Further, in some photo shoots, Dolce & Gabbana deliberately challenge Catholic sexual norms. See, for example, "Stefano and Domenico's Dolce Vita," *W* 36 (2007): 204–25.

CONCLUSION. PUTTING GOD ON A DRESS

1 Stephanie Hirschmiller, "Holy Spirit," *British Vogue* (October 2013): 239.
2 "Karla Spetic Fall 2013 Ready-to-Wear," *Style.com*, www.style.com, accessed March 30, 2015; See also "Jean-Charles de Castelbajac's Fall Winter 2010/2011," https://youtu.be/CDCGc3LTkhI, accessed March 30, 2105.
3 Alyx Gorman, "Karla Spetic Spring 2013 Review," *TheVine.com*, April 9, 2013, www.thevine.com.au.
4 Carley Drennan, "Faithful Fashion," *FortheFaithofFashion.blogspot*, October 3, 2013, http://forthefaithoffashion.blogspot.com.
5 Lou Stoppard, "Lou Stoppard Reports on the Dolce e Gabbana Show," *ShowStudio.com*, February 24, 2013, http://showstudio.com.
6 Anibundel, "Milan Fashion Week Fall 2013 RTW: Dolce and Gabbana," *Ani-Izzy.com*, March 2, 2013, http://anibundel.wordpress.com.
7 "Visual Rhetoric: Figures of Substitution," *Lambros' Visual Language Blog*, February 2, 2015, https://lambrosvisuallanguage.wordpress.com.
8 Morgan, *Visual Piety*, 124–80.

9 MacCannell, *The Tourist*, 48.

10 Morgan, *The Sacred Gaze*, 6.

11 MacCannell, *The Tourist*, 3.

12 Jerico Mandybur, "Exclusive: Karla Spetic Q&A," *Pagesdigital.com*, June 4, 2013, www.pagesdigital.com.

13 "Dolce & Gabbana: Winter Woman 2014: 'Tailored Mosaic,'" *Swide.com*, February 24, 2013, www.swide.com.

14 Nina Stotler, "Dolce & Gabbana," *WGSN Blogs*, February 24, 2013, http://test.stylesight.com.

15 For more on this collection, see Neal, "Religion Reprocessed in Dolce & Gabbana's 'Tailored Mosaic.'"

16 McCrone, Morris, and Kiely, *Scotland—the Brand*, 1, 4.

17 Ibid., 4.

18 Ibid., 1.

19 Alison Parr, "2013 MBFWA: Karla Spetic," *PopSugar.com*, April 9, 2013, www.popsugar.com.au.

20 McCrone, Morris, and Kiely, *Scotland—the Brand*, 1.

21 Ibid., 8–9.

22 Duncan and Duncan, "The Aestheticization of the Politics of Landscape Preservation," 391.

23 Hervieu-Léger, *Religion as a Chain of Memory*, 158.

24 Stallybrass and White, *The Politics and Poetics of Transgression*, 42.

25 Duncan and Duncan, "The Aestheticization of the Politics of Landscape Preservation," 387.

26 Ibid., 391.

27 Hervieu-Léger, *Religion as a Chain of Memory*, 33.

28 Pew Research Center, "'Nones' on the Rise," *Pew Research Center: Religion & Public Life*, October 9, 2012, www.pewforum.org.

29 Kimberly Winston, "The Rise of the 'Nones,'" *Christian Century*, October 31, 2012, www.christiancentury.org.

30 Cathy Lynn Grossman, "Number with No Religion Growing," *Times Recorder* (Zanesville, OH), October 9, 2012, B3.

31 Amy Sullivan, "The Rise of the Nones," *Time* 179:10 (March 12, 2012): 68.

32 Gary Laderman, "The Rise of the Religious 'Nones' Indicates the End of Religion as We Know It," *Huffington Post*, originally posted March 20, 2013, updated May 19, 2013, www.huffingtonpost.com.

33 Pew Research Center, "'Nones' on the Rise."

34 Davie, *Religion in Modern Europe*, 3, 8.

35 Wuthnow, *After Heaven*, 4; Morgan, *The Sacred Gaze*, 6.

36 Danièle Hervieu-Léger, *Religion as a Chain of Memory*, xi.

37 Ibid., 139.

38 "Katy Perry Channels a Goth Medieval Queen at the Met Gala in Dolce & Gabbana," *MTV Style*, May 7, 2013, http://style.mtv.com.

39 Katy Perry. Twitter Post. May 6, 2013, 4:42 PM. https://twitter.com/katyperry /status/331554477473685504.

40 "Marvelous Mosaics," *Dolcegabbana.com*, www.dolcegabbana.com, accessed April 1, 2015.

41 Lynn S. Neal, "Faith in Fashion Survey: 2016–2018," IRB Study #IRB00022075.

42 Suzy Menkes, "Around the World Hits from Vuitton, Lanvin, and Galliano: The Collections," *International Herald Tribune* (Paris), October 8, 2002, 14. Also see Maggie Alderson, "A Pair of Aces: Style," *The Age* (Melbourne, Victoria, Australia), October 16, 2002, 5.

43 "Sri Lanka Bans Buddha Bikinis," *Chicago Tribune*, June 18, 2004, 10; Dennis Coday, "Protests Halt Swimsuit Sales," *National Catholic Reporter* (Kansas City), May 7, 2004, 7.

44 Lindsay Goldwert, "Swimsuit Designer Outrages Hindus by Depicting Goddess Lakshmi on Bikinis," *Daily News* (New York), May 9, 2011, www.nydailynews. com; "Lakshmi Swimwear Designer: I Have Learned My Lesson from Hinduism," *National Turk*, July 18, 2011, www.nationalturk.com.

45 Duncan and Duncan, "The Aestheticization of the Politics of Landscape Preservation," 389.

46 MacCannell, *The Tourist*, 10.

BIBLIOGRAPHY

Albanese, Catherine L. "From New Thought to New Vision: The Shamanic Paradigm in Contemporary Spirituality." In *Communication & Change in American Religious History*, edited by Leonard I. Sweet, 335–54. Grand Rapids, MI: Wm. B. Eerdmans Publishing Co., 1993.

Allitt, Patrick. *Religion in America Since 1945: A History*. New York: Columbia University Press, 2003.

Appadurai, Arjun, ed. *The Social Life of Things: Commodities in Cultural Perspective*. Cambridge: Cambridge University Press, 1986.

Arthur, Linda B., ed. *Religion, Dress, and the Body*. Oxford: Berg, 1999.

Barber, Bernard, and Lyel S. Lobel. "'Fashion' in Women's Clothes and the American Social System." *Social Forces* 31:2 (December 1952): 124–31.

Barnard, Malcolm. *Fashion as Communication*. London: Routledge, 1996.

Baucom, Ian. *Specters of the Atlantic: Finance Capital, Slavery, and the Philosophy of History*. Durham: Duke University Press, 2005.

Bedell, Rebecca. "What Is Sentimental Art?" *American Art* 25:3 (Fall 2011): 9–12.

Benjamin, Walter. *Illuminations*. Edited and with an introduction by Hannah Arendt. New York: Shocken Books, 1969.

Besecke, Kelly. "Seeing Invisible Religion: Religion as a Societal Conversation about Transcendent Meaning." *Sociological Theory* 23:3 (June 2005): 179–96.

Blum, Edward J., and Paul Harvey. *The Color of Christ: The Son of God and the Saga of Race in America*. Chapel Hill: University of North Carolina Press, 2012.

Braham, Peter. "Fashion: Unpacking a Cultural Production." In *Production of Culture/Cultures of Production*, edited by Paul Du Gay, 119–76. London: SAGE Publications, 1991.

Braude, Ann. "Women's History *Is* American Religious History." In *Retelling U.S. Religious History*, edited by Thomas A. Tweed, 87–107. Berkeley: University of California Press, 1997.

Bucar, Elizabeth. *Pious Fashion: How Muslim Women Dress*. Cambridge, MA: Harvard University Press, 2017.

Burke Smith, Anthony. *The Look of Catholics: Portrayals in Popular Culture from the Great Depression to the Cold War*. Lawrence: University Press of Kansas, 2010.

Charles-Roux, Edmonde. *Chanel and Her World: Friends, Fashion, and Fame*. New York: Vendome Press, 2005.

Cohen, Erik. "Authenticity and Commoditization in Tourism." *Annals of Tourism Research* 15: (1988): 371–86.

Coleman, Simon. "Mary: Images and Objects." In *Mary: The Complete Resource*, edited by Sarah Jane Boss, 395–410. New York: Oxford University Press, 2007.

Conklin, Beth A. "Body Paint, Feathers, and VCRs: Aesthetics and Authenticity in Amazonian Activism." *American Ethnologist* 24:4 (November 1997): 711–37.

Connerton, Paul. *How Societies Remember*. Cambridge: Cambridge University Press, 1989, 2007.

Cook, James W. *The Arts of Deception*. Cambridge, MA: Harvard University Press, 2001.

Davie, Grace. *Religion in Modern Europe*. Oxford: Oxford University Press, 2000.

Davis, Fred. *Fashion, Culture, and Identity*. Chicago: University of Chicago Press, 1992.

Davison Hunter, James. *Culture Wars: The Struggle to Define America*. New York: Basic Books, 1991.

De la Haye, Amy, and Shelley Tobin. *Chanel: The Couturiere at Work*. Woodstock, New York: Overlook Press, 1996.

Demerath, N. J., III, "Cultural Victory and Organizational Defeat in the Paradoxical Decline of Liberal Protestantism." *Journal for the Scientific Study of Religion* 34:4 (December 1995): 458-69.

Dillon, Stephen. "'It's Here, It's That Time:' Race, Queer Futurity, and the Temporality of Violence in *Born in Flames*." *Women & Performance: A Journal of Feminist Theory* 23:1 (2013): 38–51.

Duncan, James S., and Nancy G. Duncan. "The Aestheticization of the Politics of Landscape Preservation." *Annals of the Association of American Geographers* 91:2 (June 2001): 387–409.

Durkheim, Émile. *The Elementary Forms of Religious Life*. New York: Free Press, 1915, 1969.

Dwyer-McNulty, Sally. *Common Threads: A Cultural History of Clothing in American Catholicism*. Chapel Hill: University of North Carolina Press, 2014.

Ellwood, Robert S. *1950: Crossroad of American Religious Life*. Louisville, KY: Westminster John Knox Press, 2000.

———. *The Fifties Spiritual Marketplace: American Religion in a Decade of Conflict*. New Brunswick, NJ: Rutgers University Press, 1997.

Entwistle, Joanne. *The Fashioned Body: Fashion, Dress and Modern Social Theory*. Cambridge: Polity Press, 2000.

Eskridge, Larry. *God's Forever Family: The Jesus People Movement in America*. New York: Oxford University Press, 2013.

Farrell-Beck, Jane, and Jean Parsons. *20th-Century Dress in the United States*. New York: Fairchild Books, 2007.

Fessenden, Tracy. *Culture and Redemption: Religion, the Secular, and American Literature*. Princeton, NJ: Princeton University Press, 2007.

Finch, Martha L. "'Fashions of Worldly Dames': Separatist Discourses of Dress in Early Modern London, Amsterdam, and Plymouth Colony." *Church History* 74:3 (September 2005): 494–533.

Finkelstein, Joanne. *Fashion: An Introduction*. New York: New York University Press, 1998.

Forbes, Bruce. *Christmas: A Candid History*. Berkeley: University of California Press, 2007.

Freedberg, David. *The Power of Images*. Chicago: University of Chicago Press, 1989.

Geary, Patrick. "Sacred Commodities: The Circulation of Medieval Relics." In *The Social Life of Things: Commodities in Cultural Perspective*, edited by Arjun Appadurai, 169–91. Cambridge: Cambridge University Press, 1986.

Gilbert, Roger. "Awash with Angels: The Religious Turn in Nineties Poetry." *Contemporary Literature* 42:2 (Summer 2001): 238–69.

Grazian, David. "Demystifying Authenticity in the Sociology of Culture." In *Handbook of Cultural Sociology*, edited by John R. Hall, Laura Grindstaff, and Ming-Cheng Lo, 191–200. New York: Routledge, 2010.

Greeley, Andrew. *The Catholic Myth: The Behavior and Beliefs of American Catholics*. New York: Collier Books, 1990.

Haas, Katherine. "The Fabric of Religion: Vestments and Devotional Catholicism in Nineteenth-Century America." *Material Religion* 3:2 (July 2007): 190–217.

Hansen, Regina, ed. *Roman Catholicism in Fantastic Film: Essays on Belief, Spectacle, Ritual and Imagery*. Jefferson, NC: McFarland & Co., 2011.

Hendershot, Heather. *Shaking the World for Jesus*. Chicago: University of Chicago Press, 2004.

Herberg, Will. *Protestant, Catholic, Jew: An Essay in American Religious Sociology*. Garden City, NY: Doubleday, 1955.

Hermkens, Anna-Karina, Willy Jansen, and Catrien Notermans, eds. *Moved by Mary: The Power of Pilgrimage in the Modern World*. Burlington, VT: Ashgate Publishing Company, 2009.

Hervieu-Léger, Danièle. *Religion as a Chain of Memory*. New Brunswick, NJ: Rutgers University Press, 1993, 2000.

Hutchison, William R. *The Modernist Impulse in American Protestantism*. Cambridge, MA: Harvard University Press, 1976.

Jenks, Chris. *Transgression*. London: Routledge, 2003.

Jenß, Heike. "Dressed in History: Retro Styles and the Construction of Authenticity in Youth Culture." *Fashion Theory* 8:4 (2004): 387–404.

Jewelry: Ancient to Modern. New York: The Viking Press, 1979.

Jhally, Sut. "Advertising as Religion: The Dialectic of Technology and Magic." In *Cultural Politics in Contemporary America*, edited by Lan Angus and Sut Jhally, 217–29. New York: Routledge, 1989.

Jones, David Albert. *Angels: A History*. New York: Oxford University Press, 2010.

Joselit, Jenna Weissman. *A Perfect Fit: Clothes, Character, and the Promise of America*. New York: Henry Holt & Co., 2001.

Jouve, Marie-Andrée. *Balenciaga*. New York: Universe Publishing/Vendome Press, 1997.

Kawamura, Yuniya. *Doing Research in Fashion and Dress: An Introduction to Qualitative Methods*. Oxford: Berg, 2011.

Keenan, William J. F. "From Friars to Fornicators: The Eroticization of Sacred Dress." *Fashion Theory* 3:4 (1999): 389–410.

———. "Of Mammon Clothed Divinely: The Profanization of Sacred Dress." *Body & Society* 5:1 (1999): 73–92.

Klassen, Pamela E. "The Robes of Womanhood: Dress and Authenticity among African American Methodist Women in the Nineteenth Century." *Religion and American Culture* 14:1 (Winter 2004): 39–82.

Koda, Harold, and Andrew Bolton, et al. *Chanel*. New York: Metropolitan Museum of Art, 2005.

Laski, Marghanita. "Advertising—Sacred and Profane." *Twentieth Century* 165 (February 1959): 118–29.

Lears, T. J. Jackson. *Fables of Abundance: A Cultural History of Advertising in America*. New York: Basic Books, 1994.

Lee, Raymond L. M. "The Globalization of Religious Markets: International Innovations, Malaysian Consumption." *Sojourn: Journal of Social Issues in Southeast Asia* 8:1 (February 1993): 35–61.

Lofton, Kathryn. *Oprah: The Gospel of an Icon*. Berkeley: University of California Press, 2011.

Lowden, John. *Early Christian & Byzantine Art*. London: Phaidon, 1997.

Luckmann, Thomas. "Shrinking Transcendence, Expanding Religion?" *Sociological Analysis* 51:2 (Summer 1990): 127–38.

MacCannell, Dean. "Staged Authenticity: Arrangements of Social Space in Tourist Settings." *American Journal of Sociology* 79:3 (November 1973): 589–603.

———. *The Tourist: A New Theory of the Leisure Class*. New York: Schocken Books, 1976.

Mackrell, Alice. *Fashion and Art*. London: BT Batsford, 2005.

Marchand, Roland. *Advertising the American Dream: Making Way for Modernity, 1920–1940*. Berkeley: University of California Press, 1985.

Martin, Richard H. *Gianni Versace*. New York: Metropolitan Museum of Art, 1997.

———. "Sailing to Byzantium: A Fashion Odyssey, 1990–1991." *Textile and Text* 14:2 (February 1991): 3–12.

Mauriès, Patrick. *Jewelry by Chanel*. Boston: Bulfinch Press, Little, Brown and Company, 1993 and 2000.

Mayo, Janet. *A History of Ecclesiastical Dress*. New York: Holmes & Meier Publishers, Inc., 1984.

McCrone, David, Angela Morris, and Richard Kiely. *Scotland—the Brand: The Making of Scottish Heritage*. Edinburgh: Edinburgh University Press, 1995.

McDannell, Colleen. *Material Christianity*. New Haven, CT: Yale University Press, 1995.

McLeod, Hugh. *The Religious Crisis of the 1960s*. New York: Oxford University Press, 2010.

Mendes, Valerie, and Amy de la Haye. *Fashion Since 1900, Second edition*. London: Thames and Hudson, 1999 and 2010.

Merlo, Elisabetta, and Francesca Polese. "Turning Fashion into Business: The Emergence of Milan as an International Fashion Hub." *Business History Review* 80:3 (Autumn 2006): 415–47.

Meyer, Birgit. *Mediation and the Genesis of Presence: Towards a Material Approach to Religion*. Utrecht: Universiteit Utrecht, 2012.

———. "'Praise the Lord': Popular Cinema and Pentecostalite Style in Ghana's New Public Sphere." *American Ethnologist* 31:1 (February 2004): 92–110.

Moffitt, Peggy, and William Claxton. *The Rudi Gernreich Book*. Köln: Taschen, 1999.

Monk, Maria, Theodore Dwight, J. J. Slocum, and William K. Hoyte. *Awful Disclosures of Maria Monk, or, The Hidden Secrets of a Nun's Life in a Convent Exposed!* Philadelphia: T. B. Peterson, 1836.

Moore, R. Laurence. "Religion, Secularization, and the Shaping of the Culture Industry in Antebellum America." *American Quarterly* 41:2 (June 1989): 216–42.

———. *Selling God: American Religion in the Marketplace of Culture*. New York: Oxford University Press, 1994.

Moore, Tara. *Christmas: The Sacred to Santa*. London: Reaktion Books, 2014.

Morgan, David. "Art and Religion in the Modern Age." In *Re-Enchantment*, edited by James Elkins and David Morgan, 25–45. New York: Routledge, 2009.

———. *The Sacred Gaze: Religious Visual Culture in Theory and Practice*. Berkeley: University of California Press, 2005.

———. *Visual Piety*. Berkeley: University of California Press, 1998.

Nakahara, Tamao. "Barred Nuns: Italian Nunsploitation Films." In *Alternative Europe: Eurotrash and Exploitation Cinema Since 1945*, edited by Ernest Mathijs and Xavier Mendik, 124–33. London: Wallflower Press, 2004.

Neal, Lynn S. "OMG: Authenticity, Parody, and Evangelical Christian Fashion." *Fashion Theory* 21:3 (2017): 223–44.

———. "Religion Reprocessed in Dolce & Gabbana's 'Tailored Mosaic.'" In *Fashion and Contemporaneity*, edited by Laura Petican, 228–46. Leiden: Brill, 2019.

O'Hara Callan, Georgina. *The Thames and Hudson Dictionary of Fashion and Fashion Designers*. London: Thames and Hudson, 1998.

Ortner, Sherry B. "On Key Symbols." In *A Reader in the Anthropology of Religion*, edited by Michael Lambek, 158–67. Malden, MA: Blackwell Publishers, 2002.

Payne, Blanche, Geitel Winakor, and Jane Farrell-Beck. *The History of Costume: From Ancient Mesopotamia through the Twentieth Century*. New York: HarperCollins Publishers, 1992.

Payne, Leah. "'Pants Don't Make Preachers': Fashion and Gender Construction in Late Nineteenth and Early Twentieth-Century American Revivalism." *Fashion Theory* 19:1 (2015): 83–113. https://doi.org/10.2752/175174115X14113933306860.

Pelikan, Jaroslav. *Mary through the Centuries: Her Place in the History of Culture*. New Haven, CT: Yale University Press, 1996.

Phillips, Clare. *Jewelry: From Antiquity to the Present*. London: Thames and Hudson, 1996.

Pieto, Rick. "'The Devil Made Me Do It:' Catholicism, Verisimilitude and the Reception of Horror Films." In *Roman Catholicism in Fantastic Film: Essays on Belief, Spectacle, Ritual and Imagery*, edited by Regina Hansen, 52–64. Jefferson, NC: McFarland & Co., 2011.

Plate, S. Brent. *A History of Religion in 5 ½ Objects*. Boston: Beacon Press, 2014.

Porterfield, Amanda. *The Transformation of American Religion: The Story of the Late Twentieth-Century*. Oxford: Oxford University Press, 2001.

Pountain, Dick, and David Robbins. *Cool Rules: Anatomy of an Attitude*. London: Reaktion Books, 2000.

Rabine, Leslie W. "A Woman's Two Bodies: Fashion Magazines, Consumerism, and Feminism." In *On Fashion*, edited by Shari Benstock and Suzanne Ferriss, 59–75. New Brunswick, NJ: Rutgers University Press, 1994.

Radway, Janice A. "Reading Is Not Eating: Mass-Produced Literature and the Theoretical, Methodological, and Political Consequences of a Metaphor." *Book Research Quarterly* 2 (1986): 7–29.

Restad, Penne L. *Christmas in America: A History*. New York: Oxford University Press, 1995.

Roof, Wade Clark. "God Is in the Details: Reflections on Religion's Public Presence in the United States in the Mid-1990s." *Sociology of Religion* 57:2 (1996): 149–62.

———. "Religious Kaleidoscope: American Religion in the 1990s." *Temenos* 32 (1996): 183–93.

———. *Spiritual Marketplace: Baby Boomers and the Remaking of American Religion*. Princeton, NJ: Princeton University Press, 1999.

Saler, Michael. "Modernity and Enchantment: A Historiographic Review." *American Historical Review* 111:3 (June 2006): 692–716.

Sanders, Theresa. *Approaching Eden: Adam and Eve in Popular Culture*. Lanham, MD: Rowman & Littlefield, 2009.

Seebohm, Caroline. *The Man Who Was Vogue: The Life and Times of Condé Nast*. New York: Viking Press, 1982.

Sheffield, Tricia. *The Religious Dimensions of Advertising*. New York: Palgrave Macmillan, 2006.

Simmel, Georg. "Fashion." *American Journal of Sociology* 62:6 (May 1957): 541–58.

Smith, Erin A. *What Would Jesus Read?: Popular Religious Books and Everyday Life in Twentieth-Century America*. Chapel Hill: University of North Carolina Press, 2015.

Spooner, Brian. "Weavers and Dealers: The Authenticity of an Oriental Carpet." In *The Social Life of Things: Commodities in Cultural Perspective*, edited by Arjun Appadurai, 195–235. Cambridge: Cambridge University Press, 1986.

Stallybrass, Peter, and Allon White. *The Politics and Poetics of Transgression*. Ithaca, NY: Cornell University Press, 1986.

Stearns, Peter N. *American Cool*. New York: New York University Press, 1994.

Sturken, Marita. *Tangled Memories: The Vietnam War, the AIDS Epidemic, and the Politics of Remembering*. Berkeley: University of California Press, 1997.

Styers, Randall. *Making Magic: Religion, Magic, and Science in the Modern World*. New York: Oxford University Press, 2004.

Sutcliffe, Steven J., and Ingvild Saelid Gihus, eds. *New Age Spirituality*. Durham, UK: Acumen Publishing, 2013.

Tarlo, Emma. *Visibly Muslim: Fashion, Politics, Faith*. London: Bloomsbury Academic, 2010.

Tortora, Phyllis, and Keith Eubank. *Survey of Historic Costume: A History of Western Dress*, 5th ed. New York: Fairchild Books, 2010.

Tweed, Thomas A. *Our Lady of the Exile: Diasporic Religion at a Cuban Catholic Shrine in Miami*. New York: Oxford University Press, 1997.

Twitchell, James B. *Lead Us into Temptation: The Triumph of American Materialism*. New York: Columbia University Press, 1999.

Van de Port, Mattijs. "Visualizing the Sacred: Video Technology, 'Televisual' Style, and the Religious Imagination in Bahian Candomblé." *American Ethnologist* 33:3 (2006): 444–61.

Vanderlaan, Eldred C., Compiler. *Fundamentalism versus Modernism*. New York: H. W. Wilson Company, 1925.

Vloberg, Maurice. "The Iconographic Types of the Virgin in Western Art." In *Mary: The Complete Resource*, edited by Sarah Jan Boss, 537–85. New York: Oxford University Press, 2007.

Wuthnow, Robert. *After Heaven: Spirituality in America since 1950s*. Berkeley: University of California Press, 1998.

INDEX

The color insert image pages are indicated by the figure number, *1f, 2f*, etc.

ABOUT THE AUTHOR

Lynn S. Neal is Professor of Religious Studies at Wake Forest University. An award-winning teacher, Neal's work focuses on the mediation of religion, with special attention to popular culture. Previous publications include *Romancing God: Evangelical Women and Inspirational Fiction* (2006) and *Religious Intolerance in America* (2010, co-edited with John Corrigan), as well as articles on religion and fashion, and religion and television.

Printed and bound by CPI Group (UK) Ltd, Croydon, CR0 4YY

13/04/2025

14656577-0001